IBN KHALDŪN IN EGYPT

WALTER J. FISCHEL

IBN KHALDŪN IN EGYPT

His Public Functions and His Historical Research (1382–1406)

A Study in Islamic Historiography

1967
UNIVERSITY OF CALIFORNIA PRESS
BERKELEY AND LOS ANGELES

University of California Press
Berkeley and Los Angeles, California

Library of Congress Catalog Card Number: 67-11200

PREFACE

In submitting this study, which is a summation of research on Ibn Khaldūn that has occupied me for many years, I am fully aware of the difficulties of any attempt to penetrate into the complexities of Ibn Khaldūn's life and work, and to unravel the peculiarities of his Arabic language and terminology. I can do no more than take refuge in Ibn Khaldūn's own statement in the *Muqqadimah* (I, 8; quoted according to *Proleg.*, I, 14), namely,

> The capital of knowledge that an individual scholar has to offer is small.
> Admission [of one's shortcomings] saves from censure.
> Kindness from colleagues is hoped for.
> It is God whom I ask to make our deeds acceptable in His sight.
> He suffices me—He is a good protector.

It gives me pleasure to acknowledge my gratitude to the many libraries here and abroad that so readily cooperated in my search for manuscripts and books during my repeated travels to Europe and the Middle East.

I want, also, to acknowledge my indebtedness to the Bollingen Foundation, and to its President and Board of Trustees for their continued interest in my Ibn Khaldūn studies and for the support rendered so generously.

This book is dedicated to my dear wife, Irene Jerukhim, and our daughter, Corinne Zipporah—a token of gratitude for their patience and understanding.

W. J. F.

Berkeley, California
March 1967

CONTENTS

Preface v

List of Abbreviations xi

Introduction 1

Primary Sources 7

  Ibn Khaldūn's Works 7

  Translations of the *Muqaddimah* 9

  External Arabic Sources 10

PART ONE: IBN KHALDŪN'S LIFE AND PUBLIC FUNCTIONS IN MAMLŪK EGYPT

1 Arrival in Egypt in 1382 15

2 Protégé of Sultan Barqūq 20

3 The "Maghribī Consul" in Cairo 23

4 Teacher and Educator in Cairo 26

5 Mālikite Chief Cadi in Cairo 30

  First appointment as Chief Cadi (1384–1385) 30

  Ibn Khaldūn and the Fetwā against Barqūq (1389) 34

  Second appointment as Chief Cadi (1399–1400) 39

6 Meeting with Tamerlane in Damascus (1401) 42

  Journey to Damascus 42

  From the walls of Damascus to the camp of Tamerlane 44

  The topics of Ibn Khaldūn's discussions with Tamerlane 48

7 Last Phase of Public Activities in Cairo (1401–1406) 66

PART TWO: IBN KHALDŪN'S HISTORICAL RESEARCH IN EGYPT

I Historian of Mamlūk Egypt of His Time

1 As Historian of Sultan Barqūq 71
The challenge 71
Biographer of Sultan Barqūq (1382–1399) 73
Critical observation and evaluation 78
2 As Historian of the Tatars and the Mongols 82
Sources for the history of Jenghiz Khān and his descendants 84
From Jenghiz Khān to the Il-Khān dynasty 87
3 As Historian of the Mamlūk-Mongol Conflict under Tamerlane 93
Historian of Tamerlane's siege and conquest of Damascus 94
Recorder of the diplomatic activities of this period 100
Portrayer of Tamerlane's personality 103
The historiographical significance of Ibn Khaldūn's account of Tamerlane 105

II Historian of Non-Islamic Monotheistic Religions

1 Historiographical Introduction 109
Ibn Khaldūn and al-Mas'ūdī 111
The multiplicity of his sources 114
Ibn Khaldūn's methodological approach 119
2 Ibn Khaldūn on the Religious Manifestations of Ancient Iran 121
Hebrew-Iranian synchronisms 122
Zoroaster and the "Dīn al-Majūsīya" 123
Conversions and dissensions 127
3 Historian of Early Christianity 130
From Jesus to the apostles 130
The Christian Canon 132
The ecclesiastical history of Eastern Christianity 133

4 Historian of Biblical and Post-Biblical Judaism 138
Biblical history 138
Post-biblical history: Ibn Khaldūn and *Yosiphon* 139
Ibn Khaldūn and the Hebrew Scriptures 144
His critical approach to the Bible 148
His approach to ancient chronology 151
Application of his socio-philosophical views to Jewish history 152

PART THREE: IBN KHALDŪN AND HIS "AUTOBIOGRAPHY"

His *Ta'rīf* and Its Evaluation 159

Chronological Table of Major Events in Ibn Khaldūn's "Egyptian Phase" 167

Ibn Khaldūniana: A Bibliography of Writings on and Pertaining to Ibn Khaldūn 171

Index 213

LIST OF ABBREVIATIONS

B.S.O.A.S.	Bulletin of the School of Oriental and African Studies
E.I.	The Encyclopedia of Islam
G.A.L.	Brockelmann, C. Geschichte der arabischen Litteratur (Supplementbände)
I.C.	Islamic Culture
I.B.L.A.	Institut des Belles Lettres Arabes
I.L.	Islamic Literature
J.A.	Journal Asiatique
J.A.O.S.	Journal of the American Oriental Society
J.E.S.H.O.	Journal of the Economic and Social History of the Orient, Leiden
J.Q.R.	Jewish Quarterly Review, Philadelphia
J.R.A.S.	Journal of the Royal Asiatic Society of Great Britain and Ireland
M.W.	Muslim World
O.L.Z.	Orientalistische Literaturzeitung
R.A.A.	Revue de l'Académie arabe
R.E.I.	Revue des Études Islamiques
R.E.J.	Revue des Études Juives
R.S.O.	Rivista degli Studi Orientali
S.I.	Studia Islamica
Z.A.T.W.	Zeitschrift für die Alttestamentalische Wissenschaft
Z.D.M.G.	Zeitschrift der Deutschen Morgenländischen Gesellschaft

INTRODUCTION

The great scholarly legacy that Ibn Khaldūn bequeathed to posterity has given him an exceptional place in the annals of Islamic historiography. This renown is based on his monumental "Universal History" (*Kitāb al-'Ibar*) in seven volumes, the first volume of which constitutes the famous "Introduction to History" (*Muqaddimah* or *Prolegomena*); on his "Autobiography" (*Ta'rīf*); and on some other smaller works, which have become known only recently.[1]

Ever since the days of the European discovery of Ibn Khaldūn in the nineteenth century, his profound socio-philosophical ideas, as embedded in his *Muqaddimah,* have been expounded and made the subject of a great number of valuable and thorough studies and monographs. Very eloquently have these ideas been evaluated by a galaxy of great Orientalists and historians.

R. Nicholson characterized Ibn Khaldūn's work by asserting that "no Muslim had ever taken a view at once so comprehensive and so philosophical; none had attempted to trace the deeply hidden causes of events, to expose the moral and spiritual forces at work beneath the surface, or to divine the immutable laws of national progress and decay. Ibn Khaldūn stood far above his age, and his own countrymen have admired rather than followed him . . ."[2] G. Sarton regarded Ibn Khaldūn as "the greatest theoretician of history, the greatest philosopher of man's experience, not only of the Middle Ages, but the whole period extending from the time of the great class-

[1] See the list of "Ibn Khaldūn's Works," following Introduction.

[2] *A Literary History of the Arabs,* pp. 438–439.

Full bibliographical details of works cited briefly in the notes are given in the "Ibn Khaldūniana" bibliography at the end of the book, or in the list of "External Arabic Sources," following the Introduction.

ical historians down to that of Machiavelli, Bodin and Vico . . ."[3] A. Toynbee did surely not exaggerate when he declared that Ibn Khaldūn's *Muqaddimah* is "the greatest book of its kind that has ever yet been created by any mind in any time or place."[4]

The renewed and revived interest in Ibn Khaldūn's legacy in our own time has centered again mainly on his sociological and philosophical ideas as manifested in the abundance of publications in this field and, in the many translations of the *Muqaddimah* from Arabic into other languages, such as Turkish, Persian, Hindu, Urdu, French, Portuguese, German, Hebrew, and above all English.[5] The prevailing concentration on Ibn Khaldūn as the author of the *Muqaddimah,* as a philosopher of history, and as a sociologist of culture tends, however, to narrow down his scope and to provide but a partial picture of his scholarly contribution, just as an undue stress on Ibn Khaldūn as the authority of Western Islam would limit his work to but one region of the vast Islamic civilization.[6]

In order to evaluate and appraise Ibn Khaldūn's total contribution to history and to place him properly in the annals of Islamic and general historiography, the totality of his writings must be taken into consideration. It must be born in mind, also, that Ibn Khaldūn is one of the historians whose life is closely interwoven with his scholarly work and that a clear distinction must be made between the two major phases into which Ibn Khaldūn's activities have to be divided, namely into the "Maghribī" period in North Africa and Spain, which extended from his birth in 1332 until his departure from Tunis in 1382, and into the "Egyptian" period, which lasted from 1382 until his death in 1406.

By correlating and viewing his research in conjunction with his manifold personal experiences, it becomes evident that Ibn Khaldūn was more than the author of the *Muqaddimah* and more than the unquestionable authority on Western Islam, and that his scholarly research encompassed also the history of Eastern Islam and the history of the non-Islamic peoples of the East.

While his life and research in the Maghrib have been thoroughly and

---

[3] *Introduction to the History of Science,* III, 1770, 1775–1776

[4] *A Study of History,* III, 322 ff.

[5] For these, see "Translations of the *Muqaddimah,*" following Introduction.

[6] Ibn Khaldūn's history of the Berbers was the first part of his *Kitāb al-'Ibar* which became known to Western scholars through de Slane's edition, *Kitāb al-Duwal al-Islāmīya bi-l-maghrib,* and his French translation, entitled *Histoire des Berbères et des dynasties musulmanes de l'Afrique septentrionale.* This fact may be responsible for the over-emphasis of Ibn Khaldūn's contribution to Western Islam.

adequately investigated, the "Egyptian" phase of Ibn Khaldūn has thus far remained largely unexplored and has not yet been subjected to a thorough critical analysis in all its facets.[7]

The present study concentrates, therefore, deliberately and intentionally on Ibn Khaldūn's "Egyptian" phase and tries to present Ibn Khaldūn in his two-fold role, first as a public figure in the service of the Mamlūk state, and secondly as an author and historian during his twenty-three-years' stay in Cairo. The first part focuses on all the various aspects of purely biographical relevance. It will be shown how Ibn Khaldūn, after his arrival in Cairo, was again drawn into the public arena and became involved in political entanglements which he had so fervently hoped to avoid in his new environment. Though he was determined to devote his time in Egypt to scholarship and research, matters turned out differently. He suffered also in Egypt, as he did during his stay in the Maghrib, from an inner conflict between an urge for action and the wielding of power and influence on the one hand, and a devotion to learning, research, and scholarship on the other. It was a conflict which continued to remain the typical feature of his complex personality. The temptation of a public career and a leading position in the ruling circles was too strong to let him remain too long, or exclusively, in the seclusion and isolation of academic life in Egypt.

In Part One, his various public and official assignments during his stay in Egypt are unfolded, with all the ups and downs of his public career, as recorded by himself and by external Arabic sources:[8] his association with Sultan Barqūq, whose protégé he became; his role as a Maghribī consul; his activities as educator and professor at many educational institutions in Cairo; his function as a Mālikite Chief Cadi, to which post he was appointed at various periods not less than six times; and last, but not least, his diplomatic activities which culminated in his dramatic meeting with the great Mongol conqueror, Tamerlane, outside the gates of Damascus in January, 1401.

The great variety of Ibn Khaldūn's official public functions in Egypt had undoubtedly absorbed a large amount of his time and effort. Yet they occupied only a fraction of the twenty-three years of his stay in Egypt, and Ibn Khaldūn was actually free from any official responsibilities and political involvements for almost fifteen years. He was out of office as a Mālikite Chief Cadi from 1385 to 1399 and, in particular, did not hold any official position during the whole

[7] For some preliminary studies on this topic, see my publications as listed in the "Ibn Khaldūniana" bibliography.

[8] See the list of "External Arabic Sources," following the Introduction.

decade from 1389 to 1399, during which time he wore the "mantle of retirement," disappeared from the public eye, and lived in solitude and isolation. How did he use his leisure and free time, how did he fill those intervals between dismissal from one and appointment to another official position? We can hardly assume that a man of his caliber, with his scholarly ability and creativity, would sit idle and just enjoy life on the banks of the Nile. Ibn Khaldūn himself gives us an answer and allows us to recognize that he used every free moment during his stay in Egypt to devote himself to historical research and writing. This is attested by himself in such frequent statements scattered throughout his writings during his stay in Egypt as, "I devoted my time to research"; "I have not ceased to apply myself to scholarship, writing and teaching"; and "from now on I shall devote all my time to research." [9]

Ibn Khaldūn did nowhere explicitly indicate what was hidden behind these all-too-general phrases, and what was specifically meant by his repeatedly proclaimed intention of returning to his research and to scholarly writings. In combing the totality of his writings it becomes evident that his major scholarly activities in Egypt were directed toward two major fields: first, to a revision and supplementation of those of his works which he had brought along from North Africa and which had been written or drafted in the Maghrib, in particular his *Muqaddimah;* and second, to the investigation and study of new fields of historical research which had not fully engaged his attention in the Maghrib.

In regards to the revision of his "Maghribī" writings, there can be no doubt that Ibn Khaldūn had incorporated into various sections of the original North African draft of his *Muqaddimah* new material based on sources and information which became available to him only in Egypt and during his travels to the libraries in Mecca and Damascus. This is, indeed, clearly indicated by Ibn Khaldūn himself when he stated at the beginning of his *Prolegomena,* "Later on there was my trip to the East [Egypt] . . . as a result I was able to fill the gaps in my historical information about the non-Arab [Persian] rulers of those lands, and about the Turkish dynasties in the regions over which they ruled. I added this information to what I had written here [before in this connection]." [10] He alluded again at the end of his *Muqaddimah* to the additions and changes to his *Kitāb al-'Ibar* by stating, "Thereafter [while in Egypt] I revised and corrected the

[9] For references to this effect, see *Ta'rīf,* pp. 260, 278, 284, 285, 311, 347, 350 and others.

[10] *Muq.,* I, 7; *Proleg.,* I, 12.

book, and added to it the history of the [various] nations, as I have mentioned and proposed to do at the beginning of the work." [11]

This steady process of correcting and revising, adding and supplementing, carried out in Egypt, effected not only the *Muqaddimah* but also the other volumes of his history, *Kitāb al-'Ibar,* which contain many references to events and happenings which had occurred long after his departure from the Maghrib. These references and insertions, scattered all through his writings, show that there is a considerable "Egyptian stratum" mingled with the original "Maghribī stratum" in his writings.[12] It was also in Egypt that Ibn Khaldūn could penetrate into new fields and topics of historical research and to add new studies of great significance to those which had already established his fame in the Maghrib. What were these new fields and topics to which Ibn Khaldūn devoted himself in Egypt? [13]

An answer to this question is being offered in the second part of my study. In it I try, by going beyond the purely biographical aspect, to elucidate the impact which Ibn Khaldūn's long stay in Egypt had on his scholarly productivity, to examine the "Egyptian stratum" in his writings, and to deal with those specific themes within his historical writings that could be reasonably regarded as a distinct and typical "Egyptian" contribution. It will be shown that the peculiar political situation in which Ibn Khaldūn found himself throughout his career in Egypt and his proximity to the scene of great historical events confronted him with new scholarly challenges and opened new vistas for him in dealing with hitherto untouched topics of historical scholarship. Among those new fields belong his account of contemporary Mamlūk Egypt and its internal aspects, and, in particular, the biography of Sultan Barqūq which constitutes a complete life-story of the Sultan, covering his career from youth until death. He also turned his attention to the external front of the Mamlūk state and, especially, to the Mamlūk-Mongol conflict which had reached its climax in Ibn Khaldūn's own days with the appearance of the world

[11] *Muq.,* III, 434; *Proleg.,* III, 481.

[12] On the kind of insertions and additions made by Ibn Khaldūn, see my last chapter on his "Autobiography." Here it may suffice to mention that the latest date in his *'Ibar* relates to events of the year 1396–1397—twelve years after his departure from the Maghrib, while the latest date in his *Muqaddimah* deals with events of the year 1400—eighteen years after he had left Tunis.

[13] Though it was assumed by some scholars that many chapters in Ibn Khaldūn's *Muqaddimah* could not have been written by him during his Maghribī period and that for chronological reasons alone they must have been composed during his stay in Egypt, a thorough investigation of the Egyptian stratum in his writings has not been carried out.

conqueror, Tamerlane, on the scene of history. Under the impact of the actuality of the Mongol threat to Mamlûk Egypt, he, the historian, delved first of all into the past of the Mongol and Tatar tribes which had come out of Asia under their leader, Jenghiz Khān, and he produced a historical survey of the events from the time of Jenghiz Khān on until Tamerlane's siege of Damascus in 1401, thus becoming the historian and biographer of Jenghiz Khān and his descendants, as well as of Tamerlane.

Ibn Khaldûn's contribution to historical scholarship while in Egypt went even beyond the confines of Islam and encompassed also a part of the non-Islamic world, the history of non-Arabic and pre-Islamic peoples in the East. Based on the many sources which became available and accessible to him in Egypt, Ibn Khaldûn gave considerable attention to the three pre-Islamic monotheistic religions: Judaism, Zoroastrianism, and Christianity. His approach to this topic indicates that he was particularly aware of the cultural and religious highlights in the history of the non-Islamic peoples, of the decisive books and ideas that molded and shaped the spiritual history of these nations, and of the great religious personalities who made history. In his survey of ancient Israel and Judaism, of ancient Iran and of early Christianity, he therefore laid much stress on the Holy Books of the monotheistic religions, their translation and transmission; on the religious leaders and personalities; on the religious institutions; and also on the heresies and dissensions, and the sectarian movements and formations of every kind.

The last, but by far not the least important, of his original accomplishments in Egypt was the composition and conclusion of his own life-story, his "Autobiography" (*Ta'rîf*), which, in its complete form has become available only recently.

In investigating all those aspects of his research which can be credited to his Egyptian stay, Ibn Khaldûn emerges as a most prolific and creative author during his twenty-three-year stay in Egypt, who, despite his many public and official duties, was also able to penetrate into new fields of historical research and make, with them, a unique contribution of great significance to Islamic and general historiography.

PRIMARY SOURCES

Ibn Khaldūn's Works

A. 'IBAR

'Ibar=Kitāb al-'Ibar wa-Dīwān al-Mubtada' wa-l-Khabar fī Ayyām al-'Arab wal-'Ajam wal-Barbar wa man 'aṣarahum min dhawī as-Sultān al-Akbar.
Edited by Shaikh Naṣr al-Hūrīnī.
Būlāq, 1867–1868. 7 vols.

For further texts see:
Ta'rīkh Ibn Khaldūn al musammā bi-Kitāb al-'Ibar. . . .
By 'Alāl al-Fāsī and 'Abd al-'Azīz b. Idrīs, and edited by Emīr Shakīb Arslān. (Only vol. II and part of vol. III, pp. 1–189 of Būlāq text with a separate volume of Appendices.)
Cairo, 1936. 3 vols.

Ta'rikh al-'Allāmah Ibn Khaldūn.
By Joseph A. Dāghir.
Beirut, 1956–1959. 7 vols.

B. MUQADDIMAH

Muq.=Muqaddimat Ibn Khaldūn.
Edited by E. Quatremère. (*Les Prolégomènes d'Ebn Khaldoun.*) *Notices et Extraits des Manuscrits, de la Bibliothèque Impériale.*
Paris, 1858. Vols. XVI, XVII, XVIII.

Of many other texts of the *Muqaddimah* published in Beirut, Cairo, and Būlāq, see:
Kitāb al-'Ibar.
Edited by Hūrīnī.
Būlāq, 1867. Vol. I.

Ta'rīkh al 'Allāma, Ibn Khaldūn.
By J. A. Dāghir.
Beirut, 1956. Vol. I.

Muqaddimat Ibn Khaldūn.
By Wāfī, 'Alī 'Abd al-Wāḥid. With notes and introduction.
Cairo, 1957–1962. 4 vols.

C. TA'RĪF

Ta'rīf=at-Ta'rīf bi-Ibn Khaldūn wa-riḥlatuhu gharban wa-sharqan.
Edited by aṭ-Ṭanjī, Muḥammad b. Tāwīt.
Cairo, 1951.
Republished by J. Dāghir in *Ta'rīkh al-'Allāmah,* at the end of Vol. VII.
Beirut, 1960, pp. 793–1224.

D. SMALLER TREATISES

Lubāb al-Muḥaṣṣal fī Uṣūl ad-Dīn (*de Ibn Jaldun*), Arabic text of his *Treatise on Logic.*
Edited by P. Luciano Rubio.
Tetuan, 1952. Vol. I.

Shifā' as-sā'il litahdhībia'l-masā'il.
Edited by Muḥammad b. Tāwīt aṭ-Ṭanjī.
Istanbul, 1958.
Another edition by Ignace Abdo Khalifé, *Recherches de l'Institut de Lettres Orientales de Beyrouth,* XI. Beirut, 1959.

See also:
Revue de l'Institut des Manuscrits Arabes.
Cairo, 1958, IV, 355. 1959, V, 167, no. 88. See also p. 178, no. 50; *cf. ibid.*

Translations of the Muqaddimah

French:

by William MacGuckin, Baron de Slane.
Les Prolégomènes d'Ibn Khaldoun, Notices et Extraits des Manuscripts de la Bibliothèque Imperiale.
Paris. 1863, 1865, 1868. Vols. XIX, XX, XXI. Reproduction photomécanique, Paris, 1934–1938. 3 vols.

Turkish:

by Mehmed Pīrī Zādeh (1725 ff.) and Aḥmed Jewdet Pāshā.
'Unwān as-siyar, Tarjumen muqaddamat Ibn Khaldūn.
Constantinople, 1860 ff. 3 vols.

by Zakir Kadiri Ugan.
Ibni Halduni Mukaddime.
Ankara-Istanbul. 1954–1957. 3 vols.

Urdu:

by Aḥmad Ḥusain Allāhābād and 'Abdu-r Raḥmān Shams al-Ulemā'.
Ibn Khaldūn's Muqaddimah.
Lahore, 1924, 1932. 3 vols.

Persian:

by M. Parvīn Gonābādy.
Muqaddimah.
Teheran, 1957–1959. 2 vols. New revised edition, Teheran, 1966–1967.

Portuguese:

by José Khoury e Angelina Bierrenbach Khoury.
Ibn Khaldūn, Os Prolegômenos ou Filosofia Social. Introdução por J. Almansur Haddad.
Publicação Instituto Brasileiro de Filosofia, São Paulo. 1958–1960. 3 vols.

Hindi:

by Rizvi Athar Ahbas.
Ibnī Khalādūna Kā Mukaddama.
Lucknow, 1961.

Hebrew:
by Immanuel Kopilewitz.
Ibn Khaldūn: Aqdamot la-Historia. With notes and introduction.
Bialik Institute, Jerusalem. 1967.

English:
by Franz Rosenthal.
The Muqaddimah, An Introduction to History.
Bollingen Series. New York, 1958. 3 vols.
(Quoted as *Proleg.* in notes in this study.)

EXTERNAL ARABIC SOURCES

Ibn al-Khaṭīb, Lisān ad-Dīn (d. 1374).
al-Iḥāṭah fī Akhbār Gharnāṭah.
Cairo, 1901. See s. v. Maqqarī.

Ibn al-Furāt, Nāṣir ad-Dīn Muḥammad (d. 1404).
at-Ta'rīkh, The History of Ibn al-Furāt. Vol. IX. Edited by C. K. Zurayk and Nejla Izzedin.
Beirut, 1936–1938.

Qalqashandī, Aḥmad b. 'Alī (d. 1418).
Ṣubḥ al- A'shā.
Cairo, 1913–1919. 14 vols.

Maqrīzī, Taqī ad-Dīn Aḥmad b. 'Alī al- (d. 1442).
al-Khiṭaṭ: al-Mawā'iẓ wa-l-I'tibār bi-Dhikr al-Khiṭaṭ wa-l-Āthār.
Būlāq, 1270, H. (1853). 2 vols.

Kitāb as-Sulūk li-ma'rifat duwal al-mulūk.
Ms. Paris, no. 1728.

Ibn Qāḍī Shuhbah, Taqī ad-Dīn (d. 1448).
adh-Dhail 'alā Ta'rīkh al-Islām.
Ms. Paris, no. 1599.

Ibn Ḥajar al-'Asqalānī, Shihāb ad-Dīn (d. 1449).
al-Durar al-kāmina fī a'yān al-mī'a ath-thāmina.
Hyderabad, 1929–1930. 4 vols.

Ibn Ḥajar al-'Asqalānī, Shihāb ad-Dīn (d. 1449).
Inbā' al-Ghumr bi-abnā' al-'umr.
Ms. Paris, nos. 1603–1604.

Ibn 'Arabshāh, Aḥmad b. Muḥammad (d. 1450).
Kitāb 'Ajā'ib al-maqdūr fī akhbār Tīmūr (*Ahmedis Arabsiadae, Vitae et rerum gestarum Timuri, qui vulto Tamerlanes diciture, Historia*). Edited by Jacob Golius.
Leyden, 1636. 2 vols.

Kitāb Fākihat al-khulafā' (*Fructus Imperatorum*). Edited by G. Freytag.
Bonn, 1832–1852. 2 vols.

'Ainī, Badr ad-Dīn al- (d. 1451).
'Iqd al-Jumān fī Ta'rīkh ahl az-Zamān.
Ms. Paris, no. 1544.

Ibn Taghrī Birdī, Abu l-Maḥāsin Yūsuf (d. 1469).
an-Nujūm az-Zāhira fī Mulūk Miṣr wal-Qāhirah. Edited by William Popper. University of California Publications in Semitic Philology.
Berkeley–Los Angeles. Vol. V, 1932–1936; Vol. VI, 1915–1923.

Al-Manhal as-Ṣāfī wa'l Mustaufī ba'd al-wāfī.
Ms. Paris, no. 2069.
See Gaston Wiet, "Les biographies du Manhal Sāfī," *Mémoires présentés à l'Institut d'Egypte.*
Cairo, 1932. Vol. XIX.

Sakhāwī, Muḥammad b. 'Abd ar-Raḥmān as- (d. 1487).
aḍ-Ḍau' al-lāmi' li-ahl al-qarn at-tāsi'.
Cairo, 1353–1355 H. 12 vols.
(Quoted as *Ḍau'* in this study.)

Sakhāwī, Muḥammad b. 'Abd ar-Raḥmān as- (d. 1487).
al-I'lān bi-t-tawbīkh li-man dhamma ahl at-ta'rīkh.
Damascus, 1349 H.

Suyūṭī, 'Abd ar-Raḥmān Jalāl ad-Dīn as- (d. 1505).
Kitāb Ḥusn al-Muḥādarah fī Akhbār Miṣr wa-l-Qāhirah.
Cairo, 1321 H. 2 vols.

Ibn Iyās, Muḥammad b. Aḥmad (d. 1524).
Badā'i' az- Zuhūr fī Waqā'i ad-Duhūr.
Būlāq, 1311–1312 H. 2 vols.

Al-Maqqarī Aḥmad b. Muḥammad (d. 1632).
Nafḥ aṭ-Ṭīb min Ghuṣn al-Andalus ar-Raṭīb
Būlāq, 1311–1312 H. Vol. IV, 414–426.

Ibn al-'Imād, Abu l-Falāḥ (d. 1679).
Shadharāt adh-Dhahab fī Akhbār man Dhahab.
Cairo, 1350–1351 H. 8 vols.

PART ONE:

Ibn Khaldūn's Life and Public Functions in Mamlūk Egypt

1

ARRIVAL IN EGYPT IN 1382

On December 8, 1382, there arrived in the harbor of Alexandria, Egypt, a boat from Tunis from which disembarked, among others, a North African Muslim scholar by the name of Abū Zayd 'Abdu-r-Raḥmān Walī ad-Dīn al-Ḥaḍramī, known as Ibn Khaldūn, who, then fifty-two years of age, left behind him in the Maghrib a remarkable and illustrious career as a statesman, historian and scholar.

His ancestors, the Banū Khaldūn, hailed from South Arabia, Ḥaḍramaut, from where they emigrated in the eighth century to Spain and lived in Seville for many centuries, there rising to power and influence. In the early part of the thirteenth century the Banū Khaldūn moved to Tunis, the capital of the province of Ifrīqiya where they played a significant role in the political arena of their time. It was in Tunis that Ibn Khaldūn was born on May 27, 1332.[1] There he acquired a thorough education under the guidance of prominent Shaikhs and teachers in such fields as Qur'ān, Tafṣīr, Ḥadith, grammar, syntax, and poetry.

He began his political and public activities in Tunis[2] before he even reached the age of twenty with his appointment to the office of seal-bearer and secretary by the Ḥafṣid Sultan, Abū Isḥāq of Tunis.

In 1355 he was called to the court of the Merinid ruler, Abū 'Inān Fāris in Fez, and served at the latter's invitation as his secretary. Having lost favor in the court because of his friendship and sympathy

[1] The Muslim date of his birth is Ramaḍān 1, 732 H.

[2] For a full account of Ibn Khaldūn's life, background, education, and activities in the Maghrib, in North Africa, see *Ta'rīf*, ed. Ṭanji, pp. 1–245. Since this "pre-Egyptian" phase of Ibn Khaldūn's life, until 1382, has been investigated and presented in all its details, it will suffice here to give only the general outlines as but an introduction to his "Egyptian" phase.

with this ruler's Ḥafṣid rival, Abū Sālim, Ibn Khaldūn was imprisoned on February 10, 1357, for almost twenty-one months, but after his release, following the death of Abū 'Inān on November 27, 1358, he was appointed by the new Merinid Sultan Abū Sālim in Fez to be his confidential secretary (*kātib as-sirr*). Later, in 1359, he was assigned to the office of the "Maẓālim," in charge of jurisdiction over complaints.

When Abū Sālim was killed in 1362 as the result of a revolt, Ibn Khaldūn did not feel safe in Fez and left for Spain. He crossed the Straits of Gibraltar and arrived in Granada on December 26, 1362. There he was welcomed by King Muḥammad V of Granada and his vizier, Lisān ad-Dīn Ibn al-Khaṭīb,[3] a close friend of Ibn Khaldūn. The king entrusted him with a special mission to the then most powerful Christian ruler of Spain, Pedro of Seville, to conclude a peace treaty between them. At this dramatic meeting[4] between Pedro and Ibn Khaldūn (1363–1364)—a highlight of his colorful career in the political arena in the Maghrib—Pedro, impressed by Ibn Khaldūn, invited him to stay with him and offered him as an inducement the return of the property of his ancestors in Seville.[5] Ibn Khaldūn declined this offer, however, and returned to Granada. Due to a conflict with the vizier Lisān ad-Dīn Ibn al-Khaṭīb Ibn Khaldūn decided to leave and he returned again to North Africa in February, 1365.

In this period, Ibn Khaldūn was involved in tribal politics. He was assigned to rally the tribes under the flag of Sultan 'Abd al-'Azīz, and in Bougie he had to collect taxes from the Berber tribes on behalf of Abū'l-'Abbās. In subsequent years, Ibn Khaldūn stayed in Biskra, Bougie and Tlemcen, returning in 1372 to Fez. He made a second visit to Granada in 1374, returning to North Africa in 1375. In the course of his manifold activities in the Maghrib, Ibn Khaldūn had met with most of the contemporary Arab and Berber rulers and high officials and served many of them in one or another capacity.[6]

---

[3] He was one of the most distinguished poets, historians, and statesmen of his time. Many of the letters exchanged between these two scholars, preserved in the "Autobiography," testify to their friendship. See Sakhāwī, *Ḍau'*, IV, 147.

[4] Ibn Khaldūn was introduced to Pedro the Cruel by his Jewish Court-Physician, Ibrāhīm b. Zarzar; about him, see later.

[5] *Ta'rīf*, pp. 84 ff.; for a description in European literature of this historic meeting with Pedro—Ibn Khaldūn's first contact with Christian Europe—see Sanchez-Albornoz, *Ben Jaldūn ante Pedro El Cruel*, II, 422–23; Pons-Boignes, *Ensayo Bio-Bibliográfico*, pp. 353–354; Irving, "Peter the Cruel and Ibn Khaldūn," in *I.L.*, XI, 5–17.

[6] For the various rulers and their dynasties in whose service Ibn Khaldūn stood, see E. von Zambaur, *Manuel de Généalogie et de Chronologie pour l'Histoire de l'Islam* (Hanover, 1927), reprinted 1955.

This turbulent period of his life in the Maghrib, lasting over a decade, was terminated by his retreat in 1375 to Qal'at Ibn Salāmah, a village in the province of Oran. He stayed there four years until 1378, detached from all political activities and devoting his time exclusively to research and writing, the result of which was the composition of his famous *Muqaddimah* (*Prolegomena*), the first volume of his great "Universal History," the *'Ibar*.[7]

In order to continue his research in a place with greater library facilities he decided, after recovering from an illness, to leave Qal'at Ibn Salāmah in 1378 and to return to his birthplace, Tunis, which was then ruled by the Ḥafṣid Sultan Abu'l-'Abbās. From the winter of 1378 until 1382 he continued his research in Tunis. During the last years of Ibn Khaldūn's stay in Tunis he met with increasingly severe opposition, with the enmity and intrigues of court officials who, being jealous of his standing, incited even the Sultan against him. Leading in these intrigues was the Imām of the mosque of Tunis, the Mālikite Judge, the Mufti Ibn 'Arafah (d. 1401). They succeeded in removing Ibn Khaldūn from the Sultan's court.[8]

Ibn Khaldūn intended to abandon public life in North Africa completely, even though it had brought him to the pinnacle of leadership and influence, and had established his fame as a statesman, diplomat, and historian. He now yearned to free himself from political involvements and responsibilities. Tired of being subjected to the whims and moods of the ruler and to the machinations of the jealous courtiers around him, he conceived the plan of leaving the Maghrib, his native land, and of changing the geographical scene of his activities by emigrating to Egypt and devoting himself there exclusively to scholarly activities. Under the pretext of making the pilgrimage to Mecca, he finally received permission from the Sultan of Tunis, Abu'l-'Abbās, to leave for the East. Ibn Khaldūn himself says: "I begged the Sultan [of Tunis] to free me and to permit me to fulfill my religious duty [to go on a pilgrimage], [a request] which he granted me."[9]

[7] *Ta'rīf*, pp. 229–230; *Proleg.*, I, 53. He stated, "I completed the *Muqaddimah* in that remarkable manner to which I was inspired by that retreat, with words and ideas pouring into my head like cream into a churn, until the finished product was ready."

[8] *Ta'rīf*, pp. 232, 244. Ibn 'Arafah and Ibn Khaldūn were the most representative personalities of the Ḥafṣid dynasty in the Maghrib of the fourteenth century. The jealousy and hatred of Ibn 'Arafah toward Ibn Khaldūn may well be regarded as a major cause of Ibn Khaldūn's departure for Egypt. See Sakhāwī, *Ḍau'* IX, 240–242; IV, 146; and Brunschvig, *La Berbérie orientale*, II, 391 ff.

[9] *Ta'rīf*, pp. 245–246. Some regard Ibn Khaldūn's departure from Tunis as a real flight from his homeland. See Ibn Ḥajar, Ms. Arabe, Paris, no. 1603, fol. 223; Ibn al-'Imād, *Shadharāt-adh-Dhahab*, III, 77.

In the harbor of Tunis at that juncture there happened to be anchored a ship belonging to Alexandrian merchants, which was about to sail for Alexandria, and on which Ibn Khaldūn embarked on October 24, 1382, leaving his homeland Tunis, and his family behind him. After about forty days of a stormy and dangerous sea journey, he arrived in Alexandria on December 8, 1382, finding the city in a festive mood since it was only twelve days after the coronation of the new Circassian Mamlūk Sultan of Egypt, al-Malik aẓ-Ẓāhir Abū Sa'īd Barqūq (1382–1399). Ibn Khaldūn remained in Alexandria for a full month, planning to embark on his pilgrimage to Mecca, but owing to circumstances, the nature of which is not reported, he decided to postpone his pilgrimage and go on to Cairo where he arrived on January 6, 1383.

While still in the Maghrib, Ibn Khaldūn had, of course, heard much about Cairo as a great cultural and economic center from merchants, travellers, and pilgrims returning from Egypt. On one occasion he stated: "At this time, we hear astonishing things about conditions in Cairo and Egypt as regards luxury and wealth in the customs of the inhabitants there. Many of the poor in the Maghrib even want to move to Egypt on account of that and because they hear that prosperity in Egypt is greater than anywhere else. The common people believe that this is so because property is abundant in those regions, and [their inhabitants] have much property hoarded, and are more charitable and bountiful than the inhabitants of any other city. [However] this is not so, but, as one knows, the reason is that the civilization [population] of Egypt and Cairo is larger than that of any other city one might think of. Therefore [the inhabitants of Egypt] enjoy better [living] conditions." [10] He also expressed the view while still in the Maghrib that "Today, no [city] has a more abundant sedentary culture than Cairo. It is the mother of the world, the great center of Islam, and the mainspring of the sciences and the crafts." [11] He remembered that one of the scholars of the Maghrib on his return had remarked, "Whoever has not seen Cairo has not seen the glory of Islam."

The immediate impression that Cairo made on Ibn Khaldūn must have been indeed overwhelming. He eloquently expressed his admiration for this great capital and describes in glowing terms the beauty and grandeur of this city, its buildings and bazaars, the crowded streets, the great material prosperity, the luxury of its inhabitants, the castles and

---

[10] Of his many references to Cairo as a cultural and scientific center, see in particular *Muq.*, II, 238, 309, 338, 339, 345, 380–384.

[11] *Muq.*, III, 274, quoted as translated in *Proleg.*, III, 315.

palaces, schools and workshops. "I saw there moons and stars shining among its scholars: on seeing the Nile, I thought I was seeing the river of paradise; one would say that its waters came from heaven, and spread everywhere good health, as well as fruits, flowers, and riches. I saw the city filled with passers-by, and its bazaars of merchandise. We did not stop talking about this city for a long time and admiring its great and beautiful buildings." [12] It must have been indeed a great and new experience for Ibn Khaldūn, who until then had never been outside of the region of the Maghrib and southern Spain.

From the moment Ibn Khaldūn set foot on Egyptian soil he made Cairo his new home, and except for a few short journeys, including the pilgrimage to Mecca in September, 1387, he remained in Cairo until his death in the month of March, 1406, and never returned to his native land, the Maghrib. The "Egyptian phase" of his life and activities [13] thus comprised over twenty-three years under the rule of the Mamlūk Sultan Barqūq and under the early reign of Barqūq's son and successor, Faraj.

[12] *Ta'rīf*, pp. 246–247.

[13] The major source for Ibn Khaldūn's "Egyptian phase" is his own account in *Ta'rīf*, ed. Ṭanjī, pp. 246–384. This account has to be supplemented, however, by two other categories of biographical relevance, firstly by those many biographical data scattered throughout his *Muqaddimah* and other volumes of his *Ibar*, and secondly by external Arabic sources which contain relevant data on his life and activities in Egypt, which have not been recorded by himself. See the list of "External Arabic Sources."

2

PROTÉGÉ OF SULTAN BARQŪQ

Shortly after his arrival in Cairo, Ibn Khaldūn came into contact with a most influential personality at the court of Sultan Barqūq, namely the Emir Alṭunbughā al-Jūbānī (d. 1395),[1] who occupied, during the early rule of Barqūq, the high office of Emir of the Council (*emīr al-majlis*), and was the second-ranking official at the court of Barqūq. Ibn Khaldūn became a close friend of al-Jūbānī, who was instrumental in opening for Ibn Khaldūn the road to influence and official standing by introducing him to Sultan Barqūq. If not for this Emir, Ibn Khaldūn might never have risen to that standing which he finally attained in his public career during his stay in Egypt. Whether the Sultan, always interested in supporting scholars of fame and known for his patronage of "men of the pen," asked to make his acquaintance, or whether he himself made known his desire to be presented to him, we are not told. In any event, the first meeting between Barqūq and Ibn Khaldūn resulted immediately in a close and intimate friendship which endured, with one, rather long and sad, exception, throughout the Sultan's life and rule.

Ibn Khaldūn's whole life in Egypt and all his further activities were determined and influenced by the confidence Sultan Barqūq had in him. This relationship was indeed a turning point in Ibn Khaldūn's life and the very key for the understanding of his subsequent activities in Egypt. He had free access to the Sultan, had many private audiences with him, and throughout his stay in Egypt found in Barqūq a protector and patron who overwhelmed him with favors and kindness, who granted him generous allowances and afforded him moral support in all his undertakings. According to Ibn Khaldūn's own record, Barqūq made his stay pleasant, consoled him in his for-

[1] About him see later, note 18, chapter 5, Part One.

eignness and remoteness from his homeland, and enlarged his stipend according to his habit with scholars.[2]

One of the first manifestations of Barqūq's interest in Ibn Khaldūn was the Sultan's intervention on behalf of his family, his wife and children, who were left behind in Tunis when he departed hurriedly for Egypt. In Cairo, Ibn Khaldūn waited impatiently for their arrival, but the Sultan of Tunis refused to let them go and prevented their departure so as to force Ibn Khaldūn to return to him.

Very little is known about Ibn Khaldūn's immediate family. His father had died in 1348, a victim of the Black Plague, as was probably the case with his mother, who is nowhere mentioned by him. Of his two brothers, Muḥammad and Abū Zakarīyā' Yaḥyā, only the latter became prominent as a historian and a statesman in his own right.[3] Ibn Khaldūn married, in the Maghrib, the daughter of Muḥammad b. al-Ḥākim (d. 1343), the Ḥafṣid general and minister of war,[4] but her name and the names of their children are not mentioned by him. External sources inform us, however, that he had five daughters and two sons, and that the names of the latter were Muḥammad and 'Alī.[5] No sources have yet been found to shed light on these two sons and the role they played, if any.

Ibn Khaldūn mentioned his family only in a general way. His many travels and adventures in North Africa and Spain caused frequent separations from them. Sometimes they were put into the care of relatives, such as a maternal uncle in Constantine, or relatives in other places such as Tlemcen and Biskra.[6]

Being most anxious to bring his family from Tunis to Cairo, and encouraged by the friendly attitude of Sultan Barqūq toward him, Ibn Khaldūn asked his royal protector to intervene on their behalf and to request the Sultan of Tunis to permit his family to leave for Cairo. The Sultan agreed and wrote a letter, on April 8, 1384, to Abu'l-'Abbās, the Sultan of Tunis, full of flattery and exaggeration, in which the Sultan of Tunis is informed that "the great, the noble, the learned, the illustrious, the honorable, respected and erudite 'Abdu-r-Raḥmān Ibn Khaldūn al-Mālikī, the friend of kings and sultans, the

---

[2] Many such expressions of gratitude towards Barqūq's generosity and kindness can be found all through his writings.

[3] Ibn Khaldūn mentioned his ancestors, as well as his father and his brothers in various places in his *Ta'rīf*. On his brother Yaḥyā, the historian, see Brockelmann, *G.A.L.* II, 240–241; Suppl. II, 340; and Sarton, *Introduction to the History of Science,* III, part 2, p. 1766.

[4] See *Muq.,* I, 326.

[5] Ibn Qāḍī Shuhbah, Ms. Paris, fol. 181.

[6] See *Ta'rīf,* passim, and *'Ibar,* V, 420, 440, 479–480, 501, etc.

teacher of students, has come to our noble country and preferred to stay with us in Egypt, not because he decided to renounce his country, but due to his love for us and closeness to our desire, since we found in him more than one can expect . . . He has been praising your Royal Highness [the Sultan of Tunis] since his arrival, enumerated your noble character, which led us to love you more and more." The letter goes on to say that since this Ibn Khaldūn wished to have his wife and children, at present in Tunis under the Sultan's protection, with him all the time he spends here (Cairo), "we decided to write to your Royal Highness to give order for the family of the above-mentioned great scholar, to remove all the obstacles and to prepare them to be received honorably by the bearer of our message . . ." Barqūq sent this letter through a special messenger and asked to send the family on one of the royal ships so that they would arrive safely in his country.[7]

The intervention of Barqūq in favor of Ibn Khaldūn's family proved to be successful, and the Sultan of Tunis permitted them to sail for Egypt. Ibn Khaldūn was most grateful for Barqūq's interest in his family. However, the ship on which his wife and five daughters travelled ran into a violent storm near the harbor of Alexandria (in August, 1384) and was wrecked. All its passengers, except one, drowned in the Mediterranean Sea. This great misfortune which befell Ibn Khaldūn was a terrible blow to him—a loss from which he never recovered.[8]

[7] For the complete text, see *Ta'rīf*, pp. 249–253.

[8] This tragic end of most of his family is repeatedly mentioned by Ibn Khaldūn. See *Ta'rīf*, especially pp. 259, 285, 311, and 332.

3

THE "MAGHRIBĪ CONSUL" IN CAIRO

With Ibn Khaldūn's departure from Tunis, and the tragic death of his wife and daughters, his connections with North Africa and Spain were by no means severed. He remained in correspondence with his friends in the Maghrib and in Spain, and visitors from the Maghrib, pilgrims and merchants, whenever passing through Cairo at that time used to call on Ibn Khaldūn, their distinguished native son, now living in the land of the Nile. It was through them that Ibn Khaldūn was kept steadily informed about the events of the West, just as during his former stay in the West, it had been the returning Maghribī pilgrims and merchants who had brought him news about the state of affairs in the East.

Ibn Khaldūn's attachment to the Maghrib while in Cairo is illustrated by the fact that Maghribī personalities coming to Cairo during this period used to call first on Ibn Khaldūn and were then introduced by him to the Sultan. Once, when a Maghribī pilgrim caravan, on its way to Mecca, was attacked by robbers, the help of the Sultan was solicited through the medium of Ibn Khaldūn. On another occasion, when the well-known Shaikh Yūsuf b. 'Alī b. Ghānem fled from the Maghrib to Cairo, and asked for the intervention of Barqūq on his behalf with the Sultan of Tunis, it was Ibn Khaldūn who took charge of the matter, since Barqūq was at that time in Damascus. Upon the Sultan's return to Cairo, Shaikh Yūsuf was presented to him by Ibn Khaldūn. Barqūq agreed to comply with the Shaikh's desire and wrote a letter of intercession in favor of the Shaikh to the Sultan of Tunis.[1]

[1] *Ta'rīf,* pp. 339–340.

During his pilgrimage, on which he embarked on September 27, 1387, with the permission of the Sultan, Ibn Khaldūn associated himself mainly with other pilgrims from the Maghrib, renewing his contacts and exchanging with them views about the situation in the West.[2]

It is worth noting that shortly after Ibn Khaldūn arrived in Cairo and was warmly received by Barqūq, he wrote to the Sultan of Tunis, probably at the suggestion of Barqūq, that Barqūq admired pedigreed horses from the Maghrib, because of their strength and resistance, and urged him therewith to send such horses to Barqūq.[3] The Sultan of Tunis, responding to this suggestion, sent five of his best horses to Barqūq on the same ship which was also to bring Ibn Khaldūn's wife and daughters to Egypt, and which sank shortly before its arrival in Alexandria and thus, Ibn Khaldūn recounts, "perished the horses with all that the ship contained."

Barqūq decided then to send some of his own emirs to Tunis to buy horses for him. Before dispatching these emirs in person, Barqūq consulted with Ibn Khaldūn as his expert and advisor in Maghribī affairs. Ibn Khaldūn helped to arrange the itinerary of the emirs' journey and also advised Barqūq to write letters to the Sultan of Tunis, the Sultan of Tlemcen and the Sultan of Fez in Morocco. For each of these sultans the envoys carried gifts, comprising cloth, perfume and sabres as suggested by Ibn Khaldūn.

The fact that Ibn Khaldūn continued his contacts with the leading circles in North Africa was regarded by Sultan Barqūq as a useful asset. It appeared that the unswerving and favorable support which the Sultan accorded to Ibn Khaldūn was motivated not only by the Sultan's usual patronage of scholars but, in this case, also by his desire to avail himself of Ibn Khaldūn's diplomatic skill, qualifications and manifold connections with the ruling class of the Maghrib.

Ibn Khaldūn thus became virtually the "Maghribī Consul" for Barqūq, the interpreter and mediator between the Maghrib in the East and Mamlūk Egypt in the West. He functioned as an advisor to Barqūq in all matters pertaining to Maghribī affairs and particularly to Maghribī visitors to Cairo, and thus strengthened further the con-

[2] *Ta'rīf*, pp. 261–278. During Ibn Khaldūn's pilgrimage to Mecca, a letter from the vizier and poet, Ibn Zamrak of Granada, was delivered to him, together with a poem written in honor of Barqūq, for the Sultan. This poem, written in Maghribī Arabic, was transliterated by Ibn Khaldūn himself into the Mashriqī script and presented to Barqūq. It is significant that Ibn Khaldūn was asked by the vizier to send him some scholarly books from Egypt.

[3] About the procurement of horses from the Maghrib for Barqūq, a great lover of horses, see *'Ibar*, V, 420–425, 440–442, 479–480.

nections between Fez and Cairo. Ibn Khaldūn seemed to have been very conscious of this diplomatic service that he could render to Barqūq (and later also to Faraj) as the link, the mediator, between East and West, Egypt and the Maghrib, and affirmed that he gained in all this a good reputation because he succeeded in establishing a good and permanent relationship between the two rulers.

The attachment that Ibn Khaldūn felt to the Maghrib while in Egypt was exhibited by him also outwardly by his stubbornly clinging to his Maghribī garb,[4] for he never wore the customary robe of an Egyptian judge. This was scornfully emphasized by his contemporary enemies, "because he was fond of behaving and appearing different in everything." He remained throughout his life a Maghribī and, indeed, a foreigner in Egypt, ostentatiously exhibiting by his attire and attitude that he belonged to the West.[5] So anxious was Ibn Khaldūn to stress always his Maghribī origin that he asked to be introduced to Tamerlane at his memorable meeting in Damascus, as we shall see, as a "Maghribī Mālikite Cadi."

His Maghribī background, his continuous attachment to the Maghrib, even in Egypt, undoubtedly explain some of the difficulties which Ibn Khaldūn encountered under the new social and political conditions in Egypt. He could not free himself entirely from his "African" heritage, and despite his adaptability to changing situations, it was this "African" heritage which prevented him from being completely assimilated to the new Mamlūk-Egyptian society within which he lived during the last twenty-three years of his life.

[4] See chapter 5, Part One, on his function as a Mālikite Chief Cadi.

[5] This continuous feeling of kinship to the Maghrib resulted also in an important literary transaction. It was in conjunction with the exchange of goods and presents of the Sultan that Ibn Khaldūn sent in 1396, through messengers of Barqūq, a greatly revised and augmented copy of part of his *Kitāb al-'Ibar,* to the sultan of the Merinid dynasty at Fez, where it is still housed in the library of the Qarawīyīn Mosque; see Lévi-Provençal, *J. A.*, 1923, pp. 161–168; and A. Bel, *Catalogue,* p. 6, n. 4, and nos. 1266–1271.

4

TEACHER AND EDUCATOR IN CAIRO

When Ibn Khaldūn arrived in Cairo, his reputation as a historian, as the author of the *Muqaddimah* and of a history of the Berbers and the Zanātah, and above all as a leading figure in the political arena of the West had undoubtedly preceded him. No wonder, therefore, that the news of the arrival of a scholar of his caliber spread quickly in Cairo and attracted the attention of scholarly circles. He was soon invited to lecture at the famous al-Azhar mosque,[1] and he accepted this invitation, delivering a series of lectures, attended by many scholars and court officials. The lectures most probably dealt with his philosophy, his theory of *'aṣabīyah* and his concepts of the rise, development and decline of states and societies as expounded by him in his *Muqaddimah*.[2]

After his debut on the intellectual stage of Cairo, Ibn Khaldūn was appointed by Sultan Barqūq to the position of a professor at the Qamḥīya Madrasah (college) in Old-Cairo in 1384, to teach Mālikite jurisprudence (*fiqh*).[3] He must have felt quite privileged to be connected with so famous and ancient a college, established by Sultan Ṣalāḥ ad-Dīn and to serve there as director of courses and teacher of jurisprudence. His inaugural lecture, attended by many notables of the court, undoubtedly was quite a literary event. In it he gave a historical survey of the spread and expansion of Islam, the glory of Egypt and its ruler; he praised the Turkish Mamlūk dynasty

[1] See *Ta'rīf*, p. 248. It was probably the above-mentioned Emir al-Jūbānī who was instrumental in inviting Ibn Khaldūn. About the history of this famous educational and theological institution, see B. Dodge, *Al-Azhar, A Millenium of Muslim Learning* (Washington, 1961).

[2] For this concept, see later, note 33, chapter 6, Part One.

[3] *Ta'rīf*, p. 253.

and especially Barqūq, who "has honored me despite the inadequacy of my person, and who has magnified my ability." [4]

Ibn Khaldūn's next appointment in the educational field, as teacher of Mālikite law was that to the *madrasah* in the Bayn Qaṣrain Street in Cairo, also called al-Barqūqīya or aẓ-Ẓāhirīya, a college built by Barqūq himself.[5] From this post, however, Ibn Khaldūn was soon removed through the pressure of some of the notables at the court. The nature of the quarrel between Ibn Khaldūn and some of the notables, and the kind of intrigues behind the scene, are not indicated. The exact date of his dismissal from the Barqūqīya also is not given, but it must have taken place before Ibn Khaldūn's pilgrimage to Mecca, which he began in September, 1387. After Ibn Khaldūn's return, having been absent from Cairo for about eight months, Barqūq appointed him in January, 1389, as a professor of *hadīth* (science of tradition) at the Ṣarghitmishīya Madrasah, named after the Emir Sayf ad-Dīn Ṣarghitmish, who had established this college as a pious foundation (*waqf*).[6] The inaugural lecture which Ibn Khaldūn gave and whose full text is preserved, was chiefly devoted, after the usual praise of his protector, Barqūq, to the great theologian and jurist, Mālik ibn Anas (d. 795) and his famous work *al-Muwaṭṭa,* which Ibn Khaldūn had already studied in his youth under prominent teachers in Tunis. Ibn Khaldūn felt that his first appearance at this school before a distinguished audience was a great success. With no lack of modesty he flattered himself; "Their looks followed me with admiration and respect, and many foresaw high positions for me thanks to my abilities." [7]

He occupied the position at the Ṣarghitmishīya Madrasah until the Sultan appointed him, it seems in addition to this, to another college in April, 1389, namely to the Baybarsīya Khānqa (college). This *khānqa* in Cairo, built by Sultan Baybars (1305) and established as a *waqf,* was one of the most important ones in Cairo. When the controller and head of this *khānqa,* the Imām of Barqūq, died shortly after Ibn Khaldūn's return from his pilgrimage to Mecca, the Sultan appointed Ibn Khaldūn in his place as controller and overseer.

[4] For the full text of his inaugural lecture, see *Ta'rīf,* pp. 279–285.

[5] *Ta'rīf,* pp. 286 ff.

[6] *Ta'rīf,* pp. 293–294. See Ibn Khaldūn's special chapter on "The Direction of Instruction and the Khānqa," which reveals a sound understanding of the educational and cultural background of the Mamlūk society. For the topography and history of the various educational institutions with which Ibn Khaldūn was associated during his stay in Cairo, see, apart from Ibn Khaldūn's own references, al-Maqrīzī, *Khiṭāṭ,* II, 256–258, 364–374.

[7] *Ta'rīf,* pp. 296–310; *Muq.* III, 4–6.

There was, however, one condition of the *waqf*-deed which Ibn Khaldūn could not fulfill at the outset. The endowment deeds of this *khānqa* demanded that the controller and other officials must be one of the Ṣūfis. Ibn Khaldūn, therefore, had to enter the college as a Ṣūfi and was present there for just one day in order to become eligible and to qualify for the position to which Barqūq had appointed him.

It seems that no other assignment in the educational field had been as highly valued by Ibn Khaldūn as this. Apart from the prestige attached to this position, the *waqf* yielded a great revenue and the allowances for the controller and the overseer were exceedingly high. Ibn Khaldūn must have been very pleased with this appointment and expressed his feelings of gratitude to the Sultan in the highest terms. He remained in this post at the Baybarsīya Khānqa, however, only a little over one year, "until the rebellion of an-Nāṣirī occurred." [8]

The many courses and lectures which Ibn Khaldūn gave in his various educational posts and assignments on jurisprudence, tradition, and history, must have attracted many students and scholars. Ibn Khaldūn himself referred only in general terms to the large attendance at some of his public lectures and audiences, and mentioned nowhere any single person as a student or disciple of his by name. We learn, however, from external Arabic sources, that Ibn Khaldūn could count among his students in Cairo a galaxy of important scholars and historians of his time, some of whom were most favorably impressed by his lectures and regarded him as highly competent.[9]

Muḥammad b. 'Ammār,[10] who studied the principles of jurisprudence under him and attended his lectures on history, praised Ibn Khaldūn most highly and said: "The 'Muqaddimah' comprises all branches of learning, and similar stylistic perfection has not yet been achieved by anybody, and cannot be attempted to be achieved. Indeed, it is one of the works whose titles are not descriptive of their contents." Taqī ad-Dīn al-Maqrīzī (d. 1442), the famous Mamlūk historian, was also a great admirer of Ibn Khaldūn [11] and, having attended his lectures (on problems of the *Muqaddimah*), said: "Nothing like it has ever been done [before] and it would be difficult for

[8] All the details concerning his affiliation with the Baybarsīya Khānqa are presented by Ibn Khaldūn in a special chapter entitled, "Appointment to the Baybarsīya and dismissal from it"; *Ta'rīf*, pp. 311–313, and pp. 330 ff.

[9] The views of some of Ibn Khaldūn's students, who later became famous historians themselves, have been collected by Sakhāwī, in *Ḍau'*, IV, 147 ff., and in his *I'lān*. For the following quotations see F. Rosenthal, *A History of Muslim Historiography*, pp. 40, 419–420.

[10] Sakhāwī, *Ḍau'*, VIII, 232–234.

[11] Ibn Khaldūn's influence on Maqrīzī would deserve a special study.

anyone who might try, to achieve something like it [in the future] . . ." According to him, "It is the cream of knowledge and sciences and the pleasure of sound intellects and minds. It informs about the reality of happenings and events. It refers to the representatives of everything in existence in a style which is more brilliant than a well-arranged pearl and finer than water fanned by a zephyr." Ibn Ḥajar, al-'Asqalānī, (d. 1449), another leading historian of Mamlūk Egypt,[12] who knew him personally, admitted as others have done that his lecturing was extremely good, fluent and interesting.[13]

[12] Ibn Ḥajar voiced his view, however, that Ibn Khaldūn had not acquired through his studies a precise knowledge of historical events (*akhbār*), in particular those concerned with the East.

[13] For references to other students of Ibn Khaldūn's in Egypt, such as Ibn Damamīnī, al-Bisāṭi, al-Biskrī, and others, see Sakhāwī's *Ḍau'*, VII, 172, 186; X, 195, 312; and Ben Cheneb, *Etude sur les personnages . . .*, pp. 514–515.

5

MĀLIKITE CHIEF CADI IN CAIRO

First Appointment as Chief Cadi (1384–1385)

Important as Ibn Khaldūn's activities were as professor and teacher at various colleges in Cairo, and significant as his role was as Maghribī Consul for Barqūq, his major assignments to which he was appointed in Egypt were in the legal field, in the administration of justice. In the course of his stay in Egypt he was appointed no fewer than six times to the office of the Mālikite Chief Cadi, the official legal rite of the Maghribites.[1]

In Egypt, jurisdiction rested in the hands of the four Chief Cadis, one for each legal school or rite (*madhbab*),[2] a practice established in the time of the Mamlūk Sultan Baybars (d. 1277). Priority was given, however, to the Chief Cadi of the Shāfi'ite rite, since it was the official legal rite in Egypt. The Shāfi'ite Chief Cadi had greater influence than the other judges and enjoyed special privileges such as the right of supervision of the foundations for orphans, of wills and testaments. According to Islamic theory and practice, the appointment of a Chief Cadi of any rite was a royal act and entirely in the hands of the supreme ruler. Barqūq's close friendship with Ibn Khaldūn may explain the fact that as soon as a vacancy had occurred, he appointed Ibn Khaldūn to fill the post of a Mālikite Chief Judge in Cairo.[3]

---

[1] On all the questions connected with the institution of the cadi in Islamic society and particularly in Mamlūk Egypt, see Tyan, *Histoire de l'organisation judiciare;* Annemarie Schimmel, *Kalif und Kadi im spätmittelalterlichen Ägypten, in Die Welt des Islams* (Berlin, 1942), XXIV, 1–128; *Law in the Middle East,* ed. Majid Khadduri and Herbert J. Liebesny, 100 ff.

[2] Ibn Khaldūn discusses the four legal schools in *Muq.* III, 6–14.

[3] His various appointments as Mālikite Chief Judge are, of course, mentioned in all the contemporary Arabic sources. See Ṣalība, *Listes Chronologiques,* pp. 112–115.

With Ibn Khaldūn's appointment to the Chief Cadiship of the Mālikites on August 11, 1384, Ibn Khaldūn was again drawn into public life which he had hoped, according to his own statement, to abandon. During his stay in the Maghrib, Ibn Khaldūn had acquired some practical experience in the judicial field. In 1359 the Merinid ruler, Abū Sālim, appointed him to be "Examiner of Complaints" (*an-nāẓir fi'l maẓālim*),[4] an office which had belonged to the functions of a cadi, but Ibn Khaldūn had actually never been a cadi in the Maghrib. His official functions at the courts of various Maghribī rulers had certainly afforded him some insight into the methods of the administration of law. More than the practical experience, he had sufficient theoretical knowledge since he had studied assiduously the legal treatises of earlier Muslim jurists and theologians, in particular al-Māwardī (d. 1058).[5] Ibn Khaldūn knew very well what was expected of a cadi, having expounded in great detail the qualifications and duties of a cadi in the Islamic state.

When Sultan Barqūq offered him the cadiship, Ibn Khaldūn tried at first to evade the appointment and the great honor accorded to him by his protector Barqūq, but Barqūq refused to yield and Ibn Khaldūn finally, apparently gladly, complied with his royal friend's insistence and request. He was invested with the cadi's "robe of honor" as part of the official inauguration of a Chief Judge in the reception hall of the Palace of the Sultan and began to exercise his juridical function from his office in the Ṣālaḥīya Madrasah, in the Bayn Qaṣrain quarter (between the two palaces in Cairo.) [6]

Ibn Khaldūn entered upon his new role with the best of intentions and with a high degree of idealism, fully aware of his responsibility to the people and to the Sultan, his protector. He tried to justify to the utmost the confidence the Sultan had in him and stated: "I applied the Law of God with impartiality and without consideration of rank and power, putting the opposing parties always on the same footing, helping the weak to regain his rights, trying to learn the truth of the matter and rendering justice." In explaining the principles which guided him in the administration of justice, as well as the difficulties which he encountered he confessed that he was particularly stubborn against yielding to illegal practices, corruption and bribery and that

---

[4] *Ta'rīf*, p. 77. See also *Muq*. I, 399–400, where Ibn Khaldūn explains the duties of his office.

[5] The classical account on all these matters is al-Māwardī's *Aḥkām-as-Sulṭanīya;* see H. F. Amedroz, "The Office of the Cadi according to al-Māwardī," in *J. R. A. S* (London, 1910), pp. 761–796; see also *J. R. A. S.* (1911), pp. 635–674.

[6] The subsequent account and quotations pertaining to his first appointment as Chief Cadi are derived from *Ta'rīf*, pp. 254–260.

he refused honors which other cadis used to accept. The main obstacles in his administration of justice were the *shuhūd,* the notaries, some of whom were either dishonest or under the influence of the officials of the court and misused their functions for selfish and partisan purposes.[7]

He resented also those incompetent *muftis,* who assumed the function of judges and issued decisions contrary to the position taken by the court. Ibn Khaldūn was particularly enraged by those officials who evaded the conditions laid down in the *waqf* deeds and used their authority for their own personal advantage. His account of the reforms which he deemed necessary, such as the abolition of certain abuses and the reform of the prevailing corrupt practices of the notables and emirs shed important light on the legal aspects of that period of Mamlūk history. He realized that favoritism was so widespread in the time of Barqūq, that even high emirs permitted themselves to interfere in the legal field and bear pressure on judges and witnesses.

It seems that from the very outset the appointment of Ibn Khaldūn to the Chief Judgeship had been viewed with amazement and resentment by some of the notables. That he was appointed lecturer at the Azhar Mosque or professor at the Qamḥīya College or at other educational institutions in Cairo was, even in their view, fitting and suitable for a man of Ibn Khaldūn's qualities. But that a "foreigner," recently arrived from the Maghrib, should be called upon to occupy one of the highest judicial offices in Cairo and should even dare to introduce reforms and abolish illegal practices and conventions of long standing, could hardly remain unchallenged.

Soon Ibn Khaldūn learned a bitter lesson. His reforms were vehemently resented and aroused antagonism and discontent in influential circles. His opponents were probably jealous of him because he was persona grata with the Sultan and because they were afraid of losing their long-established, but illegally obtained, prerogatives. They reacted to his rigidness in matters of justice by slandering him, marring his reputation by lies, rumors and false accusations; they even plotted against him before the Sultan and accused him of issuing unjust decrees and of being ignorant of the law. The opposition reached such a point that a petition was sent to Barqūq demanding his investigation. Ibn Khaldūn was, indeed, summoned before the *Ḥājib al-Kabīr,* the Grand Chamberlain, and the judges and *muftis* assembled to examine "his case."

Ibn Khaldūn himself seemed to regard the opposition of a clique

[7] About the meaning and function of these various officials see the literature listed in note 1 of this chapter and the respective articles in E.I.

of high officials against him as motivated by his refusal to accept bribes [8] in accordance with previously established conventions, and by his strict insistence on rendering justice on the basis of the merits of each case. He felt himself surrounded by venom and envy and in a very bitter tone stated: "Then enmity on every side increased and the atmosphere became dark between me and the government officials." Despite the pressure of the court circles on Sultan Barqūq to dismiss Ibn Khaldūn, Barqūq seems to have firmly backed his protégé as long as it was possible. It was this moral support which, in all probability, caused Ibn Khaldūn to believe that "I acquitted myself of the obligation of a judge to the satisfaction of the Sultan."

Ibn Khaldūn succumbed finally to the pressure of the court and decided to resign on June 17, 1385. At this juncture he received word that the ship on which his wife and daughters were travelling had sunk in a heavy storm, and his desire to resign was strengthened. He writes: "My sorrow was intense and my spirit became troubled. I wished to retire . . ." Barqūq finally "allowed" him to resign and the office of the Mālikite Chief Cadi was returned to its previous holder. Ibn Khaldūn stated that Barqūq took pity and permitted him to withdraw, thus "releasing me from the chains of the office."

The news of Ibn Khaldūn's appointment as a judge, the difficulties he encountered, and his final resignation reached the West, the Maghrib, also. His activities in Egypt were closely followed by his Maghribī friends, and it is no wonder that his dismissal from the judgeship found an echo in the West. The Chief Cadi of Granada, an old friend of Ibn Khaldūn, wrote him: "I have heard that you have been dismissed from the Cadiship which you had occupied, whereby you have suffered . . . I heard that your resignation was approved." [9]

On the other side, there was also a different reaction among certain persons in the Maghrib. Resentment against him was voiced in the following terms: "The office of a judge was considered to be the highest of all offices, but when it was occupied by this one [Ibn Khaldūn] it became just the opposite." Sakhāwī, who had included this statement in his biographical sketch of Ibn Khaldūn, added: "and the people of the Maghrib when they heard of Ibn Khaldūn's activities as a judge were puzzled and considered the Egyptians to be of little knowledge and culture." [10] This view loses much of its validity, however,

[8] See in this connection the illuminating study by F. Rosenthal, "Gifts and Bribes: The Muslim View," *Proceedings of the American Philosophical Society* (Philadelphia, 1964) CVIII, 135–144.

[9] *Ta'rīf*, pp. 274–276.

[10] Sakhāwī, *Ḍau'*, IV, 146 ff.

when it is realized that it was expressed by Muḥammad b. 'Arafah, the Grand Mufti of Tunis, who had long been a personal enemy of Ibn Khaldūn and who could hardly be credited with fair and objective judgment in matters pertaining to him.[11]

In any case, Ibn Khaldūn's administration of justice as a Mālikite Chief Cadi must have been one of the most controversial issues of his time. His own conduct was vehemently criticized by some contemporary Egyptian writers. Thus, Sakhāwī expressed his discontent with Ibn Khaldūn's conduct as a judge and remarked: "Ibn Khaldūn treated the people very severely and arrogantly. He offended them for he did not stand up for any of the judges when they entered to greet him; when he was criticized for that he would offer a general apology to all. . . . He was harsh and maltreated many of the important secretaries and notaries, punishing them with slapping, which he called 'sticking' [hitting with a spear] and when he was angry with anyone he would say, 'stick him' and they would be slapped until their neck was red."

Other critics, however, opposed Ibn Khaldūn on the grounds of ignorance and incompetence in legal matters and lack of knowledge of usage and conventional practice. Another charge voiced was the fact mentioned above that Ibn Khaldūn as a cadi always wore his Maghribī garb [12] and never wore the customary robe of an Egyptian judge, because as they said, he liked to appear different in every respect.

However, so objective an historian and chronicler as Ibn Taghrī Birdī confirms that Ibn Khaldūn performed his duty as a judge with dignity and ability, though with strictness. He stated: "Ibn Khaldūn was exceedingly strict. He administered the office with great honor and exceedingly great regard; his conduct was praised. He rejected the requests of the high-ranking people of the government and refused to hear the appeals of the rich men. For that reason they began to speak against him [before the Sultan] until the Sultan dismissed him . . ." [13]

IBN KHALDŪN AND THE FETWĀ AGAINST BARQŪQ (1389)

Despite his removal from the Chief Cadiship, Ibn Khaldūn continued to enjoy the favor and undiminished support of the Sultan

[11] See note 8, chapter 1, Part One; and Sakhāwī, *Ḍau'*, IV, 146; IX, 240 ff.

[12] About his Maghribī affiliation, see above. On the garb of a cadi, see L. A. Mayer, *Saracenic Costumes* (Genève, 1952); and Tyan, *Histoire*, I, 288–312.

[13] al-Manhal aṣ-Ṣāfī, Ms. Paris, fols. 49–50.

who appointed him to the professorship for Mālikite law at the Ẓāhirīya school and later to other educational tasks. After having served as professor at the Ṣarghitmishīya Madrasah, he was put in charge of the Baybarsīya Khānqa in 1389. He was, however, dismissed from the educational post "after a year or so" and remained, then, without any public office for almost a decade. This retirement from public life during this decade, was connected with his participation in a legal decision (*fetwā*) against his protector, Sultan Barqūq—a topic to be clarified here because it sheds light on Ibn Khaldūn's complex and complicated personality in a crucial moment of his career.

When, in 1389, a rebellion against *Barqūq* had forced the Sultan to relinquish the throne, at least temporarily, the leaders of the rebellion, Minṭāsh and Yalbughā an-Nāṣirī, having proclaimed Malik al-Manṣūr Ḥājjī as a new Sultan, were most anxious to dispose definitely of Barqūq. They, however, could not reach agreement whether to recommend Barqūq's death or imprisonment and in order to settle this issue once and for all, a State Council was summoned by the rebels to come to a decision.[14]

On November 11, 1389, Minṭāsh summoned the State Council, which included the Caliph, the four cadis and other scholars, to secure a legal decision (*fetwā*) regarding Barqūq and a declaration of war against him. In the decision which was drafted a few days later, Barqūq was accused, among other things, of having deposed the Caliph and the Sultan, of having killed a descendant of the Prophet in the month of Muḥarram and in the sacred city, despite the fact that he was sacrosanct (the reference was to Aḥmad. b. 'Ajlān, the ruler of Mecca), of having unlawfully appropriated men's property, and of being guilty of murder and various other charges. In the final draft, submitted to the State Council, a new statement was inserted, according to which Barqūq had enlisted in his army about 600 Christians to fight against the Mohammedans. Although this, too, was not true and was only meant to deceive the scholars—as Ibn al-Furāt asserts [15]—all those present signed the decree.

The list of those present differs slightly in the accounts of the contemporary and later Arab historians, but they all confirm the presence of Ibn Khaldūn at these meetings and concur in the fact that in the presence of the Caliph, the new Sultan and the four cadis, he put,

---

[14] For the historical background of these events, see chapter 2, Part One, on Barqūq.

[15] Ibn al-Furāt, IX, 160. Ibn Khaldūn had already taken part in another *fetwā* in that year, in which the case of a person charged with heresy (*kufr*) had to be decided. See Ibn al-Furāt, IX, 112.

together with the rest, his signature on the *fetwā* against Barqūq. Thus, Ibn Khaldūn, though not being a cadi at that time and only a director of the Baybarsīya Khānqa, entered this conflict and sided voluntarily or forcibly with the rebels against Barqūq, his great benefactor, through whom he had obtained his standing and prestige in Egypt.

When the rebellion was successfully quelled and Barqūq was restored to his sultanate on February 1, 1390, Barqūq became well acquainted with the action of the emirs, cadis, and scholars in regard to the *fetwā* against him. Despite their attitude toward him, he did not deal harshly with them and ordered the freeing of some of the emirs. He released Yalbughā an-Nāṣirī and al-Jūbānī from their imprisonment in Alexandria and even reappointed al-Jūbānī Grand Head of the Guards and then Viceroy of Syria in February, 1390, and commissioned him, together with an-Nāṣirī, the commander of the armies, to march against Minṭāsh who, despite Barqūq's victory, was persistent in his revolt against Barqūq in Syria.

It was only natural that Barqūq wished to reward those few who had remained loyal and faithful to him. He therefore reappointed as Viceroy of Egypt, Emir Sūdūn ash-Shaikhūnī, who held the position of a *nāẓir* (supervisor) at the Baybarsīya Khānqa and appointed to the office of Mālikite Chief Cadi, Shams ad-Dīn Muḥammad b. ar-Rakrākī, who had refused to sign the *fetwā* and was punished bodily by Minṭāsh for his refusal and for his loyalty to Barqūq.[16]

Barqūq must have felt, however, particularly bitter about the attitude against him by one of his protégés, namely Ibn Khaldūn. Considering all the benefits he had received from Sultan Barqūq, the many signs of his generosity and benevolence, the many appointments in the educational and juridical fields, it is indeed astonishing that Ibn Khaldūn had joined in the condemnation of Barqūq and did not, like his colleague ar-Rakrākī, refuse or abstain. Barqūq, apparently full of wrath about Ibn Khaldūn's behavior, dismissed, therefore, Ibn Khaldūn from the only office that, by the grace of the Sultan, he had held during the very time of the civil war, namely the office of the controller and overseer of the Baybarsīya Khānqa.

Ibn Khaldūn and Emir Sūdūn

His dismissal from the office he held at the Baybarsīya Khānqa caused Ibn Khaldūn greater concern than any other change in his

[16] For details about ar-Rakrākī (d. 1391), see Ibn Taghrī Birdī, *Nujūm*, ed. Popper, V, 522; Ibn al-Furāt, IX, 204, 290.

public career, so rich in ups and downs, in appointments and dismissals. This is indicated by the fact that Ibn Khaldūn has devoted a special and rather lengthy chapter to this matter in which he tried to reveal the web of circumstances which, to his mind, caused his dismissal. He puts the blame for his dismissal on the Viceroy Sūdūn ash-Skaikhūnī (d. 1396),[17] then the most influential and powerful figure at the court of the Sultan, who had been appointed a viceroy of Barqūq in December, 1382. Ibn Khaldūn linked Sūdūn's attitude toward him to certain encounters and strained relationship experienced during his first cadiship and attributes Sūdūn's animosity toward him to an act of revenge against him. Ibn Khaldūn expressed his belief that Sūdūn, who was also acting as a supervisor of the *khānqa* in which Ibn Khaldūn was employed, "felt resentment against me because of some instances of opposition to certain judicial decisions which he desired [me to make] at times when I was in charge of the Cadiship; also because of the administration activities of his *dawādār* whom he appointed as his representative over the khānqa. His heart was bitter because of this. . . . Sūdūn thus succeeded in securing the permission from Barqūq to remove me from the khānqa. Another person was appointed for the post, and I was deposed from it."

The personal displeasure of one emir, even of one as high as Emir Sūdūn would hardly have been sufficient to sway the Sultan to deprive Ibn Khaldūn of his position at the Baybarsīya Khānqa. There entered another element into the picture which alone seems to explain objectively why Barqūq, after his restoration to the throne agreed to the dismissal of Ibn Khaldūn—this was Ibn Khaldūn's attitude during the revolt against Barqūq and the *fetwā* which Ibn Khaldūn signed in the State Council, together with other high officials.

It possibly did not require much effort on Sūdūn's part to convince Barqūq that this Ibn Khaldūn, in signing the *fetwā*, had disqualified himself to occupy a position of trust and confidence from the Sultan and that in view of his breech of loyalty, he deserved to be dismissed from the only office he had still occupied during the turbulent times of Barqūq's dethronement and restoration.

Indeed, Ibn Khaldūn sensed the real reason behind the dismissal order and refers apologetically to the matter of the *fetwā* by stating, "Barqūq was angry because of the fetwas of the assembly of the jurists, which Minṭāsh had demanded from us and forced us to sign and we signed it, although we used in it ambiguous terms as far as we could. The Sultan refused to accept this [explanation] and showed discontent against him [Minṭāsh] and especially against me."

---

[17] About Emir Sūdūn, see *Ta'rīf*, pp. 330–331; *'Ibar* V, 502–503.

The excuse which Ibn Khaldūn offered, namely that he was forced to sign, seemed very unconvincing. Why then did he not act as did ar-Rakrākī, who was ready to bear the consequences of his refusal? Ibn Khaldūn undoubtedly tried in these critical months to explain, or defend, his attitude to the Sultan directly. He could evidently not get the ear of the Sultan. Such an interview, it seems was not granted to him and was probably prevented from occurring by Emir Sūdūn or other leading emirs.

Ibn Khaldūn and Emir al-Jūbānī

In his distress, abandoned and forsaken by the Sultan and deprived of the last public office he had then held, Ibn Khaldūn did remember his old friend Emir al-Jūbānī who occupied during the rule of Barqūq such high offices as Emir of the Council (*emir al-majlis*), the second ranking official at the court of Barqūq. He was *aṭābak* (viceroy) of Damascus, Commander of the Egyptian and Syrian armies against Tamerlane and was successful in saving Barqūq from death during the insurrection under an-Nāṣirī and Minṭāsh. This emir was a close friend of Ibn Khaldūn since his arrival on Egyptian soil and was instrumental in many of the appointments which Sultan Barqūq accorded to Ibn Khaldūn.

It is a strange reflection on Ibn Khaldūn's character that he did not report with one word any of al-Jūbānī's previous acts of kindness toward him. He passed with complete silence over all of his connections with al-Jūbānī, and failed to express his debt of gratitude to him anywhere earlier in his writings. Only when Ibn Khaldūn's public career came temporarily to an abrupt end, at this very critical stage after his dismissal from the Baybarsīya Khānqa, did he turn to al-Jūbānī, apparently the only remaining friend of his in the court circles, and only then does he remember him.

Ibn Khaldūn addressed a letter to al-Jūbānī in the form of a poem consisting of over fifty verses,[18] a remarkable human document which reveals in a most illuminating way Ibn Khaldūn's state of mind at this juncture. From the historical context it is clear that these verses must have been written sometime between the date of al-Jūbānī's appointment by Barqūq as Commander of the Armies and his assignment to go to Syria to fight against Minṭāsh and the date of al-Jūbānī's actual departure with the armies. This can be fairly certainly concluded from Ibn Khaldūn's reference in the poem where he

[18] On al-Jūbānī see *'Ibar* V, 471–486 and passim; *Ta'rīf*, pp. 321–327, 335. For the long poem of over fifty verses see *Ta'rīf*, pp. 331–335.

wishes al-Jūbānī success in his march against Minṭāsh "in the month of Jumādā or a little thereafter."

When we strip these verses, which make up his letter of their flowery expression, metaphorical language, and flattering attributes, we realize the purpose of Ibn Khaldūn in turning to al-Jūbānī. He appeals to him to intercede on his behalf with the Sultan and to present to him his excuses and apologies. In most flattering terms he urges al-Jūbānī—"You who are his friend and chosen companion, you the shelter, the paradise," etc.—to present his case to the Sultan, to induce him to renew the Sultan's favors toward him and "to heal my broken bones." He bitterly decries the fact that he had been deprived of his livelihood: "Why was the khānqa taken from me?" and he implores al-Jūbānī to remember him. He also tries to dissipate rumors and false statements and slander about his action in connection with the *fetwā,* and states that he was forced to sign it. "And they summoned me though I had no part in the judicial offices nor was I one who drags [on the ground] his skirts beside them. They maintained," he says, "that I have said things which none could have expected to have been said by me . . . How could I have been so ungrateful . . . ?"

What was the result of Ibn Khaldūn's appeal to al-Jūbānī? We are not told whether al-Jūbānī had a chance to fulfill Ibn Khaldūn's request to see the Sultan, but Ibn Khaldūn's own words, "that his excuses were disregarded and he was shunned for some time" indicate that the intervention proved to be unsuccessful. In any event, al-Jūbānī left for Damascus, and contrary to Ibn Khaldūn's hope for and prediction of al-Jūbānī's victory, al-Jūbānī was killed in the war against Minṭāsh toward the end of 1390.

Ibn Khaldūn, having encountered the wrath and displeasure of the Sultan because of the *fetwā,* retired from public life after his dismissal from the *khānqa.* It must have hurt a man of Ibn Khaldūn's stature and character to be deprived of the royal protection and to be without any official position and recognition for almost ten years.[19]

Second Appointment as Chief Cadi (1399–1400)

When Ibn Khaldūn had resigned from his position as Mālikite Chief Cadi in 1385, his friends and well-wishers expressed the hope that they might soon see him again in the position of the Chief Cadi. This hope for a return was, indeed, realized and fulfilled—but later than expected—not until fourteen years had passed, in 1399.

[19] According to Sakhāwī, IV, 146 ff. and VIII, 233, Ibn Khaldūn continued to hold his appointment as professor of law (*fiqh*) in the Qubbat aṣ-Ṣāliḥ in Bimāristān.

How Ibn Khaldūn filled out the years in which he wore "the mantle of retirement" and disappeared from the public eye, is one of the most obscure chapters of his life.[20] Even external sources do not help out, and leave only a vacuum which has still to be filled. The one fact we learn from his own report is that he stayed for some time in the Fayyūm [21] to look after his own estates and that he was engaged in study and research. It was after this long interval that Ibn Khaldūn appeared on the scene again when Sultan Barqūq once more showed him favor, and appointed him for the second time to the Mālikite Chief Cadiship in 1399.

The way was open for Ibn Khaldūn's reentry into the juridical field under Barqūq when some of those notables and emirs at the court, to whose simmering animosity Ibn Khaldūn had ascribed the fact of his being neglected and ignored, passed away and when the position of the Mālikite Chief Cadiship became vacant. Barqūq then sent for him in the Fayyūm, and Ibn Khaldūn could proudly record, "The Sultan put the necklace back on those who had previously worn it [restored the offices to the men as before] and he returned also to me his usual generosity, benevolence and kindness." [22]

Ibn Khaldūn was apparently only too ready to accept again the position of Chief Judge for which he had undoubtedly begun to strive ever since his first dismissal. In a self-confident mood he writes: "Sultan Barqūq would have continued to consider me the most capable person to occupy the post of judge had it not been for some of the emirs and leading courtiers." Ibn Khaldūn flattered himself, saying: "I acquitted myself of the obligations of this position according to the well-known conditions imposed by law and custom . . . and the Sultan manifested his satisfaction with what he had heard about me."

Only one month after Ibn Khaldūn's second appointment to the Mālikite Chief Cadiship, Sultan Barqūq died on June 30, 1399. According to Islamic law a Chief Cadi, a personal representative of the sultan and personally appointed by him, loses, ipso facto, his position upon the death of the ruler, unless he is reappointed upon the accession of the new ruler. Though the new sultan, Barqūq's son Faraj,

[20] It was this decade which can be regarded as the most creative period of his stay in Egypt, affording him the leisure to devote himself exclusively to his research and to accomplish much of what we may regard as his "Egyptian" contribution to scholarship. See the Part Two of this study.

[21] Apparently Ibn Khaldūn frequently attended his own lands in the Fayyūm, which he had probably received as compensation after his dismissal from the Qamḥīya Madrasah; *Ta'rīf,* pp. 254, 347.

[22] For the following account of his second cadiship, see *Ta'rīf,* pp. 347–351.

confirmed Ibn Khaldūn in his post as Chief Cadi, Ibn Khaldūn could not hold this position very long.

All through his second occupancy of the Chief Cadiship, Ibn Khaldūn again met with the same opposition and attacks on behalf of some of the emirs. The charges against him included the fact that he increased at various times the number of the deputy judges (*nuwwāb*) and notaries (*shuhūd*), a practice quite contrary to what he did during the first appointment as judge. The opposition to Ibn Khaldūn supported a candidate who, for the greater part of the time, served as a deputy for Mālikite judges and was urged by friends to aspire to and to claim the post of Chief Judge for himself. Ibn Khaldūn accused him of having given money to the important officials and emirs to intercede in his favor and plot against him. In consequence of these intrigues, Ibn Khaldūn could not hold his position very long and Sultan Faraj, yielding to the pressure, dismissed Ibn Khaldūn from his post in September, 1400.

The second resignation or dismissal of Ibn Khaldūn from the position of a Mālikite Chief Cadi did, however, by no means terminate his role as a cadi. In fact, he was called back to the judgeship after his second incumbency no fewer than four times more, as we shall see.

6

MEETING WITH TAMERLANE IN DAMASCUS (1401)

Journey to Damascus

In the West, the Maghrib, Ibn Khaldūn had led a very exciting and dynamic life. He occupied a great variety of high-ranking positions in the service of many rulers of the Ḥafṣīd and Merinid dynasties, changing his masters as frequently as his place of action. Compared with his steady movements and travels in the Maghrib, Ibn Khaldūn's external life in Egypt was relatively stable. Only three times in the course of his Egyptian sojourn of twenty-three years did he leave Cairo for a short period. His pilgrimage to Mecca, planned in 1382 and finally carried out in 1387, took him away from Cairo for about eight months. After an interval of thirteen years, in March, 1400, he went to Damascus in his official capacity as a Mālikite Chief Cadi, at the request of the young Sultan Faraj. On this occasion Ibn Khaldūn asked the Sultan for permission on his way back to Cairo to visit the Christian holy places in Palestine, Jerusalem, Bethlehem and Hebron (May, 1400), and it was granted to him.[1]

His third and last journey away from Cairo brought Ibn Khaldūn again to Damascus, toward the end of November, 1400, when an expeditionary force was sent there in order to repulse the Mongol conqueror, Tamerlane, who, after the conquest and destruction of Aleppo, had marched towards Damascus. At the time Sultan Faraj proclaimed the march of the army to Damascus, Ibn Khaldūn was "out of office,"

[1] For his first visit to Damascus and the descriptions of the Holy Places in Palestine, see *Ta'rīf*, pp. 349–350.

and was detached from the post of a Mâlikite Chief Cadi. Despite this, Ibn Khaldûn was summoned to accompany Faraj and the royal party, together with other emirs and cadis, to Damascus.

Since a cadi, even when dismissed and out of office continued, according to general practice, to be called a cadi—"once a cadi, always a cadi"—he could, always expect to be invited, even after his resignation or dismissal by the sultan, to fulfill certain official functions in the interest of the state. It was also a common practice in Mamlûk society to entrust a Chief Cadi with diplomatic or military missions, to negotiate peace treaties, and even to assign him military command and military operations.[2] It was probably due to Ibn Khaldûn's standing as a former Chief Cadi and as a man of experience and a scholar, that he was summoned by Emir Yashbak ash-Sha'bānī, a powerful figure among the emirs of the court, to join Sultan Faraj's forces.[3] Though Ibn Khaldûn was then already seventy years of age and had been in Damascus only half a year earlier, Yashbak insisted on Ibn Khaldûn's joining Sultan Faraj's party. Faraj, then about thirteen years old, could hardly have expressed such a desire, nor is it clear whether or not Ibn Khaldûn was a personal friend of Yashbak, who desired Ibn Khaldûn's presence in view of his special abilities and qualifications as a diplomat, scholar, and historian. Somehow forced by Yashbak, Ibn Khaldûn, after some pressure ("though with gentleness of speech and considerable generosity") had been put on him, agreed reluctantly to accompany Faraj and his party. Ibn Khaldûn could hardly have foreseen that this journey to Damascus would provide him with the greatest experience of his already colorful career and would climax in his dramatic confrontation with the great Mongol conqueror, Tamerlane, outside the gates of Damascus in January, 1401.

Sultan Faraj left Cairo with his regular army, the emirs, and cadis on November 19, 1400, and went to Raydānīya, the customary first encampment when an army went on a campaign, about a mile or so north of Cairo. The advance force left Raydānīya on November 26 and the Sultan followed with the main army on November 28,

[2] About the cadi in Mamlûk society, see the literature mentioned above, note 1, chapter 5.

[3] Yashbak had been, under Barqûq, Grand Treasurer (*khāzindār*), and, together with another emir, had been appointed also tutor or guardian of Barqûq's infant son, the later Sultan Faraj; his duties brought him in close relations with the Sultan, since he was charged with supervising the execution of the Sultan's orders. He was promoted to the rank of dawādār, military or executive secretary of Egypt; about this office see *Muq.* II, 24.

1400. Faraj arrived in Gaza on December 8, and after a short stay in Shaqḥab, about twenty-two miles south of Damascus, he moved on to the city, where he and his party, including Ibn Khaldūn, arrived on December 23, 1400,[4] forestalling Tamerlane's army which shortly after had reached the outskirts of Damascus.[5] Ibn Khaldūn took up his residence in the 'Ādilīya Madrasah, northwest of the Omayyād Mosque, some 650 feet east of the Citadel, where the other notables and cadis were also staying.[6]

Without going into all the military and political ramifications of the approaching Mamlūk-Mongol conflict (which will be dealt with in Part Two of this study), it might suffice for the understanding of the personal situation in which Ibn Khaldūn found himself to give here only the major outlines. Faraj did not stay more than two weeks in Damascus because rumors of a seditious plot in Cairo against him and his government, caused him to return hastily with some of his emirs to Cairo, leaving Ibn Khaldūn and other notables behind.[7] The inhabitants of Damascus were perplexed when they realized the following morning that the Sultan and most of his emirs had fled and that they were left without military command and leadership. It was in this confusion and under these unexpected circumstances that the leaders of Damascus decided, after consultation with Ibn Khaldūn, as expressly stated by him, to accept Tamerlane's previous offer of an armistice. They appointed Ibn Mufliḥ [8] as their spokesman to ask for the security of their homes and families and to negotiate a favorable peace.

From the Walls of Damascus to the Camp of Tamerlane

Ibn Khaldūn, who until then remained in his residential quarters in the 'Ādilīya Madrasah, entered the picture only when Ibn Mufliḥ,

[4] Faraj's camp was at Qubbat Yalbughā, although according to Ibn Iyās, I, 323, it was in al-Qaṣr al-Ablaq, "The Striped Palace," outside the city wall, west of the citadel.

[5] In *Ta'rīf*, p. 368, Ibn Khaldūn expressly stated that Faraj and his army had arrived in Damascus first.

[6] For all topographical questions see the studies by M. Gaudefroy-Demombynes, *La Syrie à l'époque des Mamlouks* (Paris, 1923); and by K. Wulzinger and C. Watzinger, H. Sauvaire, and J. Sauvaget.

[7] This plot in Cairo, which caused the sudden return of the Sultan Faraj and his emirs as mentioned in *Ta'rīf*, p. 367, is also described in detail by the contemporary Arabic sources.

[8] About Ibn Mufliḥ al-Ḥanbalī ad-Dimashqī, generally called not Burhān ad-Dīn, as Ibn Khaldūn does, but Taqī ad-Dīn, see Sakhāwī, *Ḍau'*, I, 167–168; for further details see part two. Sakhāwī compared Ibn Mufliḥ's mission to Tamerlane with Ibn Taymīya's visit, a century earlier, to Ghāzān in Damascus.

after his second visit to Tamerlane,[9] had returned and informed Ibn Khaldūn that Tamerlane had asked about him, inquiring whether he had left with the armies of Egypt or whether he was still in the city. How Tamerlane knew at all of Ibn Khaldūn's presence in Damascus is not quite clear. He might have gotten the information through the many spies and informers working for him in Damascus.[10] There would be, of course, no need for Tamerlane to ask about Ibn Khaldūn, had Ibn Mufliḥ told Tamerlane that Ibn Khaldūn was among the cadis and emirs who were left behind when Faraj and his party fled to Cairo and that Ibn Khaldūn was among those who, at the meeting in the 'Ādilīya Madrasah advised the leaders of Damascus to surrender and to come to terms with Tamerlane.

Be this as it may, the very fact that Tamerlane had asked about Ibn Khaldūn would imply that Ibn Khaldūn's fame had reached Tamerlane and that he had previous knowledge of Ibn Khaldūn's presence in Damascus. This fact undoubtedly must have most strongly appealed to Ibn Khaldūn's vanity, highly flattering him, and may have given him the idea and incentive to meet with the great world conqueror in person. Indeed, Ibn Khaldūn admitted quite frankly later in a letter to the Maghribī ruler that "When I heard that the Sultan Tīmūr [Tamerlane] had asked about me, I could not help seeing him and I went out from Damascus to present myself in his council." [11]

Ibn Khaldūn was motivated to go out of Damascus, not only by his curiosity and passionate desire to meet with the great world-conqueror in person; there was another reason for his decision. When, the surrender terms which the official delegation, headed by Ibn Mufliḥ, had negotiated with Tamerlane were brought back to Damascus and read in the Omayyād Mosque, a dispute arose because not all of the leaders of Damascus, nor the populace, approved the reliance on the surrender terms. Rumors of this dispute reached Ibn Khaldūn late at night at his residence and, being seized by the fear of "some rash attempt on my life," as expressly stated by him—since he was among those who advocated the acceptance of Tamerlane's peace offer—Ibn Khaldūn arose at dawn, and hastened toward a group of judges who were at the city gate, asking them for permission to let him go out, in view of the anxiety which had seized him to meet Tamerlane.

[9] This second visit of Ibn Mufliḥ to Tamerlane must have taken place on January 8, 1401. Ibn Mufliḥ returned to the city the following morning, January 9.

[10] It is well known that Tamerlane used as spies "experts in Arabic, Greek, Hebrew, and every other language and likewise in astronomy, geometry, magic and witchcraft, gifted with all of these powers." See B. de Mignanelli's "Vita Tamerlani," ed. Fischel, in *Oriens*, p. 214.

[11] *Ta'rīf*, pp. 380–381.

Since all the gates had been closed by the emirs and the Viceroy of the Citadel (*nā'ib al-qala'*) refused exit through the Naṣr Gate,[12] Ibn Khaldūn, following the precedent set by Ibn Mufliḥ and his party, left the city by letting himself down from the top of the wall of Damascus by means of a rope (*ḥabl*).[13]

When Ibn Khaldūn came down from the wall,[14] probably on Monday morning, January 10, 1401, he found one of Tamerlane's officials near the gate and was introduced to Shāh Malik,[15] one of the Banū Jaghaṭāi whom Tamerlane had designated as his Governor of Damascus. Ibn Khaldūn described his first contact with the Mongol officials as follows: "I said to them, 'May Allāh prolong your lives,' and they said to me, 'May Allāh prolong your life,' and I said, 'May I be your ransom,' and they said to me, 'May we be your ransom.' " After the customary exchange of greetings, Shāh Malik offered him a mount and sent with him one of the Sultan's retinue who conducted him to Tamerlane's camp.

Standing at the entrance of Tamerlane's tent, permission came out to seat him there in a tent adjoining his reception tent. Ibn Khaldūn was then introduced to Tamerlane with the additional title, the "Maghribī Mālikite Cadi," probably at Ibn Khaldūn's own suggestion.[16] Actually, Ibn Khaldūn had never been a cadi in the Maghrib, nor did he hold at this juncture the office of a Mālikite cadi in Egypt. Ibn Khaldūn most likely believed that Tamerlane would be more kindly disposed toward him and that his own importance would be enhanced if his Maghribī origin could be stressed and if he could disassociate himself from the Syrian Mamlūk cadis and emirs as much as possible.

Ibn Khaldūn observed when approaching the audience-tent that Tamerlane "was reclining on his elbow while platters of food were passed before him, which he was sending one after the other to groups of Mongols sitting in circles in front of his tent." Upon entering, Ibn Khaldūn spoke first, greeting him with "Peace be with you,"

[12] About the role of the viceroy, see later.

[13] From Ibn Khaldūn's own description, it is obvious that he left Damascus not in any official capacity, not as a member of a delegation, but went out of his own volition as an individual to meet Tamerlane. This has to be stressed in view of the erroneous statements of later Egyptian historians such as Ibn 'Arabshāh, Ibn Qāḍī Shuhbah, and Ibn Tagrī Birdī, who say that Ibn Khaldūn was part of the official delegation under Ibn Mufliḥ sent to Tamerlane, and that only then, when Ibn Khaldūn appeared before the world-conqueror, did the latter learn of him.

[14] The following, if not otherwise indicated, is based on *Ta'rīf*, pp. 366–382.

[15] Shāh Malik was one of the leading emirs of Tamerlane who became the Viceroy (*nā'ib*) of Damascus on behalf of Tamerlane.

[16] This is another indication of his continuous attachment to his Maghribī heritage.

and making a gesture of humility, probably by bowing his head. Thereupon Tamerlane raised his head and stretched out his hand to Ibn Khaldūn, which he kissed. He made a sign to him to sit down, which he did. Ibn Khaldūn was also asked to partake of a food called *rishta,* a kind of soup containing macaroni, which the people were "experts in preparing." [17] He describes how "some dishes of it were brought in, and Tamerlane made a sign that they should be set before me. I arose, took them, and drank, and liked it, and this impressed him favorably. I then sat down and we remained silent."

The haste with which Ibn Khaldūn had left Damascus to meet with the Mongol conqueror did not allow Ibn Khaldūn to follow the established custom of presenting Tamerlane with some gifts. Advised by one of his friends, who knew of the Mongol customs to submit to the conqueror some gift, however small its value might be. Ibn Khaldūn went out, probably after the formal and initial meeting with Tamerlane, to choose from the market in Damascus an exceedingly beautiful Qur'ān copy, a beautiful prayer rug, a copy of the famous poem *al-Burda* by al-Būṣīrī (d. 1296), and four boxes of the excellent Cairo sweetmeat (*ḥalāwa*). Ibn Khaldūn took all these as gifts to Tamerlane and entered Tamerlane's reception hall.

The presentation of the gifts [18] is described by Ibn Khaldūn as follows: "When he saw me arriving he stood up and made a sign to me to sit at his right, where I took a seat, some of the leaders of the Jaghaṭāi being on both sides of him. After having sat there for a little while, I moved over in front of him and pointed to the presents which I have mentioned and which were in my servants' hands. I set them down, and he turned toward me. Then I opened the Qur'ān, and when he saw it, he hurriedly arose and put it on his head.[19] Then I presented the *Burda* to him; he asked me about it and about its author, and I told him all I knew about it.[20] I next gave him the prayer rug, which he took and kissed. Then I put in front of him

[17] About this special dish which is described as macaroni or a soup containing it, see Ibn Baṭṭūta, *Voyages* (Paris, 1893–1914), II, 365–366; and M. Rodinson in *R.E.I.* (Paris, 1949), p. 138, note 9.

[18] Ibn Khaldūn's account of the presentation of the gifts to Tamerlane is reported by him in *Ta'rīf,* p. 377 ff., as having taken place at some subsequent meetings with him. This scene is described here in order not to interrupt the survey of the topics of their discussion.

[19] The placing of the Qur'ān, or any other holy book, on the head as a sign of reverence is a well-known custom among Asiatic rulers.

[20] The *Qaṣīdat al-Burda* is a celebrated poem in honor of Muḥammad. Its author, of Berber origin, was Sharaf ad-Dīn Abū 'Abd Allāh Muḥammad ibn Sa'īd al-Abūṣīrī (or al-Buṣīrī) (d. 1296). Ibn al-Khaṭīb, according to al-Maqqarī, *Nafḥ aṭ-Ṭīb,* IV, 419, credits Ibn Khaldūn himself with having written a commentary to the *Burda;* see later chapter on his "Autobiography."

the boxes of sweets and took a bit of them, according to the custom of courtesy, and he distributed the sweetmeats in the box among those present at his council."[21] Tamerlane accepted all this and it was Ibn Khaldūn's impression that the conqueror was pleased with it.

The Topics of Ibn Khaldūn's Discussions with Tamerlane

It seems that Tamerlane was most anxious to enter into a discussion with Ibn Khaldūn, whose reputation as a great historian and statesman in the Maghrib and in Mamlūk Egypt had undoubtedly preceded his personal appearance. Impressed by Ibn Khaldūn's personality, his "distinguished countenance and handsome appearance," and by his "eloquence, sagacity and cleverness," Tamerlane accorded him many opportunities to be with him.[22] According to Ibn Khaldūn's own statement, he was in attendance with Tamerlane and his council for thirty-five days, mornings and evenings, or went to see him on thirty-five occasions, "sometimes in the morning and sometimes in the evening," during a period which extended from his first visit on January 10, 1401, to February 25 or 27, 1401, the most likely date of Ibn Khaldūn's departure from Damascus.[23]

The frequency of these meetings and the length of their association alone are an indication and a confirmation of the interest which the great world conqueror had evinced in talking to the great scholar and historian. Within this span of time, the sessions with Tamerlane had led to a continuous chain of talks on a variety of topics and subjects.

Since Ibn Khaldūn could make himself understood only through the medium of the Arabic language, and Tamerlane, on the other hand, understood only a little Arabic, Tamerlane summoned from his retinue his official interpreter, the Ḥanafite jurist, 'Abd al-Jabbār b. an-Nu'mān, al-Khwārizmī (d. 1403), a man of great learning in all branches of scholarship, familiar with Arabic, Persian, and Turkish as well. Skilled in disputation, he conducted in Tamerlane's name

[21] Ibn Khaldūn, in tasting first of the sweetmeats, followed a custom attributed to Jenghiz Khān that no one should accept any food from the hand of another unless he who presented it ate from it first, even if the recipient is a prince. See Maqrīzī, *Khiṭaṭ*, II, 220; de Sacy, *Chrestomathie Arabe*, II, 162.

[22] Most of the later Egyptian historians, Ibn 'Arabshāh, Ibn Qāḍī Shuhhbah, Ibn Tagrī Birdī and others stress the point of Ibn Khaldūn's distinguished appearance and conspicuous attire, "together with the sweetness of his speech, his sagacity and his many sayings in extravagant praise of him," *Manhal*, fol. 49 ff.

[23] *Ta'rīf*, p. 381. This does not imply that he was in constant attendance upon Tamerlane during his stay in Damascus.

many discussions with the scholars of Aleppo and Damascus, and was one of the four scholars who were with Tamerlane day and night as his counselor and advisor. He functioned as official interpreter at all those meetings with Ibn Khaldūn.[24]

This interpreter would have been the person best qualified, apart from Ibn Khaldūn himself, to give a full and authentic account of all the topics discussed during their meetings since he, as official interpreter, was present at all the discussions of the two men. However, no such account has been preserved nor has there been left any record by Shihāb ad-Dīn b. al-'Izz, who is said to have "witnessed a part of their interview." [25]

For an investigation of the topics of their discussions, we are dependent, therefore, on Ibn Khaldūn's own and apparently authentic account, which he left for posterity. I have arranged the following account according to the six major topics as recorded by Ibn Khaldūn himself, though their conversations may have included other aspects of a much wider range, which have remained unrecorded.

1) On the Maghrib and Ibn Khaldūn's land of origin.
2) On heroes in history.
3) On predictions of things to come.
4) On the 'Abbāsid Caliphate.
5) On amnesty and security: "Concerning Myself and some Companions of Mine."
6) On Ibn Khaldūn's intention to stay with Tamerlane.

1 On the Maghrib and Ibn Khaldūn's land of origin.

The first question put to Ibn Khaldūn by Tamerlane pertained to his own person, to his origin, and his activities in Egypt. When Tamerlane asked Ibn Khaldūn from where in the Maghrib he had come and why he had come, Ibn Khaldūn replied that he had left his country in order to perform the pilgrimage and that he arrived in Egypt by sea at the Port of Alexandria "on the day of the breaking of the Fast in the year 784 (A.D. 1382), while festivities were [in progress] within their walls because aẓ-Ẓāhir [Barqūq] was sitting on the royal throne during these ten days." [26]

[24] For the interpreter 'Abd al-Jabbār, see Sakhāwī, *Ḍau'*, IV, 35; Ibn 'Arabshāh, transl. Sanders, pp. 127–129; 147–149.

[25] On Ibn al-'Izz, see Sakhāwī, *Ḍau'*, II, 220–221, X, 127–128; Ibn al-'Imād, *Shadharāt adh-Dhahab*, VII 80; and Ibn 'Arabshāh, transl. Sanders, p. 143.

[26] Actually, it was twelve days after Barqūq's coronation (November 26, 1382), but Ibn Khaldūn prefers, here as elsewhere, to give just round figures. He stayed in Alexandria about one month before moving to Cairo on January 6, 1383.

When Tamerlane continued to ask him what Sultan Barqūq had done for him he enumerated various acts of favors and kindness he was accorded by Barqūq and stressed that Barqūq gave recognition to his position, that he accorded him hospitality and supplied him with provisions for the pilgrimage, and that after his return from Mecca the Sultan allotted him a large stipend and continued to offer him his shelter and protection.

Tamerlane, knowing that Ibn Khaldūn was a Chief Cadi under Barqūq, asked him, "How did he happen to appoint you a cadi?" Ibn Khaldūn, referring here only to his second appointment as Chief Cadi in 1399, replied that when the incumbent Chief Cadi of the Mālikites had died, Sultan Barqūq saw that "I had the proper qualifications for the office—the pursuit of justice and right, and the rejection of outside influence"—and so the appointment was made. But, he continued, when Barqūq died a month later, those in charge of the government were not pleased with his position and replaced him with another cadi.

Tamerlane did not pause here, and taking up his first question, which Ibn Khaldūn had avoided answering, pressed for further details about his birthplace.[27] When Ibn Khaldūn, rather evasively and generally, replied that the "inner Maghrib" was his land and the land of his forefathers, the discussion turned to the geographical configuration and division of the Maghrib. Pressed by Tamerlane even further, Ibn Khaldūn explained that the term "inner Maghrib" means in common usage, "interior," that is, the most distant, because all of the Maghrib is situated on the southern coast of the Mediterranean Sea, and the parts of it nearest here are Barka and Ifrīqiya. The term "middle Maghrib" (*maghrib al-ausaṭ*) comprises Tlemcen, and the country of the Zanātah,[28] while the "farthest Maghrib" (*maghrib al-aqṣā*) is Fez and Morocco. Tamerlane then asked about the location of Tangier in relation to the Maghrib. Ibn Khaldūn replied, "In the corner which is between the Mediterranean Sea and the canal known as az-Zuqāq, that is, the Mediterranean Strait (Gibraltar)." Tamerlane continued to inquire about the location of Sabta (Ceuta) to which he answered, "at one day's distance from Tangier on the coast of the strait. From there one crosses to Spain, because the distance is short, about twenty miles."

---

[27] The discussion on the Maghrib is covered in *Ta'rīf*, pp. 369–370. For all the place names and their locations, see Ibn Khaldūn's *"Kitāb al-'Ibar,"* vol. VI and part of vol. VII and their French translation by de Slane, *Histoire des Berbères et des dynasties musulmanes de l'Afrique septentrionale,* (new ed.).

[28] Zanātah is the name of one of the two groups of Berber tribes in the Maghrib, the Ṣinhājah being the other tribal group.

Tamerlane continued to ask, "And Sijilmāsa?" whereupon Ibn Khaldūn replied, "On the border between the cultivated regions and the sands in the south." "And Fez?" "And I said it is not at the coast but in the center and is the residence of the Merinid kings of the Maghrib."

Despite Ibn Khaldūn's factual reply to all these questions, Tamerlane was not satisfied and evinced a most lively interest in getting further clarification of all those geographical places which Ibn Khaldūn had mentioned. He turned, therefore, to Ibn Khaldūn and told him, "All this does not convince me. It will be necessary to write a book for me on all the countries of the Maghrib, its remote parts as well as its near ones, its mountains and its rivers, its villages and its cities, so that I may clearly visualize them." Ibn Khaldūn promised him, "This will be accomplished under your auspices." [29]

After his retirement from this audience, Ibn Khaldūn wrote this account for Tamerlane. Ibn Khaldūn remained shut up in his lodgings and began working on this survey of the Maghrib which Tamerlane had requested. He wrote it within a few days in the form of a resumé filling the size of twelve booklets of half-sized format.[30] Having written so extensively on the history of the Berbers and the Maghrib in general, Ibn Khaldūn was familiar enough with the subject matter that he needed no more than just a "few days" for writing the account requested by Tamerlane. At a later meeting, Ibn Khaldūn presented it to Tamerlane, who took it from his hands and ordered his secretary to have it translated into "the Mongolian language." [31]

Whether this translation was ever carried out is not known, but

[29] Ibn Aḥmad az-Zamlakānī, a pupil of Ibn Khaldūn, left a short version (fifteen lines) of this very discussion on the Maghrib, which is almost the same as Ibn Khaldūn's own account and is probably taken from it, published by M. Kurd 'Alī in *R.A.A.* (1948), p. 159.

[30] Since a quire consisted generally of five sheets folded to make ten leaves written on both sides, the volume may have contained approximately 240 pages.

[31] With this phrase, "Mongolian language," is probably understood Eastern Turkish or Chagatai Turki, a dialect spoken throughout Central Asia and generally used by the Mongols in the Uighur writing. The extensive use of "Mongolian" as a written language in the diplomatic correspondence is indicated by the existence in the Mamlūk chancellery in Cairo of a special bureau for the translation of documents and correspondence in "Lisān al-Moghulī." According to Ibn al-Furāt, IX, 453, Tamerlane sent a letter to Barqūq in Moghulī. There seems to be some doubt in the contemporary sources concerning the extent to which Tamerlane himself knew Mongolian. According to Ibn 'Arabshāh (trans. Sanders, pp. 298 ff. and pp. 295 ff.) "Tamerlane did not know Arabic, but of Persian, Turkish, and the Moghūl language he understood enough but no more." He used in his conversations often Persian words such as "khūb khūb," and had chosen as his motto the Persian device "rāstī rūstī," meaning "truth is safety" (veritas salus). V. Barthold in "12 Vorlesungen . . .", p. 232, translated it "Gerechtigkeit ist Staerke."

the original treatise by Ibn Khaldūn, no longer extant, must be regarded as an independent separate work, produced at the request of Tamerlane, while in Damascus. Why Tamerlane was so interested in a detailed description of the Maghrib, whether it was out of pure intellectual curiosity and historical interest, or motivated by a hidden hope one day to be able to make practical use of this information, if and when he should march into North Africa, conquer it and add it to his empire, can only be surmised.

2 *On heroes in history*

It seems that one of the main topics of their discussion was centered around a well-conceived speech by Ibn Khaldūn with which he intended to flatter and exalt the conqueror and at the same time to impress on him his own qualities as a scholar and a historian. Ibn Khaldūn started out by saying, "Today it is thirty or forty years that I have longed to meet you." The interpreter immediately interrupted him and asked, "What is the reason for this?" whereupon Ibn Khaldūn gave two reasons.[32] "The first is that you are the sultan of the universe and the ruler of the world, and I do not believe that there has appeared among men from Adam until this epoch a ruler like you. I am not one of those who speak about matters by conjecture, for I am a scholar and I will explain this."

He then began to detail the first of the two reasons and indulged in a sociological-philosophical discussion on the *aṣabīyah,* that social force on which Ibn Khaldūn has based his whole concept of the process of history and society.[33] "Sovereignty," he says, "exists only because of group loyalty (*'aṣabīya*), and the greater the number in the group the greater is the extent of sovereignty." Ibn Khaldūn went on, stating: "Scholars, first and last, have agreed that most of the people of the human race are of two groups, the Arabs and the Turks.[34] You

[32] The second reason dealt with "predictions of things to come"; see next topic.

[33] According to Ibn Khaldūn, group loyalty, solidarity, or esprit de corps (*'aṣabīya*) is loyalty to a sovereign and then to the dynasty which he has founded. The maintenance of the dynasty depends upon the number of those who are willing to fight for it. This whole conception, which is the cornerstone in Ibn Khaldūn's socio-philosophical system, has been the subject of a voluminous literature. See the studies of 'Ayād, de Boer, Bombaci, Bouthoul, Flint, F. Gabrieli, Gibb, Issawi, Khemiri, Mahdi, Ritter, E. Rosenthal, F. Rosenthal, Simon, and others as listed in the "Ibn Khaldūniana" bibliography.

[34] Ibn Khaldūn follows here the view, common among Arab historians, in dividing the peoples of the East into Arabs and Turks, in a very vague and wide sense. Ibn Khaldūn chooses for his immediate purpose to emphasize the greatness of the Turks. See also *Ta'rīf,* p. 351.

know how the power of the Arabs was established when they became united in their religion in following their Prophet [Muḥammad]. As for the Turks, their contest with the kings of Persia and the seizure of Khūrāsān from their [Persian] hands by Afrāsiyāb is evidence of the origin of the Turks from royalty; and in their group loyalty no king on earth can be compared with them, not Khosraw nor Caesar nor Alexander nor Nebuchadnezzar. Khosraw [35] was the head of the Persians and their king, but what a difference between the Persians and the Turks! Caesar [36] and Alexander were the kings of the Greeks, and again what a difference between the Greeks and the Turks! As for Nebuchadnezzar, he was the head of the Babylonians and Nabaṭaeans, but what a difference between these and the Turks!"

Tamerlane listened attentively to all these historical references and was apparently very much impressed by them. Tamerlane did not notice Ibn Khaldūn's carelessness in mentioning Caesar before Alexander, nor his lack of distinction between Rome and Greece by calling both "kings of the Greeks." [37]

Tamerlane reacted only to Ibn Khaldūn's mention of Nebuchadnezzar and to Afrāsiyāb. In connection with Afrāsiyāb, Tamerlane brought into the discussion the name of Manūshihr, because he claimed, "we are related to Manūshihr on our mother's side." In the legendary history of the East. Manūshihr, a grandson of the early Persian king, Afrīdūn, lived in the time of Moses, and also in the time of Joshua, who brought the Israelites to Palestine. The power of Manūshihr was challenged by Afrāsiyāb, the king of the Turks, who after Manūshihr's death brought the Persian kingdom to ruin.[38] For Ibn Khaldūn's immediate purposes, the allusion to Afrāsiyāb was sufficient and had the effect of giving Tamerlane the opportunity to claim relationship to Manūshihr through his mother.[39]

[35] Khosraw (Kisra), known as Anūshirwān, was the twenty-first of the Sassanian kings of Persia.

[36] Caesar (*qaiṣar*) in Arabic stories denotes generally one of the Byzantine emperors; but Ibn Khaldūn here refers either to Julius Caesar (whom he calls the first of the Caesars) or to Octavius Caesar. About them, see *'Ibar*, II, 199–200.

[37] Accuracy is no concern of Ibn Khaldūn in his interview with Tamerlane; he chooses his examples without regard to their order in time. Mention should be made that Ibn Khaldūn used the term "Rūm" in a geographical sense for Asia Minor; in a historical sense, however, he denoted with it Byzantium. His failure to distinguish between Greeks and Romans, however, is merely in accordance with the Arabic conception of the Romans as a division of the Greeks.

[38] For Ibn Khaldūn's account of the legendary history of ancient Irān, see the chapter on Irān in part two.

[39] His mother's name is said to have been Takīna Khatūna. See V. Barthold, *Uluġ Beg*, p. 19.

Tamerlane was, however, more interested in Ibn Khaldūn's remarks on Nebuchadnezzar and asked him: "I see that you have mentioned Nebuchadnezzar together with Khosraw and Caesar and Alexander, although he was not of their class; they were great kings, while he was only one of the Persian generals, just as I myself am only the representative of the sovereign of the throne." [40]

Tamerlane, in order to confirm his own rank and position turned around and said, "As for the king [himself], here he is"—and he made a gesture toward the row of men standing behind him, among whom the one he meant had also been standing. This was his stepson, whose mother, he had married after the death of the boy's father, Sūyūrghatmish. But Tamerlane did not find him there, and those who were standing in that row explained that he had gone out.[41]

When Tamerlane asked Ibn Khaldūn to which of the peoples Nebuchadnezzar belonged, Ibn Khaldūn presented the various views of the scholars, of whom some say that he was of the Nabaṭaeans,[42] the last kings of Babylon, while others say of the first Persians. When Tamerlane asked Ibn Khaldūn: "Which of the two views concerning Nebuchadnezzar is weightier in your opinion?" Ibn Khaldūn gave preference to Nebuchadnezzar's descent as a Babylonian. Tamerlane, dissenting from this view, was not satisfied and it was then that Ibn Khaldūn suggested, "Let us turn to the opinion of aṭ-Ṭabarī, for he is the historian and traditioner of the people and no other opinion outweights his." [43]

Tamerlane rejected, however, the authority of aṭ-Ṭabarī and said, "We do not rely upon aṭ-Ṭabarī; let him (the interpreter) bring the histories of the Arabs and the Persians and debate with you." Ibn Khaldūn said, "And I, for my part, will debate according to the view

---

[40] Ibn Khaldūn was well aware that Nebuchadnezzar was, in fact, only a governor of one of the provinces of Persia, a satrap (*marzebān*) in command of the western borders of the empire; he called him "king" in *Muq.*, I, 417 and elsewhere in *'Ibar*, II.

[41] *Ta'rīf*, pp. 372–373.

[42] "Nabaṭaeans" is the Arabic designation of the Babylonians, the descendants of the Biblical Shem (Sam) through Nabiṭ and then Nimrod, according to one tradition; see *'Ibar*, II, 69. From Nimrod, the Assyrians (the people of Nineveh, Moṣūl, or al-Jazā'ir, Mesopotamia) were also descended, so that they too are vaguely mentioned sometimes as Nabaṭaeans.

[43] The historian Muḥammad b. Ja'far aṭ-Ṭabarī (d. 923 A.D.) is regarded by Ibn Khaldūn as "one of the few good historians" and counted among those historians of whom there are "not more than the fingers on one hand"; *Muq.* I, 3, et passim. Ibn Khaldūn leaned heavily on Ṭabarī's works and drew material from him for his history of the non-Arabic peoples; see part two.

of aṭ-Ṭabarī." [44] This ended the discussion with Tamerlane on this topic and as Ibn Khaldūn stated, "silence prevailed for a while."

It is to be noticed that this discussion centered around figures taken from the non-Islamic world, from ancient Persian, Greek and Roman history. This may have been deliberately planned by Ibn Khaldūn and the subjects carefully selected in order to avoid any reference to Islamic personalities in history to which Tamerlane might have taken exception. Ibn Khaldūn also felt on safe ground here, since he had made the history of non-Islamic peoples a topic of his research and was well-prepared to enter into a discussion with Tamerlane, being fully aware that Tamerlane was a formidable opponent in matters of historical knowledge.

3 On predictions of things to come

When Tamerlane asked Ibn Khaldūn at their first confrontation why he wanted to meet him, Ibn Khaldūn referred to two reasons which had motivated him. As the second reason, Ibn Khaldūn referred vaguely to some prognostications and predictions of Muslim scholars in the Maghrib about the occurrence of a "great event" which he had heard was to happen in his own days, and which he tried to apply through inference and allusions to the rise of Tamerlane himself.

The practice of predictions, divination and forecasting in regard to future dynastic changes in existing empires, which would affect the Muslim community as a whole, was widespread in the Maghrib of Ibn Khaldūn's time, and was known as *ḥidthān*. It was based on secret traditions, speculations and calculations of astronomers and magicians, alluding to the conjunctions of the stars and planets, which used to be collected in books called *al-malāḥim* (singular, *malḥama*).[45]

While standing before Tamerlane, Ibn Khaldūn was reminded of such predictions of a certain event which, according to astrologers,

[44] The proposed disputation is not mentioned again, since Tamerlane had rejected Ṭabarī as an authority and Ibn Khaldūn most likely did not follow up his claim.

[45] In a special chapter entitled, "Forecastings of the future of dynasties and nations, including a discussion of predictions (*malāḥim*)," Ibn Khaldūn deals with this whole aspect in great detail; see *Muq.*, II, 176–201. He traces the origin of many such predictions to Jewish converts to Islam, such as Ka'b al-Aḥbār, Wahb b. Munabbih, and 'Abdallāh b. Salām; see *Muq.*, I., 17; *Muq.*, II, 179–180, 393. For a fuller treatment of this aspect, see D. MacDonald in *E.I.*, s.v. *Malāḥim;* Renaud, in *Hespéris;* Casanova, *Mohammed,* pp. 48–50, 132–134; and his *La Malḥamat.*

was expected to occur after the conjunction of the two superior planets in the trigon. He informed Tamerlane that he met about forty years ago (1359–1360) in Fez, in the Qarawīyīn Mosque, the preacher of Constantine, Abū 'Alī b. Bādīs, who was an authority on this subject.[46] Asked about this conjunction which was to occur, and its implications, this great authority answered him, "It points to a powerful one who would arise in the northeast region of a desert people, tent dwellers, who will triumph over kingdoms, overturn governments, and become the master of most of the inhabited world." When Ibn Khaldūn asked this great preacher, "When is it due?" he was told, "in the year 784 H. (1382–1383 A.D.)—accounts of it will be widespread."

Ibn Khaldūn conveyed to Tamerlane also the view of his teacher Muḥammad b. Ibrāhīm al-Ābilī,[47] the authority on metaphysics, who told him whenever he conversed with him or questioned him about it, "This event is approaching, and if you live, you will surely witness it." Ibn Khaldūn referred also to another source of his information, namely to Ibn Zarzar, the Jewish physician and astrologer of Pedro, the son of Alfonso, the king of the "Franks," from whom Ibn Khaldūn had received a letter confirming this prediction. This Ibrāhīm b. Zarzar, who was instrumental in presenting Ibn Khaldūn to Pedro in 1363, was apparently the only Jewish scholar with whom Ibn Khaldūn had established (while still in the Maghrib) a close bond of friendship which endured all through the years and remained so deep-seated in Ibn Khaldūn's memory that he was reminded of the views of his Jewish friend even in his interview with Tamerlane forty years later.[48]

Ibn Khaldūn elaborated even further on this subject and added that the Ṣūfis in the Maghrib were also expecting this occurrence and that they believed that the agent of this event would be the Fāṭimid to whom the prophetic traditions of the Shī'a and others refer. Yaḥyā

---

[46] *Muq.*, II, 194.

[47] *Ta'rīf*, pp. 33 ff., 371. He was a teacher of Ibn Khaldūn in the Maghrib and had considerable influence on his spiritual development. Ibn Khaldūn calls him "the greatest scholar of the Maghrib, the greatest master of the sciences based on reason"; he speaks of him with great admiration in numerous places in *Ta'rīf* and *Muqaddimah*. See Nassīf Nassar, *Le Maître d'Ibn Khaldūn: al-Ābilī.*

[48] *Ta'rīf*, pp. 85, 371; *'Ibar*, VII, 304 ff. See above note 4, chapter 1. For further details about this Jewish physician in Arabic sources, see Ibn al-Khaṭīb, *al-Iḥāṭah*, I, 241; *Una versión árabe compendiada de la "Estoria de España" de Alfonso el Sabio*, ed. M.M. Antuna *al-Andalus* (Madrid, 1933), I, 105, 124, 144; J.M. Millas-Vallicrosa, *Estudios Sobre Azarquiel* (Madrid-Granada, 1943–1950), pp. 349–350; and Fischel in Goldziher volume.

b. 'Abd Allāh, the grandson of Shaikh Abū Ya'qūb al-Bādisī, foremost among the saints of the Maghrib,[49] told Ibn Khaldūn that the Shaikh had said to him one day as he came from morning prayer, "Today the Fāṭimid agent was born. That was in the fourth decade of the eighth century." Ibn Khaldūn had, of course, a purpose in telling all these predictions to Tamerlane. He wanted to flatter him and to create the impression that it was Tamerlane who was to be regarded as this "powerful one . . . who will triumph over kingdoms, overturn governments and become the master of most of the inhabited world."

4 *On the 'Abbāsid Caliphate*

At another session with Tamerlane, Ibn Khaldūn participated in a hearing which Tamerlane granted to one of the descendants of the revived 'Abbāsid Caliphate in Egypt, who had presented himself before Tamerlane and appealed to him for justice in his cause, claiming for himself the position of Caliph, since it had belonged to his ancestors.[50] This 'Abbāsid descendant stated, "This Caliphate belongs to us and to our ancestors; the tradition is sound according to which the authority (of the Caliphate) belongs to the 'Abbāsids as long as the world endures. I have a better right to the office than the one who holds it now in Cairo, since my forefathers, whose heir I am, had a just claim to it, while it came to this man without [legal] support."

Tamerlane, apparently full of respect before a scion of the Caliphate, summoned the jurists and judges, among them also Ibn Mufliḥ, the Ḥanbalite Cadi, and Ibn Khaldūn, and asked them to decide at this "court of justice" whether this claim was justified. Tamerlane turned to Ibn Khaldūn directly and asked him, "What is it that has brought the Caliphate to the 'Abbāsids until this epoch in Islam?" Ibn Khaldūn conveyed in great detail his concepts on the Caliphate and summarized them as follows: "May Allāh grant you victory! Since the death of the Prophet (may Allāh bless him and give him peace!) the Muḥammadans have differed over whether or not it is necessary for the believers to have some ruler from among themselves direct their spiritual and their world affairs. One party were of the opinion

[49] Ibn Khaldūn called him the greatest saint of the Maghrib in the fourteenth century. He did not study under Abū Ya'qūb, but learned of him through his grandson, Abū Zakarīyā' Yaḥyā. Al-Bādisī, a Ṣūfī, predicted the appearance of one who was assumed to be a descendant of the Fāṭimids and who would renew the tenets of the religion. Ibn Khaldūn presents the available traditions and views about the coming of the expected Fāṭimid Mahdī (*al-mahdī al-mustanẓar*) in a special chapter in *Muq.*, II, 142–177.

[50] See *Ta'rīf*, pp. 374–376.

—and among them were the Khārijites—that it is not necessary; the majority, however, held that it is necessary, but disagree concerning the [legal] support [in tradition] for this necessity. All the Shi'ites adhered to the tradition of testamentary designation, that the Prophet (may Allāh bless him and give him peace!) designated 'Alī to be Caliph, although the Shi'ites have more opinions than can be counted concerning the particular succession of 'Alī's descendants after him. The Sunnites were unanimous in rejecting this [principle of necessary] testamentary designation and [in holding] that the only necessity for which there is support is *ijtihād'*; they mean by this that the Muḥammadans must use extreme care to choose an honest, intelligent, and just man to whom to entrust the guidance of their affairs. . . ."

In the course of this discussion, Ibn Khaldūn outlined before Tamerlane the essential facts in the historical development of the 'Abbāsid Caliphate up to the destruction of Baghdād by Hūlāgū, and stated that the transfer of the office of the Caliphate in the time of Sultan aẓ-Ẓāhir Baybars to one of the remaining 'Abbāsids was "with the concurrence of those in power among the army and the jurists, and that the authority had been transmitted to members of his family, down to the present one who is in Cairo. Nothing is known contrary to that." Here again, Ibn Khaldūn spoke with authority since he had dealt with the various problems of the Caliphate and the Imāmate in his *'Ibar,* especially in his *Muqaddimah,* and had also listed the conditions (*shurūṭ*) for holding the position of a Caliph which, according to him, are knowledge, justice, competence, and soundness of body and senses.[51]

Ibn Khaldūn's scholarly exposé settled the dispute and Tamerlane then dismissed the claimant by stating, "You have heard the word of the jurists and judges and it appears that you have no justification before me for claiming the Caliphate—so depart—may Allāh guide you aright!"

5 On amnesty and security: "Concerning myself and some companions of mine"

Apart from discussions on historical subjects, some of the talks with Tamerlane were of a more personal nature, in which Ibn Khaldūn expressed his concern about the personal fate of some prisoners who Tamerlane had captured and about his own safety. At one occasion

[51] *Muq.,* I, 342–355 on the Caliphate: pp. 355–364 on the Imamate. See *'Ibar,* III, 540–543; *'Ibar,* V, 293 ff. On the Egyptian 'Abbāsid Caliphate see R. Hartmann, *Zur Vorgeschichte,* pp. 1–10; and Ayalon, *Studies on the Transfer,* pp. 42–59.

he expressed to Tamerlane his fear, which seized him on account of the news about the misfortune which had befallen the Chief Cadi of the Shāfi'ites, Ṣadr ad-Dīn al-Munāwī, who had been taken prisoner by those who pursued the Egyptian army when Sultan Faraj fled to Cairo. This Chief Cadi had suffered great trials and tribulations as prisoner before he was drowned in the Zāb River while being taken along by Tamerlane on his march East.[52]

On another occasion, Ibn Khaldūn in a mood of worry and weariness, somehow confused and depressed, homesick and lonely, tried to express some thoughts to Tamerlane which he had in mind, "concerning myself and some companions of mine." [53] In such a state of mind, he said to Tamerlane, "I have something which I wish to say before you." "Speak up," Tamerlane encouraged him, and Ibn Khaldūn said, revealing his inner emotions probably for the first time: "I am a stranger in this country in a double sense. First because I am away from the Maghrib, which is my homeland and my place of origin; the other [absence] is from Cairo, and my people—my race—are there. I have come under your protection, and I hope that you will give me your opinion regarding what may solace me in my exile."

Tamerlane replied, "Speak, whatever you desire I shall do for you," whereupon Ibn Khaldūn remarked, "My state of exile has made me forget what I desire; perhaps you—may Allāh aid you—will know for me what I desire." Then Tamerlane invited Ibn Khaldūn to move from the city to the camp (*urdū,* which means into the vicinity of Tamerlane's own residence) [54] and asked him to stay with him, "and if Allāh wills I will fulfill your highest aim."

Ibn Khaldūn accepted his offer but requested Tamerlane to give orders to this effect to his Viceroy Shāh Malik to prepare a pass for him to go whenever he pleased from the city to Tamerlane's camp. After the fulfillment of this request by Tamerlane, Ibn Khaldūn, apparently recovering from his depressed feelings, said to Tamerlane boldly, "I have still another request."

This time, Ibn Khaldūn did not ask for himself, but pleaded for the Damascene officials. Knowing of Tamerlane's practice of transferring skilled laborers, draftsmen and artisans from the conquered cities to his capital in Samarqand, he subtly suggested: "These Qur'ān teachers, secretaries, bureau officials and administrators, who are

---

[52] Ibn Khaldūn had mentioned al-Munāwī already in connection with the first expedition of Faraj to Syria in March, 1400. See *Ta'rīf,* pp. 349, 371.

[53] *Ta'rīf,* pp. 377–378.

[54] *Urdū* in Turkish is a royal camp, in a wider sense, the residence or the capital. Tamerlane's camp (*urdū*) was at that time in the Qaṣr al-Ablaq.

among those left behind by the Sultan of Egypt, have come under your rule. The King surely will not disregard them. Your power is vast, your provinces are very extensive, and the need of your government for men who are administrators in the various branches of service is greater than the need of any other than you."[55]

"What do you wish for them?" Tamerlane asked. Whereupon Ibn Khaldūn replied, "A letter of security to which they can appeal and upon which they can rely whatever their circumstances may be." This request, too, was answered by Tamerlane and he ordered his secretary to write "a letter of security" (*amān*) to which all these officials could appeal and upon which they could rely, whatever their circumstances might be. Ibn Khaldūn waited until the secretary had written such a letter of security and Shāh Malik had affixed to it the Sultan's seal.

When the time of Tamerlane's departure from Damascus came near, Ibn Khaldūn appeared once more before the ruler. After the exchange of the customary greetings, Tamerlane asked him on this occasion about an apparently very trivial matter, namely, about his mule (*bughla*). The mule was the riding animal of a cadi, its color was usually gray, and it was given to him at his appointment, together with a robe of honor (*khil'a*). No other official of the Mamlūk government was permitted to use a mule of a similar color. The Chief Cadi's mule was usually of great value, corresponding in this respect to the best of horses. Since the Chief Cadis were not expected to walk, their servants always kept a mule ready for them.[56]

It must have been quite surprising to Ibn Khaldūn that Tamerlane, in one of their last meetings, should have asked him, "You have a mule here? It is a good one? Will you sell it? I would buy it from you." Ibn Khaldūn must have been quite taken aback by Tamerlane's offer and replied, "May Allāh aid you! One like me does not sell to one like you, but I would gladly offer it to you in homage and also others like it if I had them." The mule was then carried to Tamerlane, whose liking for mules was well known, while Ibn Khaldūn was with him at his council; he did not see it again.

Later, back in Cairo, Ibn Khaldūn received even a payment for the mule through a certain Mamlūk official who had returned from Damascus. Ibn Khaldūn was informed through the medium of one of

---

[55] It is well-documented by Persian and European sources that Tamerlane took skilled laborers, draftsmen, weavers, bow makers, craftsmen in glass and porcelain away from Damascus to his capital in Samarqand.

[56] *Ta'rīf*, p. 378. About the mule of the cadi, see Tyan, *Histoire de l'organization*, I, 281, 307, 311. It is a curious parallel that in Ibn Khaldūn's meeting with Pedro the Cruel, the mule also was a topic of discussion.

this official's friends, "Emīr Tamerlane has sent to you by me the price of the mule which he had bought from you. Here it is—take it; because he, Tamerlane, enjoined upon us the discharge of his debt of this money of yours."

Ibn Khaldūn refused first to accept it until the Sultan, "who sent you to him, gives his permission. Otherwise I shall not." Ibn Khaldūn went to the head of the government and informed him of the matter and told him that it was not fitting for him to do so (that is, accept the money) without informing the Sultan about it. But the Sultan closed his eyes to this and sent him that amount after some time. The bearer apologized because the sum was not complete, asserting that "it was thus given to him." [57]

6 On Ibn Khaldūn's intention to stay with Tamerlane

The final topic of their discussion was related to Ibn Khaldūn's further plans, in particular whether he wanted to return to Cairo. Tamerlane put before Ibn Khaldūn squarely the question, "Are you going to travel to Cairo?" The answer of Ibn Khaldūn is as surprising as it is ambiguous. He said, "May Allāh aid you! Indeed, my desire is only [to serve] you, for you have granted me refuge and protection. If the journey to Cairo would be in your service, surely! Otherwise, I have no desire for it." [58]

This rather ambiguous reply of Ibn Khaldūn's, quite consistent, however, with his general opportunistic attitude and his repeated transfer of loyalty while in the service of the rulers of North Africa, seems to imply that he might have been willing to join Tamerlane had the latter insisted upon it. But his flattering words should not be taken too seriously; it is doubtful if, at his age, he was eager to travel any more; he had not been too eager to go even from Cairo to Damascus. In any case, Tamerlane replied unequivocally, "No, you will return to your family and to your people."

It would have been indeed a most interesting finale to Ibn Khaldūn's already colorful and exciting life had he spent its last phase in Tamerlane's service in the capital of Samarqand in Central Asia and had his experience thus extended from North Africa and Spain to Central Asia, from the Christian King, Pedro the Cruel, to Tamerlane, the Mongol conqueror!

The ambiguity of Ibn Khaldūn's reply to Tamerlane's question about his future plans, "My desire is only to serve you . . ." may

[57] *Ta'rīf*, p. 381. About this envoy called Baisaq, see later.

[58] *Ibid.*, p. 378.

have caused some later contemporary Egyptian historians to speculate about Ibn Khaldūn's real intentions. They advanced rather strange and unwarranted interpretations and maintained that Ibn Khaldūn did not want to return to Cairo but rather to join Tamerlane.[59]

According to Ibn Qāḍī Shuhbah (d. 1448),[60] Tamerlane is alleged to have invited Ibn Khaldūn, by saying, "prepare yourself to come with me to my country," upon which Ibn Khaldūn is said to have replied, "In Cairo is one who loves me and whom I love . . . in Cairo are my people, my race." [61] And Ibn Khaldūn is said to have added—leaving the way open for the future— "It is absolutely necessary that you permit me to go there, be it now or later, so as to be able to arrange my affairs, after which I shall return to put myself at your service."

The Arab historian, Aḥmad b. Muḥammad b. 'Arabshāh,[62] in his famous biographical work on Tamerlane entitled, *'Ajā'ib al-maqdūr fī akhbār Tīmūr* (completed in 1435),[63] included an account of Ibn Khaldūn's visit to Tamerlane, describing in some detail the conversations which had supposedly taken place between Tamerlane and Ibn Khaldūn in Damascus early in 1401.

[59] Thus the most important event in Ibn Khaldūn's life in Egypt, his association with Tamerlane, remained for centuries obscured and marred by confusion and contradiction.

[60] Ms. Paris, fol. 181.

[61] According to Jamāl ad-Dīn al-Bishbishī, as reported by Sakhāwī, *Ḍau'*, IV, 146 ff., Ibn Khaldūn had remarried in Cairo and it was added that his wife had a brother who was considered of mixed origin.

[62] Born in Damascus, in 1392, he spent many years in the land of Tamerlane and his successors, acquiring an intimate knowledge of Tamerlane's life and deeds. He learned Persian, Turkish, and Mongolian, and studied under various great scholars in Central Asia. He later undertook a journey to Adrianople, where he became the confidential secretary of Sultan Muḥammad I, son of Bāyazīd, and returned to Damascus in 1421, finally settling in Cairo in 1436, where he died in 1450 after a prolific literary career.

[63] The Arabic text of this biography of Tamerlane was published with the Latin translation in 1638 in Leiden by Jacob Golius; for other editions and translations see "Ibn Khaldūniana" bibliography. The publication by Jacob Golius of Ibn 'Arabshāh's Arabic biography of Tamerlane not only introduced to the Occident the first example of an Arabic text in rhymed prose, but also, and more important, introduced for the first time the name of Ibn Khaldūn to the Western world. But the name of Ibn Khaldūn did not at that juncture arouse any interest in him or his work on the part of European scholarship. In Turkey, however, parts of his works were translated into Turkish at the beginning of the eighteenth century. About the Turkish discovery of Ibn Khaldūn and its impact on Turkish historiography; see the studies of Togan, Findikoğlu, Babinger, and the article by E. Kuran, "Ottoman Historiography of the Tanzimat Period," in *Historians of the Middle East* (London, 1962), pp. 422–429.

According to Ibn 'Arabshāh,[64] Ibn Khaldūn is said to have declared, "O Lord and Amir! Egypt refuses to be ruled by any ruler but yourself or to admit any empire save yours. But I for your sake have left my wealth, ancestral and new, my family, children, fatherland, country, friends, kindred, relatives, intimates and the kings of mankind and every helper and leader . . . and I have no regret or grief except for the time which had passed in a service other than yours, nor has my eye been annointed with the light of your presence.

"Now therefore I will begin another life in your protection, will consider wicked the time of absence from your side and will pay for the loss of my past life by spending my remaining years in your service and clinging to your stirrup and will count it the most precious of times and highest of places and most eminent of my states. . . ."

Ibn Arabshāh introduced another element to which no allusion whatever is made in Ibn Khaldūn's own account. Ibn 'Arabshāh suggested that Ibn Khaldūn made his alleged intention to stay with Tamerlane somehow conditional upon a temporary return to Cairo in order to bring back his own books, which he had left behind there. He attributed to Ibn Khaldūn the statement: "Nothing breaks my back except books, in which I have spent my life and paid out the pearls of learning in composing them and have extinguished my day and made sleepless my night in writing them. I have set forth in them the annals of the world from its very beginning, and the life of the Kings of East and West, but I have made you the central pearl of the necklace and the finest part of their wealth and have embroidered the golden robes of their age with your deeds, and your empire has become a crescent moon on the forehead of their time; but those books are in the city of Cairo and if I recover them, I will never depart from your stirrup or exchange your threshold for another. And may God be praised who has given me one who knows my worth and guards my service and does not destroy dignity!"

Knowing Tamerlane's desire for books dealing with history and his love of knowledge, Ibn Khaldūn was sure to achieve his goal, and Ibn 'Arabshāh significantly states, "Tīmūr did not mark that he was deceived and carried away by the magic of this wonderful eloquence." The result, according to Ibn 'Arabshāh, was that "Tīmūr agreed with the cadi [Ibn Khaldūn] that he should go to Cairo and take his family and children and his plentiful books and should not delay any longer than to accomplish the journey and return to him with ample hope,

[64] The following quotations are based, for convenience sake, on the English translation by Sanders, pp. 296–298.

certain that he would gain his wish. So he departed to Ṣafad and rested from this affliction."

Ibn 'Arabshāh did not state the source, oral or written, from which he derived his information about the alleged content of Ibn Khaldūn's discussions with Tamerlane. He could not have known Ibn Khaldūn personally, and also had never seen or read any of Ibn Khaldūn's works, as he expressly confirmed. He had but heard of Ibn Khaldūn's "wonderful chronicle" (*at-ta'rīkh al-'ajīb*) "from a wise scholar and a true man of learning" who saw it (the chronicle) and "marked its diction and substance." His description seems to be based merely on hearsay, or at best on a loose and free embellishment of the real facts, and his contention that Ibn Khaldūn was as anxious to stay with Tamerlane as Tamerlane was eager to keep him is in no way borne out by the reliable historical facts and Ibn Khaldūn's own and authentic account.

The issue of Ibn Khaldūn's books as a primary incentive for Tamerlane's permitting him to return to Egypt has been taken up by the Turkish historian, Muṣṭafā b. 'Abdallāh, known as Ḥājjī Khalīfah (d. 1657) in his book *Kashf aẓ-Ẓunūn*.[65] According to him, Ibn Khaldūn is said to have stated: "I have composed the great history in which I have recounted all the battles. I have left it in Egypt, and it will fall into the hands of that mad one [Faraj]. . . ." Tamerlane is said to have replied: "Would it not be possible to recover these books?," whereupon Tamerlane permitted Ibn Khaldūn to return to Cairo to bring these books to him.

Ḥājjī Khalīfah added to this statement another assertion that Ibn Khaldūn was Cadi of Aleppo, when Tamerlane took that town, that he fell into the hands of the conqueror and was taken prisoner, and that Tamerlane befriended him, carried him with him to Samarqand, and later permitted him to return to Cairo—almost everything in contradiction to the real historical facts.[66]

The confusion caused by Ibn 'Arabshāh and Ḥājjī Khalīfah was

---

[65] *Lexicon Bibliographicum*, Vol. II, no. 2085, p. 101.

[66] That Ibn Khaldūn was allegedly taken prisoner by Tamerlane was uncritically accepted as a fact in many biographical sketches of Ibn Khaldūn; see, among others, de Rossi, *Dizionario Storico;* de Sacy, *Chrestomathie Arabe*, p. 393; von Kremer, *Ibn Chaldûn*, p. 584; 'Alī Pāshā Mubārak, *al-Khiṭaṭ al-Jadīda*, p. 5; Müller, *Der Islam im Morgen- und Abendland*, II, 670. Typical for the lack of exact and correct information on Ibn Khaldūn's last "Egyptian" phase is the statement by von Hammer-Purgstall in *Über die Laenderverwaltung*, p. 95, according to which Ibn Khaldūn was judge at Aleppo, at which city the conversations with Tamerlane took place.

only heightened when B. d'Herbelot (1697),[67] accepting Ḥājjī Khalīfah's mistaken views, added his own, that Ibn Khaldūn died in Samarqand in 1406. Even as late as 1834, J. Gräberg af Hemsö could state that, "Ibn Khaldūn served a short time under Tamerlane as Chief Justice at Damascus and made a journey to Samarqand."[68]

All these accounts have no basis whatsoever in history. According to Ibn Khaldūn's own account his books did not form an issue at all in his discussion with Tamerlane prior to his return to Cairo. He made it quite clear that Tamerlane did not insist on his returning to him and that the permission to depart for Cairo was given to him unconditionally and without any strings attached. The circumstances as described by Ibn Khaldūn himself hardly necessitated the use of this, or any other, ruse or excuse, as attributed to him by later Arabic historians. It is evident that discussions with Tamerlane were held in a spirit of great consideration and respect for Ibn Khaldūn and that an air of friendliness and hospitality permeated their various meetings.

At various occasions, Ibn Khaldūn stressed the cordiality and kindness of Tamerlane towards him, that Tamerlane "received me kindly" or "treated me exceptionally well" or "I obtained amnesty for the people of Damascus" or he "bade me farewell under the most pleasant circumstances." He stresses that Tamerlane granted him a "letter of safety" written in his own hand and that he furnished him with provisions for his journey back to Cairo.

In rather moving terms, Ibn Khaldūn expressed personally, before his departure from Damascus, "Is there any generosity left beyond that which you have already shown me? You have heaped favors upon me, accorded me a place in your council among your intimate followers, and shown me kindness and generosity—which I hope Allāh will repay to you in like measures."[69] The historical fact is that Ibn Khaldūn did go back to Cairo voluntarily, never to return to Damascus.

[67] *Bibliothèque Orientale*, II, 418, s.v. Khaledoun.

[68] *An Account of the Great Historical Work of the African Philosopher*, II, 387–388.

[69] Stated by Ibn Khaldūn in connection with Tamerlane's request for his mule, *Ta'rīf*, p. 378.

7

LAST PHASE OF PUBLIC ACTIVITIES IN CAIRO (1401–1406)

When Ibn Khaldūn decided to return to Cairo, Tamerlane recommended his own son to accompany him on his way.[1] The son was about to travel to Shaqḥab, to the place of the spring pasturing of his animals. Ibn Khaldūn declined this honor, however, since the journey with Tamerlane's son was not according to his planned itinerary. He preferred to go to Ṣafad under the care and guidance of a messenger who had come to Tamerlane from the Chamberlain of Ṣafad, by the name of Ibn ad-Duwaydārī.[2] Tamerlane agreed to this and Ibn Khaldūn left him with the last words recorded by Ibn Khaldūn in this connection, "so I bade him farewell and departed." On his way back, Ibn Khaldūn experienced some difficulties with this messenger from Ṣafad, which he erroneously calls "the nearest seaport," although Ṣafad is in fact sixty miles inland.[3]

Ibn Khaldūn's over-land journey from Damascus to Cairo was most adventurous and arduous. He and his friends were intercepted by a band of tribesmen, apparently Druzes, who barred their way and robbed them of all their belongings, leaving him and his friends almost naked until they escaped to the village. There they obtained some cloth in a town called aṣ-Ṣubayba, from where he travelled to Ṣafad, staying there "for a few days."

---

[1] It is not clear whether this was Mirān Shāh or Shāh Rōkh. See about them the important study by Barthold, *Uluġ Beg* and H. H. Roemer, *Šams al-Ḥusn, Eine Chronik vom Tode Timurs bis zum Jahre 1409, von Tāğ as-Salmānī* (Wiesbaden, 1956).

[2] *Ta'rīf*, p. 379. For further details about him see Ibn 'Arabshāh, trans. Sanders, p. 152.

[3] *Ta'rīf*, pp. 379–380. This must be due to inadvertence; he also failed to mention from what seaport he actually sailed along the Mediterranean coast.

From Ṣafad, Ibn Khaldūn must have gone to the Mediterranean coast, most likely 'Akkō, from where he travelled by ship along the seacoast of Palestine to Gaza. There he disembarked and using the arduous desert road across the Sinai Peninsula, finally arrived in Cairo, safe and sound, on March 17, 1401.[4]

Due to Ibn Khaldūn's long absence from Cairo—altogether about four months, from November 22, 1400 to March 17, 1401—obviously unfounded reports had spread that he had died in Damascus as a result of a heart palpitation, which afflicted him on the road.[5]

No sooner had Ibn Khaldūn returned to Cairo than he seemed to be anxious to enter public life again, and probably in recognition of the services he had rendered to the Mamlūk cause during his stay in Damascus, he was indeed appointed by Sultan Faraj to serve again as a Mālikite Chief Cadi.

During his absence from Cairo, the incumbent of the office of the Mālikite Chief Cadi in Cairo was, in 1401, Jamāl ad-Dīn al-Aqfahsī (d. 1420)—a man of great retentiveness and sagacity, upright and honest and well-known for his austerity and humility and scrupulousness in religion.[6] He had served only one month in this office when the Sultan Faraj revoked al-Aqfahsī's appointment. Turning his attention to Ibn Khaldūn, Faraj appointed him, in April, 1401, to the position of Mālikite Chief Cadi, which Ibn Khaldūn thus occupied for the third time.

In this position as a cadi for the third time, he followed the same principles which had guided him previously, and he stated that he performed his duties uprightly, avoiding consideration of special interests and exacting justice for the accused. But again he incurred the opposition of certain court circles in Cairo, "who do not render honest judgments and do not exact justice." Ibn Khaldūn mentioned that "they intervened with the Sultan to appoint a certain Mālikite Chief Cadi named Yūsuf b. Khālid al-Bisāṭī (d. 1426), who for this purpose had offered a part of his wealth as bribes to some intercessors who conspired with him and (promised them) various kinds of favoritism in his decision—may Allāh punish all of them!"[7]

Ibn Khaldūn remained for only a short time in his third appointment as a Chief Cadi and was again dismissed in February, 1402. But

[4] His arrival in Cairo on this date, or Sha'bān 3, 808 H., is confirmed by all contemporary historians.

[5] See note 10, this chapter.

[6] About him, see Sakhāwī, *Ḍau'*, V, 71.

[7] *Ta'rīf*, p. 382. See Sakhāwī, *Ḍau'*, X, 312, who quotes several critical views about him.

Faraj reconsidered his decision, "corrected his previous opposition and returned the office to me," and Ibn Khaldūn served his fourth term as judge from July 14, 1402 until September 23, 1403. Then al-Bisāṭī was restored to the position of Chief Cadi, but the authorities substituted Ibn Khaldūn again for al-Bisāṭī and Ibn Khaldūn served for the fifth time from February 11, 1405 until May 27, 1405.

With his dismissal from the Cadiship for the fifth time, his career as a judge had still not reached its end. Ibn Khaldūn was oppointed Mālikite Chief Cadi for the sixth time at the end of February or the beginning of March, 1406,[8] but he held this office only for but a few weeks, or even for only eight days, according to Ibn Ḥajar,[9] because his death occurred on Wednesday, March 17, 1406 [10] (or in Ramaḍan 25, 808 H.).

He was buried in the cemetery of the Ṣūfis outside the Bāb an-Naṣr in Cairo, but the site of his tomb is unknown today. He had reached the age of seventy-six years and twenty-five days according to the Islamic calendar, and about seventy-four years according to the Christian calendar.

---

[8] Ibn Khaldūn's six appointments to the Mālikite Chief Cadiship in Egypt were, in chronological order according to the common era, as follows:

1) August 11, 1384–June 17, 1385
2) May 22, 1399–September 3, 1400
3) May 7?, 1401–February 17, 1402
4) July 4, 1402–September 23, 1403
5) February 11, 1405–May 27, 1405
6) March 8?, 1406–March 17, 1406

[9] See Ibn Ḥajar, *Inba' al-Ghumr,* Ms. Paris, fol. 223

[10] On the last folio in one of Ibn Khaldūn's manuscripts of his *Ta'rīf,* which I found in Istanbul (Ms. Aya Sofia, Catal. no. 3200, p. 192) a note in Maghribī handwriting is inserted—probably by a copyist or an owner—which reads, "Praise be to Allāh, the author (Ibn Khaldūn) died (Allāh be merciful to him) in Cairo in the year 808. This is correct. It was also said he died in Damascus of a *rajfa* (trembling, palpitation) which afflicted him on the road, but this first statement, namely that he died in 808 H., is more sound, and Allāh, who be exalted, knows best."

PART TWO:

Ibn Khaldūn's Historical Research in Egypt

I: Historian of Mamlūk Egypt of his Time

1

AS HISTORIAN OF SULTAN BARQŪQ

The Challenge

The public arena of Mamlūk Egypt in which Ibn Khaldūn played so active a role during his twenty-three years' stay in Cairo (1382–1406) was conditioned by two decisive political factors, which had a profound effect on both the internal as well as the external affairs of Mamlūk Egypt. The first was the rise and rule of a new dynasty, the so-called Circassian Mamlūk Dynasty, under Sultan Mâlik aẓ-Ẓāhir Barqūq (1382–1399), followed by his son, Faraj (1399–1414), and the second was the appearance of Tamerlane and his army on the borders of Mamlūk Syria. These two factors confronted Ibn Khaldūn, the historian, with a great challenge and directed his scholarly curiosity and creativity into a new field of research.

During his stay in the Maghrib, Ibn Khaldūn had made the history of the Berber and the Arab dynasties and all the political events with which he was so intimately connected there, the topic of his investigation.[1] Similarly, during his stay in the Mashriq, the political, military, and diplomatic events of his time in Egypt became the subject of his writings. They must have stimulated him to leave for posterity an account of Mamlūk Egypt of this period in which Barqūq and Faraj on the one hand, and Tamerlane, the Mongol world-conqueror, on the other, were the central dramatic figures.

[1] Of his *Kitāb al-'Ibar,* the vols. VI and VII are exclusively devoted to this topic; see de Slane, *Histoire des Berbères . . . ,* text and trans.; also G. Gabrieli, "*Saggio* di bibliografia e concordanza," *R.S.O.,* X, 169–211.

While still in the Maghrib, Ibn Khaldūn had gathered information about Egypt's political, social and cultural conditions from returning pilgrims and other travellers to the East on the basis of which his views on Egypt crystallized in a rather general way. When he set foot on Egyptian soil in 1382, he was confronted with a civilization and a government which was fundamentally different in its legal, institutional and administrative patterns from anything he had experienced or had been accustomed to in the Maghrib or in Spain. The Mamlūk society, headed by a Sultan elected by the "Emirs of the Hundreds," was a military oligarchy made up of a feudal aristocracy and completely different in its ethnic composition from that of the Maghrib, which was mainly composed of Berbers and Arabs. He noted the differences in the governmental patterns and the different usage and meaning of its offices and officials. He observed that the rank of vizier, under the Turkish Mamlūk dynasty in Egypt, had lost its lofty meaning and that, compared with the Maghrib, the vizierate had become a subordinate office, designating only a person in charge of collecting a great variety of taxes. The title of *Ḥājib* was applied by the Turkish dynasty in Egypt to officials of much higher authority than was the case with bearers of this title in the Maghrib. He referred also to many other Mamlūk offices which were unknown in the Maghrib administration.[2]

He noted, also, the linguistic differences, insofar as the common language of the ruling class was primarily Turkish and not Arabic. Ibn Khaldūn refers to the Mamlūk rulers of Egypt, therefore, as "the Turks," using this term collectively without regard to the specific ethnic origin of the individual rulers.[3] Indeed, as far as the language was concerned, they nearly all spoke Turkish or Circassian and it was justifiable to apply to the Mamlūk state the official designation *ad-daula at-Turkīya* or *daulat al-atrāk.*[4]

Typically for a historian, he delved first of all into pre-Barqūqian Egypt and gave a rather detailed outline of the dynastic and political history of Egypt from the time of Saladin on. He devoted many pages to the life and activities of Salāḥ-ad-Dīn, "the first Turkish dynasty over Egypt" as he called it, and deals with his rule and his wars

[2] See *Muq.*, II, 9–21, where Ibn Khaldūn described all the terms and ranks of the governmental administration in the Maghrib.

[3] *Muq.*, I, 297; 305; *Muq.*, II, 384; *'Ibar,* V, 369 ff.

[4] See. Popper, *Egypt and Syria under the Circassian Sultans, 1382–1468* A.D.; A. N. Poliak, "Feudalism in Egypt, Syria, Palestine and the Lebanon 1250–1900," *R.A.S.* (London, 1939); and "Le Caractère Colonial de l'Etat Mamelouk, *R.E.J.* (1935), pp. 231–248; and Ayalon, "The European-Asiatic Steppe" in *Proceedings of the 25th International Orientalists' Congress* (Moscow, 1963), II, 47–52.

against the "Franks" (the Crusaders), and praised Salāḥ-ad-Dīn as "the ruler who abolished the trinity of God," who made the religion of Allāh triumph," and who "cleansed the Holy Places of infidelity." He surveyed, also, Egypt's history after Salāḥ-ad-Dīn's death, the division of his kingdom among his sons,[5] and the transfer of power through the wife of Shajar ad-Durr to Aybak and then unfolded the basic facts of the political and dynastic history of Egypt under the Baḥrī Mamlūks, especially under Baybars and the House of Qalā'ūn.[6] All this was apparently meant to serve as background only for his major task, namely the presentation of Barqūq and his time and to deal with the contemporary scene, in its internal and external aspects.

Biographer of Sultan Barqūq (1382–1399)

As a historian of Barqūq and his rule, Ibn Khaldūn was uniquely qualified. Being a friend and protégé of Sultan Barqūq, he was closely affiliated with the ruling class and the court and other associations which continued also under Barqūq's son and successor. He had thus the opportunity of acquainting himself thoroughly with the manifold happenings on the political, dynastic, military and diplomatic scene of contemporary Egypt. By virtue of his function as professor and teacher at various *madrasahs* and colleges in Cairo, Ibn Khaldūn had acquired an intimate knowledge of the cultural and educational aspects; and his several appointments as Mālikite Chief Cadi in Cairo afforded him a unique insight into the structure of the Mamlūk society and into the legal and juridical patterns of the Mamlūk administration, its abuses and corruption.

Ibn Khaldūn was, however, by no means satisfied to view the contemporary scene only as a spectrum of his own personal affiliations and experiences. He looked at Mamlūk Egypt with the eyes of a historian and tried to present an objective and factual picture of the "men who made history" in his own time.[7] For the investigation of the life and activities of Sultan Barqūq, he was not dependent on written sources

[5] On Saladin's life and activities, see the various chapters in *'Ibar,* V, between pp. 252–331; on his descendants, V, 331–363, and scattered references in *Ta'rīf,* pp. 284 ff.

[6] For the description of the pre-Circassian dynasty, in particular of Baybars and of the House of Qalā'ūn, see *'Ibar,* V, 369 ff., 394 ff., 401–412; *Ta'rīf,* pp. 317–319.

[7] The description of Barqūq's life and activities covers mainly but not exclusively *'Ibar* V, 462–505 and *Ta'rīf,* pp. 321–331. For other Arabic sources see Wiet, *Manhal,* no. 650. The following is limited mainly to Ibn Khaldūn's own account and I refrain from quoting parallel statements of later Arabic sources unless they add new facts.

—at least none are mentioned by him—since his own experience and observations during the very period he described supplied him with all the necessary facts. His presentation of Barqūq and his time is, thus, conspicuous by the absence of any quotations from or references to any written sources—quite in contrast to some other parts of his research, which are characterized by an abundant use of historical sources.

During his stay in Egypt, Ibn Khaldūn collected and recorded many of the legends and traditions which were current about Barqūq's early life. He reported the legendary claim which tried to connect the ancestors of Barqūq and the origin of the Circassian dynasty, in general, with the Ghassānids, thus placing him into a pure Arab lineage, probably in order to ascribe to Barqūq a nobler and more respectable ancestry. He mentions Barqūq's father by name, calling him Sayf ad-Dīn Ānas al-Jarkāsī (d. 1381).[8]

Ibn Khaldūn recounts how Barqūq was taken from Circassia[9] to the Crimea and was acquired there by the slave merchant Khawājā 'Uthmān, and how he was then sold (1362–1363) to the Mamlūk emir, Yalbughā al-Khāṣṣakī an-Nāṣirī, in Damascus until the slaves of this emir were ordered by the then-ruling Mamlūk Sultan, Ashraf ash-Sha'bān (1363–1376), to be sent to Cairo for the service of the Sultan's son.[10] This unexpected transfer to Cairo was a decisive turning point in Barqūq's life and opened the gates to his future public career. He got his training in the military academy, the Kitābīya, and was instructed in the various military disciplines, such as the handling of arms and horsemanship, which prepared him well for his future royal tasks.[11]

Ibn Khaldūn describes in great detail the jealousy and enmity between Barqūq and Baraka,[12] another Mamlūk slave, their hidden com-

[8] This is quite an exception since the father's name of a Mamlūk usually remained unknown or unnoticed, see *'Ibar* V, 472–473; and Sakhāwī, *Ḍau'*, III, 10–12; see Wiet, *Manhal*, no. 549.

[9] Circassia is the region lying at the eastern shores of the Black Sea. The Circassians, politically, were subjects of the Golden Horde whose ruler often sold Circassian subjects as slaves to distant lands.

[10] *'Ibar*, V, 463, 472 ff; on Yalbughā, see also *Ta'rīf*, p. 47, p. 127.

[11] Kitābīya is the military school in which the young Mamlūks were given special instruction in military and religious disciplines. See Ayalon, *L'Esclavage du Mamlouk* (Jerusalem, 1951), p. 40, note 35; p. 44, note 75, and his studies listed in the "Ibn Khaldūniana" bibliography at the end.

[12] On this Baraka al-Jūbānī al-Yalbughāwī (d. 1380) see *Ta'rīf*, p. 321 ff., *'Ibar* V, 462 ff. Baraka fled to Karak in Transjordania together with Barqūq and spent there about five years; Baraka was put to death at the instigation of Barqūq by Ibn 'Arrām, a former viceroy of Alexandria, who in turn was later executed at the command of Barqūq; see *'Ibar* V, 468–471; *Ta'rīf*, pp. 323–325.

petition for the throne, and how both were made regents for the young Sultan Malik aṣ-Ṣāliḥ Ḥājjī (1381–1382). Barqūq became Commander-in-Chief of the army with the title Aṭābak, while Baraka became Head of the Emirs. Ibn Khaldūn relates how Barqūq ultimately eliminated Baraka as competitor, in 1381, by putting him to death. He describes the deposition of the sultan, the appointment of a new Caliph,[13] and Barqūq's final rise to the throne on November 26, 1382, under the title Sayf ad-Dīn al-Malik aẓ-Ẓāhir Abū Sa'īd Barqūq.[14]

In dealing very extensively with Barqūq's turbulent rule as Sultan from 1382 until his death in 1399, Ibn Khaldūn reveals a thorough knowledge of the complexities of the situation which confronted the sultan and his court.[15] He paid thorough attention to the whole web of conspiracies, insurrections, plots and rebellions which filled the early years of Barqūq's rule. He dwells in particular on the uprising against Barqūq in 1389–1390, directed by two leading emirs of the time, Emir Tumarbughā al-Afḍalī, known as Minṭāsh (d. 1393), Viceroy of Malaṭya, and Emir Yalbughā an-Nāṣirī (d. 1391), the Viceroy of Damascus and the Commander-in-Chief. He gave the background of the civil war which led to Barqūq's temporary deposition and reports how Barqūq had to relinquish temporarily his rule over Egypt and had to go into hiding in Karak, and how a new sultan, Malik al-Manṣūr Ḥājjī, was proclaimed by the leaders of the rebellion, to whom the caliph and cadis, according to custom, swore allegiance.[16]

[13] About the role of the 'Abbāsid Caliph in Cairo at this juncture, see *Ta'rīf*, p. 336; *'Ibar*, V, 284, 382, 415, 449 ff.

[14] This was Ramaḍān 19, 784 H. The full royal name of the Sultan in the Arabic sources is al-Malik aẓ-Ẓāhir Abū Sa'īd Barqūq Sayf ad-Dīn b. Anaṣ al-Jarkasī al-'Uthmānī al-Yalbughāwī; the latter designations refer to the two slave purchasers who acquired Barqūq in his early years. His name, Barqūq, is being explained on the basis of the fact that he had squinted eyes, see Sakhāwī, *Ḍau'*, III, 10–12.

[15] Ibn Khaldūn was well aware of the fundamental differences between the Circassian dynasty founded by Barqūq and the Baḥrī dynasty (1250–1382) of his predecessors in relation to the racial and ethnic composition of its Mamlūks. External sources, especially Ibn Taghrī Birdī, stress that Barqūq ousted many of the Turkish Mamlūks replacing them with Mamlūks of Circassian origin who became the mainstay of his army. See also *'Ibar*, V, p. 371 and p. 422; Ayalon, *Ibn Khaldūn's View on the Mamlukes*, pp. 142–143.

[16] For further details see *'Ibar* V, the chapters between pp. 482–505; *Ta'rīf*, pp. 312–331. This revolt against Barqūq has been the object of many detailed descriptions in Muslim sources. For an account of a Damascus historian of these events, see Ibn Ṣaṣrā, *ad-Durra muḍī'a fil-Dawla al-Ẓāhirīya, A Chronicle of Damascus, 1389–1397*, trans., ed. and annotated by Wm. M. Brinner (Berkeley, 1963), 2 vols. For a Persian account of this revolt see H. H. Giesecke, *Das Werk des 'Azīz ibn Ārdašīr Āstarābādī*, pp. 68 ff.; 115 ff.; and 122 ff.; for a Latin Account see B. de Mignanelli, "Ascensus Barcoch," ed. Fischel, *Arabica*, 1959; and for a recent

Ibn Khaldūn records the two factions and conflicting views among the leaders of the rebellion who wanted to "dispose" of Barqūq, if and when he was captured. The one group, led by an-Nāṣirī and Minṭāsh pleaded for the death sentence of Barqūq, while another, headed by Emir Alṭunbughā al-Jūbānī recommended Barqūq's imprisonment in Karak in order to save his life and to avert a death sentence.[17]

He describes how Barqūq, after having regained the sultanate, freed himself from his enemies and secured the support of his loyal Mamlūks, who fought victoriously with him at the battle of Shaqḥab.[18] Ibn Khaldūn stresses that Barqūq forgave the emirs who voted against him by signing the *fetwā* in 1389 and returned them to their former positions. It is noteworthy that Ibn Khaldūn, who, as we have seen, was involved in the signing of the *fetwā*, refrained in this context from referring to himself and to his dismissal from the Baybarsīya Khānqa as a result of his action.[19]

Interwoven into the life-story of Barqūq are short biographical sketches of many of the leading emirs and officials of that period who held important positions.[20] Ibn Khaldūn devotes many pages in particular to Emir al-Jūbānī, the second highest ranking official at Barqūq's court, and describes his activities, his rise and fall, his imprisonment in Alexandria, his banishment to Karak, and the final phase of his life, after regaining the favor of the Sultan.[21]

He records meticulously the appointments and dismissals of the "Men of the Sword"[22] of the military oligarchy of Mamlūk Egypt and lists every important head of the military administration. Ibn Khaldūn's accumulation of names and terms is an almost dazzling and bewildering amount of facts pertaining to Barqūq and his emirs.

Turkish biography of Barqūq, see M. C. Şehabeddin Tekindağ, *Barkuk Devrinde Memlūk Sultanliği.*

17 See *Ta'rīf,* pp. 326–329.

18 It was at Shaqḥab, near Damascus, that two decisive battles took place which are fully covered by Ibn Khaldūn and other Arab sources.

19 About Ibn Khaldūn's participation in the *fetwā* against Barqūq and his subsequent dismissal from the Baybarsīya Khānqa, see Part One.

20 Among them are Kumushbughā, Aytamish, Yūnis, Tanam, Julbān, Sūdūn, Damurdāsh, Yashbak and others. About all these officials mentioned by Ibn Khaldūn in *'Ibar* and *Ta'rīf,* see Wiet, *Manhal,* Ibn Taghrī Birdī, *Nujūm,* and Popper, *Indices to Ibn Taghrī Birdī.* On the Turkish names of some of these high officials see Sauvaget, "Noms et Surnoms de Mamlouks," *J.A.*, CXXXVIII, 31–58.

21 About al-Jūbānī (d. 1390) see *'Ibar,* V, 476–478, 486, 493–497; *Ta'rīf,* pp. 248, 454, 321–334; and Wiet, *Manhal,* no. 530.

22 For this term, see *Muq.*, II, 40 ff., and W. Popper, *Systematic Notes,* I, 100 ff. and 108–119.

He praised Barqūq's character and personality, stressed his courage and devotion, his interest also in the "Men of the Pen" and lauded him for generously supporting scholars and establishing schools and colleges, so that "the nation prospered and the people were satisfied with his rule."

Ibn Khaldūn took his biography of Barqūq up to the very end and dealt also with the Last Will of Barqūq and the repercussions of its terms on the political and military scene.[23] Shortly before his death, Barqūq summoned the Caliph, cadis and emirs and requested that the eldest of his sons, Faraj, should become his successor to the throne and designated the other brothers, one after the other, after Faraj. This provision was accepted by all those present who set their signatures to this testament of Barqūq's. Mention should be made that Ibn Khaldūn also signed as a witness this Last Will of Barqūq.[24]

Barqūq also desired that Aytamish,[25] the Commander-in-Chief in Cairo be named regent or special guardian of Faraj during his sultanate, since at that time the boy was only ten years old. This request, too, was granted by all those present at the council-meeting, including Ibn Khaldūn, and "the affairs were carried on after Barqūq's death as he bequeathed them."

After Barqūq's death,[26] however, this latter provision was strongly contested by the Viceroy of Damascus, Tanam.[27] Ibn Khaldūn describes how Tanam, outraged that not he, but Aytamish, was chosen, succeeded through his courtiers at Cairo in bringing about a declaration by Faraj himself that he was mature enough to conduct the affairs of state by himself and that he should be freed from the guardianship of Aytamish. A state council, in which all the high emirs and Chief Cadis took part, among them Ibn Khaldūn, sanctioned this decision which led to Faraj's "liberation" from the guardianship of Aytamish. Thus the "rock was removed from Faraj" as the sources say.[28]

---

[23] *Ta'rīf*, p. 347; see Ibn Taghrī Birdī, *Nujūm* V, 594–595.

[24] Ibn Khaldūn's participation in this legal action indicates that he had regained the favor of the Sultan.

[25] This was Aytamish al-Asandamurī al-Bajāsī al-Jirjāwī, the Grand Emir and Commander-in-Chief of the Egyptian armies (d. 1400). See *'Ibar*, V, 500; *Ta'rīf*, pp. 326, 347–348; Wiet, *Manhal*, no. 581.

[26] He died on June 20, 1399 (Shawwāl 15, 801 H.) at the age of about sixty-three; he had ruled over Egypt and Syria as Grand Emir and Regent and as Sultan for twenty-one years and fifty-seven days. See a detailed necrology of Barqūq in Ibn Taghrī Birdī, *Nujūm*, V, 595–601.

[27] About Tanam, known as Tanbak al-Ḥasanī aẓ-Ẓāhirī, see *'Ibar*, V, 500; *Ta'rīf*, pp. 347–349; Wiet, *Manhal*, no. 787.

[28] *Ta'rīf*, p. 348.

Aytamish and his followers refused, however, to yield, and organized a rebellion against the young sultan. To quell this uprising, Faraj himself led the military expedition to Damascus, in which Ibn Khaldūn, as we have noted above, took part in his capacity as Chief Cadi at this juncture.[29]

Critical Observation and Evaluation

Ibn Khaldūn's treatment of the dynastic and political aspects of Egypt under Barqūq is basically court history, dealing with the political and military events in the capital, Cairo, as well as in the provincial centers such as Damascus, Aleppo, Tripoli, Ḥomṣ, Karak, Ṣafad, and others. It is fundamentally a history of the palace and its emirs, their uprisings and betrayals, their insurrections, intrigues and jealousies, their discords and conflicts. Whoever is mentioned by Ibn Khaldūn in his history of Mamlūk Egypt under Barqūq is closely connected with the ruling military classes.

Through his emphasis on court history, on dynastic, political and military aspects, Ibn Khaldūn neglected "the common man" and gave only little attention to the simple daily life of the Egyptian population, to the *Ahl adh-Dhimma,*[30] the living conditions of the peasants, the produce of the market, the prices of bread, meat, or barley, the movements of the Nile waters with their effect on the agricultural life of Egypt.[31] Very little can be found in his account on the economic and social problems of the Mamlūk society in general, in whose

---

[29] *Ta'rīf,* pp. 349–351; this was in September, 1400. It was at this occasion that Ibn Khaldūn was able to visit the Christian holy places in Palestine of which he gave an interesting detailed description.

[30] The non-Muslim communities in Egypt comprising Coptic and other Christian groups and numerous Jewish communities, Karaites and Rabbanites, were rather strong in Barqūq's time. For the Christian community in Egypt, see the accounts of the various Christian merchants, travellers, and missionaries, in particular L. Frescobaldi, G. Gucci and S. Sigoli, *Visit to the Holy Places of Egypt, Sinai, Palestine and Syria in 1384,* trans. from the Italian (Jerusalem, 1948); see also M. Perlmann, "Notes on Anti-Christian Propaganda in the Mamlūk Empire," *B.S.O.A.S.* (1940), X, 843–861. For the Jewish communities in Mamlūk Egypt, see L. A. Mayer, "The Status of the Jews under the Mamlūks" (in Hebrew) in *Judah L. Magnes Anniversary Book* (Jerusalem, 1938), pp. 161–167, English summary, pp. xxvii–xxviii; and E. Strauss (Ashtor), *Tōldōth ha-Yehūdim b'Mizrāyim ve Sūriya* (History of the Jews in Egypt and Syria) (Jerusalem, 1951), 2 vols.

[31] See the comprehensive monograph on this topic by W. Popper, *The Cairo Nilometer,* U.C. Publications in Semitic Philology (*Berkeley,* 1951), XII; and Kamel Osman Ghaleb Pacha, "Le Miḳyās ou Nilomètre de l'Île de Rodah," *Mémoires présentés à l'Institut d'Égypte* (Cairo, 1951), LIV.

midst he lived for so many years.[32] The famine which ravaged over Egypt in Barqūq's time was not even mentioned in Ibn Khaldūn's account.[33] Only casually does he refer to such matters as taxation, income from fiefs, and the staggering problems of the financial administration.[34] Some scattered glimpses are offered into the monetary history under Barqūq and some abuses in the financial practices.[35]

In his time a strange, but apparently widespread, custom was followed in the commercial sphere of life, namely the depositing of money, whether legally or illegally acquired, for safe-keeping in the hands of a person of trust and confidence, in order to avoid loss or confiscation by greedy officials or the state. In view of the absence of banks in the modern sense of the word,[36] this was a perfectly legal procedure, and the person most trusted in such a situation was usually the cadi, the judge.[37] Transactions of that kind were carried out in Barqūq's time by his own fiscal advisor, Jamāl ad-Dīn Maḥmūd b. 'Alī al-Ustādār, who introduced a monetary reform by issuing new coins called Maḥmūdīya dinars.

Ibn Khaldūn regarded the manipulations of Maḥmūd b. 'Alī important enough to mention them at various occasions not only in his *'Ibar* but also in his *Muqaddimah,* where he stated, "I was in Egypt in the days of al-Malik aẓ-Ẓāhir Abu Sa'īd Barqūq, when he arrested his minister of the interior, the Emir Maḥmūd, and confiscated his property. The man charged with the confiscation informed me that the amount of gold he cleaned out was 1,600,000 dinars. There was

[32] It is indeed surprising that the very scholar and historian who had earned the reputation of being one of those who so seriously took into consideration the important role which economic and social problems play in history and who so efficiently has outlined the impact of economic factors on the rise, decline, and fall of cities, states and dynasties, should have paid so little attention to the economic and social problems of Egypt of his own time.

[33] See Maqrīzī's treatise, *Ighāthat al-Umma bi Kashf al-Ghumma* (Cairo, 1940), and the French translation by G. Wiet, "Le Traité des Famines de Maqrīzī," in *J.E.S.H.O.* (1962), V, 1–85, especially 44–48.

[34] See the valuable studies on the economic and social aspects of Mamlūk Egypt by E. Ashtor, D. Ayalon, C. Cahen, A. S. Ehrenkreutz, S. D. Goitein, S. Labib, A. N. Poliak and others.

[35] For the monetary problems of that period see, Anastase al-Karmalī, *AnNuqūd al-'Arabīyah* (Baghdad, 1939), pp. 69 ff.; al-Maqrīzī, *Shudhūr al-'Uqūd,* ed. L. A. Mayer (Alexandria, 1933); and Paul Balog, "History of the Dirham in Egypt from the Fatimid Conquest until the collapse of the Mamlūk Empire (968–1517)" in *Revue Numismatique* (Paris, 1961), III, 133–146.

[36] For a comparison with the conditions in the lands of Eastern Islam of the tenth century see W. J. Fischel, "The Origin of Banking in Mediaeval Islam," *J.R.A.S.* (London, 1933), pp. 339–352; pp. 569–603.

[37] Gaudefroy-Demombynes, "Notes" in *R.E.J.,* pp. 143–144.

in addition a proportionately large amount of fabrics, riding animals, pack animals, livestock, and (grain) crops." [38]

About Barqūq's commercial policy, on the trade and commerce of Mamlūk Egypt of his time, Ibn Khaldūn is surprisingly silent. We look in vain for any reference to that powerful group, or guild, of pepper and spice merchants of Egypt, the so-called Kārimites, who precisely in this very period, during Ibn Khaldūn's stay in Egypt, under Barqūq, reached the peak of their political activities and economic prosperity in the Indian-Egyptian spice trade via Aden and Yemen. This omission is the more astounding since the activities of this group of merchants, whose headquarters was Cairo, had a direct and important bearing on the affairs of the court in the time of Barqūq. If not for the financial help of a Burhān ad-Dīn al-Maḥallī, a Shihāb ad-Dīn al-Muslim, and a Nūr ad Dīn al-Kharrūbī, the leaders of this merchant group, historical events might have taken quite a different course.[39] They advanced huge loans to the sultan, amounting to hundreds of thousands of dinars, enabling him to equip his army for the expedition against Tamerlane and so to protect the country against the Mongol threat and to stave off the march of Tamerlane to the West.

It should be stated that no other period in the history of medieval Egypt is more thoroughly covered and recorded in all its details than that of the Mamlūk rule over Egypt, and particularly that of the Burjī-Circassian dynasty, from the very time of Barqūq on. A galaxy of Muslim historians of the fifteenth century composed voluminous works on the political, military, dynastic and administrative happenings in Egypt and dealt extensively with the internal, as well as the external affairs, of this time, not only in the capital of the Mamlūk Empire, Cairo, but also in the provincial cities such as Damascus,

---

[38] Ibn Khaldūn himself was one of those cadis who was entrusted with such secret deposits. See *Muq.*, I, 326 (*Proleg.*, I, 368); *'Ibar*, V, 497–498.

[39] About these Kārimites, see W. J. Fischel, "Über die Gruppe der Kārimī Kaufleute," in *Analecta Orientalia*, (Rome, 1937), XIV, 65–82; also his "The Spice Trade in Mamlūk Egypt," in *J.E.S.H.O.* (Leiden, 1958), I, 157–174; Labīb "at-Tijāra al-Kārimīyya wa-tijārat Miṣr fi l-'uṣūr al-wusṭā," in *Bulletin de la Societé Egyptienne d'Etudes Historiques* (Cairo, 1952), IV, 5–63 and *Der Islam* (Hamburg, 1957), pp. 324–329; G. Wiet, "Les Marchands d'Epices sous les Sultans Mamlouks," *Cahiers d'histoire Egyptienne* (Cairo, 1955), pp. 81–147; E. Ashtor, "The Kārimite Merchants" in *J.R.A.S.* (London, 1956), pp. 45–56; S. D. Goitein, "New Lights on the Kārim Merchants," *J.E.S.H.O.* (Leiden, 1958), pp. 175–184. See also Miscellanea, "Les Kārimīs aux Archives de Venise," *J.E.S.H.O.* (Leiden, 1958) p. 333; J. Sublet, in Arabica (Leiden, 1962), IX, 193–196; and also Aḥmad Darrag, *L'Egypte sous le Règne de Barsbay (1422–1438)* (Damascus, 1961), esp. pp. 213–14; 233–236; and now Labīb, *Handelsgeschichte Ägyptens im Spätmittelalter (1171–1517)*.

Aleppo and others.[40] Whoever wishes to know the actual events of a certain day in a certain month of a particular year during the reigns of Barqūq and Faraj will find ample information in these historical sources, whose devotion to the most minute detail of the events of their time is astounding indeed.[41]

Yet, Ibn Khaldūn's account of Barqūq and his times differs considerably from these other sources and is distinguished by a number of very significant historiographical features. While the chronicle of Ibn Ṣaṣrā—to refer to one of the earliest Syrian Mamlūk sources—limited itself geographically to events in Damascus and this only from 1389 to 1397, offering a popular history, a mixture of stories and legends, and while the *Ta'rīkh* of Ibn al-Furāt—the other of the earlier historians of Mamlūk Egypt—dealt (at least in the available published text of his work) only with the years from 1387 to 1397, Ibn Khaldūn's account of Barqūq and his time represents a complete life-story of Barqūq and encompasses his whole career from his youth until his end. It is furthermore presented not in the form of an analistic day-by-day recording, but in a continuous, well-rounded narrative.

Above all, unlike the later Mamlūk historians of the fifteenth century who wrote their accounts of the period at least one or two generations after the occurrence of the events, Ibn Khaldūn wrote as an observer, an eyewitness of, and even an active participant in, the very events he had set out to describe. His is probably the earliest Arabic biographical sketch of the entire life and career of Barqūq, including even the early years of his son Faraj—a typical result of Ibn Khaldūn's research during his "Egyptian" phase.

[40] On all these Arab historians see the list of "External Arabic Sources," following the Introduction.

[41] There exist still some Arabic manuscripts dealing with Barqūq thus far inaccessible; according to Sakhāwī, *Ḍau'*, III, 10–12, Ibn Duqmāq is said to have composed a biography (*sīra*) of aẓ-Ẓāhir Barqūq. Sakhāwī, *Ḍau'*, VII, 18–20, refers also to a long biography (*sīrā tawīla*) of Barqūq and the men of his time by Taqī ad-Dīn al-Fāsī al-Makkī al-Mālikī (d. 1429).

2

AS HISTORIAN OF THE TATARS AND THE MONGOLS

Ibn Khaldūn by no means limited himself to the internal, dynastic and administrative affairs of Egypt under the Sultans Barqūq and Faraj. He delved, also, into the aspects of the foreign policy of contemporary Egypt and investigated and tried to understand those external factors which affected and threatened the destiny of Mamlūk Egypt beyond her borders.[1] He was mainly concerned with two fronts, the Mamlūk-Maghribī front in the West, and with the Mamlūk-Mongol conflict in the Northeast.

On the Mamlūk-Maghribī front, the "diplomatic" relationship between the rulers of North Africa and the Mamlūk Sultans in Cairo, was in those days based on mutual friendship and a "good neighbor policy." The Maghribī rulers were interested in maintaining good relations with Egypt for the sake of prestige and reputation, and out of concern for the safety of the caravans of Maghribī pilgrims travelling to Cairo on their way to Mecca. This expressed itself mainly in a regular exchange of gifts, letters, and envoys from both sides, as a sign of cordiality and as a reaffirmation of friendship.

Ibn Khaldūn, who, as a "Maghribī Consul" in Cairo, was actively engaged in fostering the Mamlūk-Maghribī contacts, became, also, the very historian of this relationship between Cairo and the Maghrib. He showed that the custom of exchanging presents between the Maghrib

[1] Some scattered references to Egypt's relations with the Yemen, Ḥijāz and the Holy Places in Arabia, with Nubia, with the Qipchaqs, with the Christian cities in the Mediterranean basin (Venice, Genoa, etc.) and with the Ottoman powers, can be found in his writings.

and Cairo was already a long-established practice from the time of Ṣalāḥ ad-Dīn on until Barqūq's time. This steady reaffirmation of friendship was the only concrete "diplomatic" issue in the relationship between Mamlūk Egypt and the West. In a special chapter entitled "Exchange of Gifts and Presents between the Rulers of the Maghrib and Barqūq," Ibn Khaldūn listed the various objects and gifts which rulers on both sides exchanged, such as garments of silk and linen, arms, horses, mules, perfumes, skins, dyes, jewelry, copper, tents, and other rare and costly articles. He also described the reception ceremonies accorded to the bearers of these gifts and the degree of hospitality accorded them during their stay in the respective capitals.[2]

Unlike the Mamlūk-Maghribī front, the Mamlūk-Mongol conflict was of utmost military and political relevance and became the major issue in Mamlūk Egypt's foreign policy even in Ibn Khaldūn's time. With the appearance of Tamerlane at the borders of the Mamlūk Empire and the actual invasion of Syria, the destruction of Aleppo and the threat to Damascus, the Mamlūk-Mongol conflict of long standing reached its climax and erupted into open warfare between the Mongol and the Syrian-Egyptian armies.

Ibn Khaldūn, the historian and statesman, attuned to the turning points in history, always fascinated by those who were destined to make history and to turn the wheels of history in one or another direction, could not remain a mere spectator and a passive eye-witness to these events. He reacted to the situation not as a politician but as a historian. Driven by a genuine interest and natural curiosity in the past of great nations and personalities in general, and motivated by a keen desire to understand the Mamlūk-Mongol conflict in Egypt's international relationship, he set out to investigate "how the kings of these Tatars from Jenghiz Khān on, happened to rule the world, much to the astonishment of the Islamic peoples." [3] He therefore delved into the origins, expansion, and conquests of those Mongol and Tatar tribes, which under their leader, Jenghiz Khān, had come out of the heart of Asia and had invaded the lands of the Eastern Caliphate at various periods.

---

[2] See *'Ibar*, V, 420–421, 440–441, 479–480, 501; *Ta'rīf*, pp. 335–351. See M. Canard, "Les Relations entre les Mérinides et les Mamelouks au XIVᵉ Siècle," V, 41–81. See Aḥmad b. Khālid an-Nāṣirī as-Salvī, "Kitāb al-Istiqçā li-Akhbār Douval el Maghrib el-Aqçā," (Histoire du Maroc), *Les Mérinides* (*Archives Marocaines*) (Paris, 1934), XXXIII. For the relationship between the Mamlūks and the Ḥafṣides in Tunis, see Brunschvig, *La Berbérie orientale*.

[3] *'Ibar*, V, 515 ff.

Sources for the History of Jenghiz Khān and His Descendants

In undertaking such a historical investigation, Ibn Khaldūn entered a field of research and a geographical area with which he was only superficially acquainted, if at all, while in the Maghrib. In order to obtain the maximum of reliable and accurate historical and geographical information on the Tatars and Mongols, on Jenghiz Khān and his descendants up to Tamerlane, he consulted and utilized as many sources and authorities as the Egyptian libraries could provide him with. The efforts he had made to ascertain a broad documentary basis for his account of the history of the Mongols and the Tatars are reflected in the frequency and multiplicity of sources, both oral and written, to which he must have had access during his stay in Egypt.

Ibn Khaldūn derived his oral information mainly from merchants, travellers, and scholars who returned from Central Asia, either China, Khwārizm, or Khurāsān. So he states in one place, "I was informed by 'people from China' whom I have met," [4] or he refers to a Burhān ad-Dīn al-Khwārizmī, one of the most eminent scholars of the time, "who informed me." [5] But his major authorities were a variety of written sources, found in Cairo, which he used most extensively for his purpose. For the geographical background of that region of Asia he used in particular the *Kitāb Rujār,* the famous geographical treatise named *Nuzhat al-Mushtāq,* by al-Idrīsī (d. 1160),[6] which was dedicated by its author to Roger, the King of Sicily. Ibn Khaldūn regarded this source as a model of geographical treatment and valued it so highly that he felt it necessary to depart from his usual method of quoting sources by elaborating on details about this author and his work, as he did, also, with another geographical work from which Ibn Khaldūn greatly benefitted to such an extent, namely, the *Riḥla* of Ibn Baṭṭūṭah (d. 1377).[7]

For the understanding of the political and dynastic background, Ibn Khaldūn made use of the *Mashārib at-Tajārib wa Ghawārib al-*

[4] *'Ibar,* V, 532. Ibn Khaldūn has very little to say about China. In speaking of the vastness of China, he remarks that it would take nine months to traverse it because China is divided according to ancient traditions into nine parts, each of which required one month of travel in crossing. Each part is ruled by a Khān, all of whom are viceroys (*nā'ib*) of the great Khān. *'Ibar,* V, 516 ff., p. 526.

[5] He referred, also, in a general way, to such sources as *Akhbār Mulūk at-Takht* (History of the Kings of Qaraqorum), and to *Khabar al-'Ajam;* see *'Ibar,* V, 530, 533.

[6] *Muq.,* I, 93 and many other references in *'Ibar,* V and VI.

[7] *Muq.,* I, 327–328. For his way of quoting these and other sources, see later.

'Arā'ib by Abu' l-Ḥasan b. Abu' l-Qāsim al-Bayhaqī (d. 1169).[8] In regards to the wars of Jenghiz Khān with the Khwārizm Shāhs, he used a work to which he refers simply as *Ta'rīkh* or *Kitāb*, composed by an-Nasawī (sometimes spelled by himself "an-Nasabī") who is none other than Shihāb ad-Dīn Muḥammad b. Aḥmad b. 'Alī al-Munshī an-Nasawī,[9] the secretary (*kātib al-inshā'*) of Jalāl ad-Dīn al-Mankobirtī. He had accompanied his master on all his campaigns and was thus able to gather at first hand the information about the dynasty of the Khwārizm Shāh and the Mongol invasion which he had recorded in his *Sīrat as-Sulṭān Jalāl ad-Dīn Mankobirtī* (concluded in 1241).[10]

An indispensable and often quoted source for Ibn Khaldūn's historical research was also the *Kāmil* of 'Izz ad-Dīn b. al-Athīr, though Ibn Khaldūn freed himself from Ibn al-Athīr's more passionate description of the Mongol invasion in its effect on the Muslim world and offered a calmer and more objective account of the events.[11] Ibn Khaldūn also refers very frequently, for this and other periods, to the *Ta'rīkh* of Mu'ayyad Ismā'īl Abu 'l-Fidā', the "Ṣāḥib Ḥamā" who had copied extensively from both Ibn al-Athīr and an-Nasawī and with whose help he could carry on the history of the Tatars up to the year 1327.[12]

Ibn Khaldūn, determined to offer a complete survey of the history of the Tatars and Mongols until his own time, was apparently not satisfied with the sources thus far mentioned. Since the account of both Ibn al-Athīr (concluded in 1233), who lived in Mesopotamia, and Abu 'l-Fidā' (concluded in 1331) were limited in time and area, Ibn Khaldūn searched in additional sources for a more complete coverage of the Mongol and Tatar history.[13] This help he found in the monu-

---

[8] *'Ibar*, V, 92. See Barthold. "Turkestan," pp. 32–33; and S. K. Husaini, *I.C.* (Hyderabad, 1954), XXVIII, 297–318, *I.C.* (1960), Vol. XXXIV, 83 ff.

[9] Ibn Khaldūn quotes an-Nasawī in innumerable places in his *'Ibar*, V.

[10] See *'Ibar*, V, 108. The Arabic text was edited with French translation by O. Houdas, "Vie de Djelal Addin Mankobirti," *Publ. de l'Ecole des langues orient. vivantes*, Ser. III (Paris, 1891–1895), IX–X.

[11] See *Kitāb al-Kāmil (Chronican)*, ed. C. J. Tornberg (Leiden, 1851–1876), esp. vols. XI and XII, very frequently quoted in his *'Ibar*, V, but significantly not mentioned in his *Muqaddimah;* see, however, *Muq.*, II, 128–129 and *Proleg.*, II, 139, note 751. In comparing Ibn Khaldūn with Ibn al-Athīr, Barthold ("Turkestan," p. 4) remarked that "for the history of Central Asia Ibn Khaldūn, who lived in Spain and Africa, gives little that is new compared with Ibn al-Athīr, of whom he evidently made use . . ." Much more to the point however is le Strange, *The Lands of the Eastern Caliphate*, p. 17 when he says: "the Universal History of Ibn Khaldūn is often of use to supplement the meager chronicle of Ibn al-Athīr."

[12] *'Ibar*, V, 383, 525, 534, and in many other places.

[13] Abu 'l-Fidā' also is not expressly mentioned by Ibn Khaldūn in his *Muqaddimah*, which tends to support our contention that this and other sources used by

mental work entitled *Masālīk al-Abṣār fī Mamālik al-Amṣār* by Aḥmad b. Yaḥyā b. Faḍl-Allāh Shihāb ad-Dīn al-'Umarī ad-Dimashqī, the famous Damasene historian, al-'Umarī (d. 1348).[14] Ibn Khaldūn used al-'Umarī's *Masālīk al-Abṣār* extensively as his guide and major source, and indicated in each instance the authorities on which al-'Umarī had based his information. Many statements concerning Jenghiz Khān, his sons and descendants are attributed by Ibn Khaldūn to a Shams ad-Dīn al-Iṣfahānī (d. 1348) whom he called "the Imām of the intellectual sciences (*ma'qulāt*) in the East" and who belonged to the circle of Naṣīr ad-Dīn aṭ-Ṭūṣī.[15]

References are made by Ibn Khaldūn, often simultaneously with the former, to another authority on which al-'Umarī greatly relied, namely, to Nizām ad-Dīn Yaḥyā b. al-Ḥakīm Nūr ad-Dīn 'Abdar-Raḥmān aṣ-Ṣayādī (d. ca. 1369),[16] who according to Ibn Khaldūn was the *kātib*, the secretary, of Abū Sa'īd, the last of the Il-Khān rulers.

Ibn Khaldūn's linguistic limitations excluded his using Persian sources for his topic, and he could, therefore, not avail himself of the valuable material embodied in the works of Nāzir al-Jūzjānī (d. 1260), Rashīd ad-Dīn (d. 1318), Waṣṣāf (d. 1327), and other Persian historians.[17]

One of the few Persian works to which Ibn Khaldūn referred as his source of information is that of 'Alā ad-Dīn 'Aṭā Juwaynī (d. 1257), whose *Ta'rīkh i Jahān Gushāy* (*History of the World Conqueror*)[18] he knew through the medium of quotations found in the Arabic work of al-'Umarī.

Ibn Khaldūn seems to have grasped the major contribution made to history by the greatest of the Persian historians, namely Abū Ṭayyib

by him in his outline of the history of the Mongols and Tartars were available to him only in Egypt.

[14] This important work remains still to be published in toto; see Wiet, *Manhal,* no. 333. How extensively Qalqashandī has used al-'Umarī's works is discussed by Björkman, *Beiträge zur Geschichte der Staatskanzlei,* pp. 75–76.

[15] *'Ibar,* V, 525, 527, 529. See Ibn Ḥajar, *Durar al-Kāmina,* III, 107; IV, 327–328 and Ibn al-'Imād, *Shadharāt adh-Dhahab,* VI, 165, 231, 255.

[16] See *'Ibar,* V, 527, 534; Ibn Ḥajar, *Durar al-Kāmina,* IV, 417–418; Quatremère, *Notices et Extraits,* XIII; Tiesenhausen, *Recueil de matériaux,* Part I, pp. 213, 217.

[17] For details on these Persian authors, see E. G. Browne, *Persian Literature under Tartar Dominion* (Cambridge, 1920, ff.); C. A. Storey, *Persian Literature: a Bibliographical Survey* (London, 1936).

[18] *'Ibar,* V, 526. For the Persian text, see *History of Jenghiz Khān and his Successors,* ed. Muḥammad Qazvīnī, Gibb Memorial Series, O.S. (Leiden, 1913) XVI, translated into English by J. A. Boyle as *The History of the World Conqueror by 'Ala-ad-Dīn 'Aṭā Malik Juwaynī* (London, 1958), 2 vols.

Rashīd ad-Daula Faḍl-Allāh b. Yaḥyā al-Hamadhānī, known as Rashīd ad-Daula or Rashīd ad-Dīn (d. 1318), the author of the Universal History *Jāmi' at-Tawārīkh,* who found his tragic end under Abū Sa'īd, the last of the Il-Khān rulers of Persia.

Though Ibn Khaldūn could not use the work of Rashīd ad-Dīn, he made a very illuminating statement about his work and life, indicating how close an affinity he felt to the great Persian historian of the fourteenth century and stated: "He had composed a history [*Ta'rīkh*] in which he gathered the accounts of the Tatars [*Akhbār Tatar*], their genealogy and their tribes and presented it in the form of a [genealogical] tree as in this our book, [*kama fī kitābina hādha*]." [19]

Despite his intensive research in Egypt, Ibn Khaldūn admitted in some cases his lack of knowledge in regard to certain genealogical and historical aspects of the Tatar tribes, and more than once he stated, "I do not know," "I cannot explain," "I do not know from what tribe these kings descended," "I do not know how correct the genealogists are . . ." etc., indicating in all this his scholarly integrity, scrutiny and reliability.[20]

From Jenghiz Khān to the Il-Khān Dynasty

Thus equipped with a great abundance of facts and data derived from reliable and authentic sources, most of which became accessible to him in Egypt, Ibn Khaldūn unfolded the history of the Tatars and Mongols and the rise of Jenghiz Khān and his descendants.[21] For Ibn Khaldūn, the Tatars belong to the Turkish tribes and he reiterates that genealogists and historians agree that most of the people of the inhabited world belong to one of two groups: either to the Arabs or to the Turks, and that there is no nation in the world which would excel them in numbers; the former one living in the southern part

[19] *'Ibar,* V, 549; on Rashīd ad-Dīn's work and significance see the editions and valuable studies by K. Jahn. Ibn Khaldūn does not refer to Rashīd ad-Dīn's Jewish origin; for this see W. J. Fischel, "Azarbaijān in Jewish History," in *Proceedings of the American Academy of Jewish Research* (New York, 1953), pp. 13–18, where most of the relevant Arabic and Persian sources concerning this aspect have been discussed.

[20] *'Ibar,* V, 506, 516, 527, 532.

[21] Ibn Khaldūn's major presentation about Jenghiz Khān and his descendants is covered in *'Ibar,* V, 515–527 and *Ta'rīf,* pp. 360–362. There are innumerable scattered references to him, and the Tatars and Mongols in general, in earlier parts of *'Ibar,* V, see also *'Ibar,* III, 15, 534–535.

of the earth, the other in the northern part of the earth, they ruled successively over the world.[22]

In a special chapter entitled "The Rule of the Tatars of the Turkish Tribes and how they became victorious over the Islamic Kingdoms and overthrew the throne of the Caliphate in Baghdād . . . and how they became Muslims . . ." [23] Ibn Khaldūn tried to unfold all the genealogical and historical ramifications. He records some of the legendary features surrounding Jenghiz Khān's birth, and traces his genealogy back to the descendants of Qūmar, the son of Yāfith, as mentioned in the *Taurāt*.[24] He also gave his original name, Tamücin, and assigned to Jenghiz Khān invariably such titles as the "Emir," "Malik," "Khān," or "Sultan" of the Mongols when he began to rule independently from the year 610 H. (1213 A. D.) onward.

In turning, first of all, to "the biography of Jenghiz Khān," Ibn Khaldūn described how, after having unified the Mongols and Tatars under his supreme leadership, Jenghiz Khān embarked on his military campaigns, the invasion of the territories of the Khwārizm Shāh dynasty [25] and his campaigns of Turkestān, Khurāsān, Māzandarān and Persia. Ibn Khaldūn stated: "These Tatars are those who came out of the desert beyond the Oxus, between it and China in the six hundred twenties under their king, Jenghiz Khān. He conquered the entire East up to 'Irāq al-'Arab from the hands of the Seljūqs and his vassals . . ."

Ibn Khaldūn gave considerable attention also to the sons of Jenghiz Khān. He had many children due to the Bedouin life he led and to his *'aṣabīyah*. Ibn Khaldūn dealt, as most of the historians did, chiefly with the four famous sons of Jenghiz Khān, namely, (1) Ṭūlī, (2) Dūshī Khān, (3) Jaghaṭāi and (4) Ogotāi. He then turned to the history of each of his sons and their respective descendants, their conquests and invasions.[26]

He dwelt at length on the division of Jenghiz Khān's empire among

[22] *Ta'rīf*, p. 351; *'Ibar*, V, 2–5, 182, 396 ff., 515 ff.; most of the medieval Muslim sources consider the Mongols to be Turks.

[23] *'Ibar*, V, 515.

[24] For the legend of his birth and his descent from priests (*kāhin*), see *'Ibar*, V, 506; *Ta'rīf*, p. 360; and *Encyclopedia of Islam*, s.v. Činghiz Khān, by Barthold.

[25] For his detailed account of Jenghiz Khān's wars against the dynasty of the Khwārizm Shāh, see *'Ibar*, V, 66–145; 379–388.

[26] The many variants and divergencies pertaining to the exact names of his sons, as Ibn Khaldūn found them in his sources, caused even him some confusion. In some places he mentioned only three sons as Jenghiz Khān's descendants, namely, Ṭūlī, Dūshī, and Jaghaṭāi, omitting Ogotāi, altogether; see, however, for all four, *Ta'rīf*, pp. 360 ff., and 381.

his sons and on the geographical extent of the respective territories which were assigned by Jenghiz Khān to each of his sons,[27] thus conveying the ramifications of the Tatar rule after the death of Jenghiz Khān.[28]

Ṭūlī, whose sons were Qubilāi and Hūlāgū, received as his portion the provinces of Khurāsān, 'Iraq al-'Ajam, Ray up to 'Irāq al-'Arab, Fārs, the land of Sijistān, and Sind; Dūshī Khān received the country of the Qipjāq, including Sarāi, and the country of the Turks as far as Khwārizm.

Ogotāi, called "the Khān," was the possessor (*ṣāḥib*) of the throne, which Ibn Khaldūn explained as "the equivalent in position to the caliph in the realm of Islam." He made Qarakorum the central residence of his empire. When he died without descendants, the Khānate passed to Qubilāi Khān and later to the sons of Dūshi Khān, the rulers of Sarāi.

Jaghaṭāi received as his share Turkestān, Kāshghar, aṣ-Ṣaghūn, ash-Shāsh, Farghāna, and the rest of the lands beyond the Oxus.

Glimpses into the Mongolian civilization

Ibn Khaldūn's history of the Mongol and Tatar tribes is not only an account of the military, dynastic and political events of Central Asia and the Eastern lands of the Caliphate; throughout his survey, Ibn Khaldūn showed a special interest also in the religious and legal aspects of the Mongolian civilization. He mentioned that Jenghiz Khān, his forefathers, and his people were at first adherents of the *Dīn al-Majūsīya*[29] before they became Muslims, and that a Muslim scholar, Shams ad-Dīn al-Bākharzī, had been instrumental in converting the grandson of Jenghiz Khān to Islam.[30] Ibn Khaldūn applied to Jenghiz Khān's religious affiliation also the expression *Dīn an-Nigushīya,* (*nagōsha* or *nigūshak*), a Pehlewi term, designating the "auditores," the Sāmi'ūn, of the Manichaean hierarchy in Samarqand.[31]

---

[27] For a detailed account of Jenghiz Khān's sons and for the territories assigned to them, see *'Ibar,* V, 526–542, and *Ta'rīf,* p. 361 ff.

[28] Ibn Khaldūn's passes over with silence the date of Jenghiz Khān's death in his account of *'Ibar,* while in his *Ta'rīf,* p. 361, he mentions the year 625 H-1227. A.D.

[29] *'Ibar,* V, 103, 526 ff., p. 532. About this term in Ibn Khaldūn's usage see later on "Ancient Iran."

[30] *'Ibar,* V, 534.

[31] *'Ibar,* V, 532. Ibn Khaldūn's does not indicate the specific source from which he derived this term, it may have been from al-'Umarī. For details about this term see V. Minorsky, *Ḥudūd al-'Ālam,* Gibb Mem. Ser. (London, 1937), p. 113, where it is stated: "In Samarkand stands the monastery of the Manichaeans, who are called nughushak ('auditores')"; see also his, "Addenda to the 'Ḥudūd al-'Ālam'"

Ibn Khaldūn's presentation of Jenghiz Khān and his time contained also a revealing observation on the "Great Yāsā" of Jenghiz Khān, the supreme law of the united Mongol tribes. It was believed that the Mongols, before the time of Jenghiz Khān, had no written documents and when they adopted the Uigur alphabet, they used it first of all for the codification of the so-called "regulations of Jenghiz Khān," the observance of which was obligatory not only for all inhabitants of the Empire, but also on the Khāns themselves. It was stated that on the occasion of the ascension of a new Khān, or of the dispatch of a large army, or of a convocation of the assembly of princes, the leaves on which these laws were written were produced and matters were decided according to their content.

Ibn Khaldūn, however, informs us—without giving his source—that "Jenghiz Khān wrote for his people a book in which he mentions 'The Great Politic' (*as-Siyāsa al-Kabīra*), the principles of politics in government and in wars, and the general rules similar to the law of the Sharī'a. He ordered it to be placed in his library so that it be . . . a special prerogative for his family; and there was nothing produced like it. . . ." [32] The custodians of the Yāsā, the tribal law of the Mongols, were the Banū Jaghaṭāi, who by virtue of this task, occupied, as Ibn Khaldūn recorded, a special privileged position at the court of Tamerlane.

The ever-changing picture of the religious affiliation of the later Il-Khān rulers also attracted Ibn Khaldūn's keen mind and he never passed up an opportunity to comment on this aspect. He stressed the fact that Hūlāgū was an adherent of the *Dīn al-Majūsīya,* that Abaghā Khān and Arghūn Khān adhered to the *Dīn al-Barāham,*[33] worship-

in *B.S.O.A.S.* (London, 1955), pp. 250–270. *Encyclopedia of Islam,* IV, 302, s.v. Shaman; and F. Steingass, *A Comprehensive Persian-English Dictionary* (London, 1957) p. 1413, s.v. Naghosā, Nighoshā.

[32] *'Ibar,* V, 526 ff. See Barthold, "Turkestan," pp. 41–42; C. Aligne, "Mongolische Gesetze," *Leipziger Rechtswissenschaftliche Studien,* (Leipzing, 1934), Heft 87; V. A. Riasanowsky, *Customary Law of the Mongol Tribes* (Harbin, 1929); G. Vernadsky, "The Scope and Content of the Yāsā," in *Proceedings of the 20th International Congress of Orientalists* (Louvain, 1940), pp. 219–221, and his "The Problem of the Reconstruction of Chenghiz Khān's Yāsā," in *Harvard Journal of Asiatic Studies* III (1937), 337–360; see, also, A. N. Poliak, "The Influence of Chenghiz Khān's Yāsạ upon the General Organization of the Mamlūk State," *B.S.O.A.S.* (London, 1942), X, 862–876.

[33] See Maqrīzī, *Khiṭaṭ,* II, 220–222 and the French translation in de Sacy, *Chrestomathie Arabe,* II, esp. pp. 161–163. Ibn Khaldūn's reference to the Yāsā precedes thus the observation of al-Maqrīzī on the Yāsā, who maintained that he met a scholar who saw a copy of the Yāsā in a library in Baghdād, thus indicating the existence of a written codex of the Yāsā. *'Ibar,* V, 546.

ping idols, and that Arghūn Khān had employed as his vizier a Jew by the name of Sa'd al-Yahūdī al-Moṣulī [34] and that, finally, under Ghāzān Khān,[35] Islam was established as the official state-religion, accepted then by all the subsequent Il-Khān rulers, until the last of them, Abū Sa'īd.

From Hūlāgū Khān to Tamerlane

To an Egyptian historian, such as Ibn Khaldūn, the life and activities of Hūlāgū, the grandson of Jenghiz Khān must have had a special appeal and significance. It was due to Hūlāgū, the founder of the Il-Khān dynasty, that the first Mongol-Mamlūk confrontation took place and Ibn Khaldūn therefore elaborated on this Mongol conqueror of Baghdād. Among the many biographical details,[36] Ibn Khaldūn refers to the controversial view that Hūlāgū was not a king but only a representative (*nā'ib*) of his brother Mangū Khān and that, therefore, no coins were struck in his or his son's name. He describes in detail Hūlāgū's conflicts with the descendants of Jenghiz Khān, his military campaigns, the conquest of the seat of the Assassins (*mulāḥid*) at Alamūt, the abolition of the 'Abbāsid Caliphate, his atrocities in Baghdād,[37] the alleged destruction of the literary treasures found in Baghdād by throwing the "Books of Knowledge" into the Tigris.[38] Ibn Khaldūn must have been well-aware that despite the defeat of Hūlāgū's army at 'Ayn Jālūt in 1260 by the Egyptian forces, his successors contemplated a renewal of the military invasion of the Mamlūk possessions. It was in particular Arghūn Khān, the grandson of Hūlāgū, who tried to win over the Christian rulers of Europe for a joint attack on the Mamlūk domain in order to rescue the Holy Land from the hands of the "infidels," the Mamlūks of Egypt. Through special messengers and correspondence, Arghūn Khān suggested to the

---

[34] *'Ibar,* V, 546. This is the well-known Jewish vizier Sa'd ad-Daula (d. 1291) of the time of Arghūn Khān; on him see W. J. Fischel, *Jews in the Economic and Political Life of Medieval Islam,* R. A. S. Monographs (London, 1937), pp. 90–117.

[35] On Ghāzān Khān see *'Ibar,* V, 412–415; 547–549.

[36] The specific chapters dealing with Hūlāgū are *'Ibar,* V, 364 ff., 379 ff., 542–545; *Ta'rīf,* p. 318, 326, 361–362, 381, and *Muq.,* II, 117, 192 and many scattered references in *Ta'rīf* and *Muq.*

[37] Ibn Khaldūn's account of Hūlāgū's conquest of Baghdād should be added to and compared with the list of those many descriptions available in Arabic sources such as adh-Dhahabī, Ibn al-Jauzī, Ibn Tiqtaqā, as-Subkī, Ibn al-Fūṭī and others.

[38] The story of the destruction of the scientific books by Hūlāgū is mentioned in *Muq.,* II, 192 and *Muq.,* III, 89–90. For a parallel account to *'Ibar,* V, 542–543, see *'Ibar,* III, 537.

Christian powers in Europe and to the Pope nothing less than a Mongol-Christian alliance, a crusade against Islam—a suggestion which failed, however, to become a reality. Even though the last attempt of the Il-Khān rulers under Ghāzān Khān to invade Syria was repelled at Shaqḥab in 1303 the Mamlūk-Mongol conflict came but to a temporary standstill.[39]

Ibn Khaldūn was conscious of the fact that the ever-latent threat to Mamlūk Egypt by the Mongols which had hung over the political horizon, ever since Hūlāgū and Ghāzān, simmered on until it erupted again into open warfare with the arrival on the scene of history of the last and greatest Mongol conqueror, Tamerlane, and with his invasion of Mamlūk Syria in the time of Sultan Faraj.[40]

---

[39] For the rulers of the Il-Khān dynasty from Abaghā until Abū Sa'īd, see *'Ibar,* V, 545–551; *Ta'rīf,* pp. 361–362 and scattered references.

[40] Ibn Khaldūn added also a short account on the rule of the Muzaffarid dynasty of Shaikh Ḥasan al-Buzurg, the founder of the Jalā'ir dynasty in Baghdād, and his son Aḥmad b. Uways, who fled from Baghdād when Tamerlane conquered the city, and found refuge at the court of Barqūq in Cairo in the years 1393. *'Ibar,* V, 556 ff.

3

AS HISTORIAN OF THE MAMLŪK-MONGOL CONFLICT UNDER TAMERLANE

It is apparent that Ibn Khaldūn's excursion into the history of Jenghiz Khān and his descendants, and their relation to the Islamic world was conditioned by the actuality and topicality of the Mongol threat and was meant to be but a prelude for the understanding of the background of the Mamlūk-Mongol conflict of his own time. Ibn Khaldūn tried to link the culmination of this conflict with the chain of events which were initiated by Jenghiz Khān and his descendants and stressed very clearly this continuity by stating, "When the rule of the sons of Jenghiz Khān vanished, there appeared in Transoxania, in Turkestān and Bukhāra, a king from among the descendants of the Banū Jaghaṭāi by the name of Tīmūr [Tamerlane]. . . ." [1]

In turning to Tamerlane, his spectacular rise to power and his amazing victories and campaigns, Ibn Khaldūn could not have used any written sources. The epoch-making events were too recent to have found a chronicler or recorder. In that early phase of Ibn Khaldūn's research on Tamerlane, he depended, therefore, exclusively on oral information. He might have gathered details on Tamerlane from the Sultan of Baghdād, Aḥmad b. Uways, who had fled to Cairo after Tamerlane's capture of Baghdād (1393).[2] Eager to learn and collect every piece of information about Tamerlane, he registered whatever he had heard from "trustworthy merchants" and travellers, who had returned to Egypt from the East, about Tamerlane's career and his

[1] *Ta'rīf*, pp. 363–364.

[2] *Ibar*, V, 577. Ibn Khaldūn stated expressly that Aḥmad b. Uways stayed with Barqūq in Cairo "at the present time."

conquests of Khwārizm, Khūrāsān, Tabāristān, Māzandarān, Iṣfahān, Shīrāz, Tabrīz, until his conquest of Baghdād. This is indeed substantiated by the Egyptian historian, Ibn Qāḍī Shuhbah, according to whom Ibn Khaldūn is credited with having stated before Tamerlane (1401): "I have also written your biography (*tarjumataka*) and I wish to read it before you so that you can correct the inaccuracies." Tamerlane, it is said, gave him permission, and when he heard Ibn Khaldūn's account of his own genealogy he asked him how he had learned it, whereupon Ibn Khaldūn responded that he had obtained it from "trustworthy merchants who had come into his country [Egypt]. . . ." [3]

All this information was, however, rather sketchy and fragmentary, as admitted by Ibn Khaldūn himself when he stated, "I do not know his lineage," or "I do not know if he was related to Jaghaṭāi." [4] When, however, fate or fortune had brought Ibn Khaldūn, as we have seen, with the expeditionary forces of Faraj to Damascus, he was not dependent any more on hearsay, but on his own direct inquiries and experiences. It was in Damascus that the rather unexpected opportunity was given to him to observe, on the very scene of the events, all the political, military, and diplomatic factors surrounding the climax of the Mamlūk-Mongol conflict and to become the first Arabic chronicler of these events.[5]

In examining all the utterances of Ibn Khaldūn on Tamerlane and the Mamlūk-Mongol conflict, we can classify them under three aspects to which he paid particular attention, namely, 1) Tamerlane, the conqueror, the besieger of Damascus, 2) Tamerlane, the negotiator, and 3) Tamerlane, the person.

Historian of Tamerlane's Siege and Conquest of Damascus

Ibn Khaldūn opens his account of the political and military situation with a description of the first direct contact between Tamerlane and Barqūq in 1397. Pretending to conclude a treaty of friendship with Barqūq of Egypt, Tamerlane had sent messengers to Cairo for this purpose. Barqūq first entertained the Mongol ambassadors and showed them hospitality, but then angered by some of their attitudes,

[3] Ms. Paris, fol. 181.

[4] *'Ibar,* V, 508, 532 ff., 555–561. It is in this part, probably concluded in 1397, that Ibn Khaldūn recorded the early campaigns of Tamerlane in the East. In his *Ta'rīf,* pp. 364–365, he gives an account of Tamerlane's movements after the conquest of Baghdād.

[5] See Part One of this study.

ordered them killed.[6] Ibn Khaldūn reported that Barqūq, anticipating Tamerlane's move against him, left Egypt and marched toward Damascus and Aleppo, and sent his army to the banks of the Euphrates. Tamerlane, who was then already en route to Syria decided, however, while at ar-Ruhā' (Edessa), to avoid, at this juncture at least, an encounter with the Mamlūk army on the Euphrates. Tamerlane did not dare challenge Barqūq, and therefore, retreated and marched with his army instead against India, where he was called for help by some of the rulers of India, whose capital, Delhi, he conquered in the year 1399.

With the death of Barqūq, and the ascent of his son Faraj[7] (d. 1412), the Mamlūk-Mongol conflict entered a new and decisive phase. When Tamerlane heard, while in India, of the death of Barqūq, he deemed this an opportune time for his long-contemplated attack on Syria and marched, after his return to Samarqand, through Khurāsān, 'Irāq, Armenia, Arzanjān and Asia Minor until he reached Sīwās, which he subdued, and then moved on to Aleppo, which he conquered.

It is to Tamerlane's "return" to Syria in the fall of 1400 and the approaching confrontation of the Syrian-Egyptian and Mongol armies that Ibn Khaldūn paid attention. Ibn Khaldūn was fully aware of the mounting threat to Damascus and of the long period of hesitancy and procrastination by the Cairo Sultan and emirs who were slow in recognizing the danger after Tamerlane's destruction of Aleppo. Despite repeated warnings of the Syrian leaders, no preparations for a war against Tamerlane were seriously considered in Cairo until the report of Tamerlane's capture of Aleppo on November 13, 1400, reached Cairo. Even this was at first not believed; only when a special messenger of Faraj, Emir Asanbughā, returned to Cairo, confirming the disastrous news that Tamerlane's troops had indeed entered Aleppo, and in the words of Ibn Khaldūn, "robbed and plundered, violated the women, and committed atrocities the like of which had never been heard of before," was a holy war proclaimed against Tamerlane and an expeditionary force finally dispatched from Cairo to Damascus "to repulse the Mongols and their king, Tamerlane."[8]

Ibn Khaldūn summed up this period of hesitancy caused by the Sultan and the emirs in Cairo in one compressed sentence: "When the news had reached Egypt that Tamerlane had conquered Asia Minor,

---

[6] About this first contact with Barqūq see *Ta'rīf*, pp. 364–365 and *'Ibar*, V, 555.

[7] On Sultan Faraj's life and career, see the sources listed in Wiet, *Manhal*, no. 1789.

[8] *Ta'rīf*, p. 365; see Ibn Taghrī Bīrdī, *Nujūm*, VI, 46 ff.

had destroyed Sīwās, and had returned to Syria, Sultan Faraj gathered his armies, opened the Bureau of Stipends, and commanded the march of his troops to Syria." [9]

Soon after his arrival in Damascus Ibn Khaldūn, staying at the 'Ādilīya College, was witnessing the early clashes and skirmishes outside of Damascus in which, as Ibn Khaldūn stated, "the two opposing armies were engaged three to four times with varying success." Despite certain setbacks during the initial battles and clashes, the main Egyptian forces were confident of Tamerlane's ultimate defeat. In fact, there was evidence that some of Tamerlane's forces were tired of the long campaign [10] and that, in the words of Ibn Khaldūn, "Tamerlane was despairing of taking the city by assault." Tamerlane, sensing the military situation and anxious to return to the East, repeatedly offered an armistice to the people of Damascus; it is reported that Tamerlane had sent two of his messengers to the walls of Damascus who shouted from a distance below the walls: "The Emir desires peace [*ṣulḥ*], so send an intelligent man to discuss it with him." [11]

The forces of the Mamlūk defenders of Damascus that were immediately involved in skirmishes with the Mongol army, might have been able to contend with Tamerlane's forces militarily for a considerable time, had they not unexpectedly suffered a great moral blow—as reported by Ibn Khaldūn—in the sudden and secret flight from Damascus, by night, of Sultan Faraj and his chief emirs, including Yashbak, probably between January 6 and 7, 1401. They hurried back to Cairo after a stay of but two weeks in Damascus upon hearing rumors from the capital of an impending seditious plot, which planned to overturn the government, to depose Faraj, and to proclaim a certain Shaikh Sayf ad-Dīn Lājīn al-Jarkāsī as his successor.[12]

It was described before, how, after the flight of Sultan Faraj and his party, the civilian leaders of Damascus agreed to ask Tamerlane for

---

[9] *Ta'rīf*, p. 366. With the term "Stipend" (*dīwān al-'aṭā*), Ibn Khaldūn seems to refer to the expense money (*jāmakīya*) given usually to the armed forces when going on a campaign.

[10] Among some of the deserters to the Egyptians was Tamerlane's own grandson, Sultan Ḥusain, and some of his followers.

[11] Tamerlane made it known to the leaders of Damascus that he would leave Syria and free his Syrian captives if Aṭlmish, one of the emirs who had been taken prisoner in Aleppo, was released.

[12] For this flight back to Cairo, see *Ta'rīf*, p. 367. As to the route which Faraj and his emirs took, Ibn Khaldūn mentioned that they were "riding up Mount aṣ-Ṣāliḥīya and descending by its passes, then they travelled along the seacoast to Gaza." Tamerlane's men chased after them and captured among others, the Cadi Ṣadr ad-Dīn al-Munāwī.

peace.[13] They had chosen as their negotiator and spokesman the Chief Cadi of the Ḥanbalites, Taqī ad-Dīn ibn Mufliḥ, who enjoyed the confidence of all groups and was also well-versed in the Turkish and Persian languages.[14] Ibn Mufliḥ went out of the city to Tamerlane on January 7, 1401, to make a formal acknowledgment of submission. After having been well received, he returned the following morning to the city of Damascus (January 8, 1401) with a "letter of safety" from Tamerlane and urged the military leaders there to cease the fighting and highly praised Tamerlane's intentions for the peaceful surrender of the city.

According to the terms of the amnesty, "the city should be opened the next day, that the people should go about their affairs, and that an Emir should enter the city, reside in its place of government, and rule over them by the force of his authority." [15] Disregarding, however, the agreement and the promise of security and safety for the inhabitants of Damascus, Tamerlane turned against them and under all kinds of pretexts, extorted tremendous amounts of money from them.

Ibn Khaldūn compressed the long and sad story of the suffering and torture of the people of Damascus by Tamerlane in a few terse sentences by stating: "From the inhabitants of the town he confiscated under torture hundred-weights of money which he seized after having taken all the property, mounts and tents which the ruler of Egypt had left behind. Then he gave permission for the plunder of the houses of the people of the city, and they were despoiled of all their furniture and goods."

Tamerlane, not satisfied with the ransom of one million dinars, which the cadis had agreed to pay in exchange for the safety of the city, contented that the promised sum was one thousand tomans, the toman being the equivalent of 10,000 dinars, and the total payment amounted, therefore, to ten million dinars, which Tamerlane exacted by force from the inhabitants of Damascus. Ibn Mufliḥ succeeded in

[13] The only opposition to any negotiation or truce with Tamerlane came from the Viceroy of the Citadel, who (as all the viceroys of the citadels of the Syrian provincial cities—such as Aleppo, Damascus, and Karak) was appointed by the Sultan in Cairo directly and thus was independent of the Viceroy and other officials in the city itself. The disapproval and objection of the viceroy to a truce with Tamerlane was, however, disregarded. Due to the refusal of the viceroy to open the Naṣr Gate just below the citadel, the delegation of the notables of Damascus to Tamerlane was compelled to scale down from another part of the wall of the city by using ropes.

[14] For Ibn Mufliḥ, see above in Part One.

[15] For the following account see *Ta'rīf*, p. 368.

collecting this ten million dinars, partly by resorting to physical force applied to the inhabitants of Damascus; yet, Tamerlane, using a pretext, claimed that because of the difference in exchange rates, this sum represented only three million dinars and that the shortage was seven million dinars.

The money which had thus far been collected and submitted to Tamerlane was regarded as that imposed on the inhabitants of Damascus only. Tamerlane then demanded in succession the money, baggage, and weapons left in Damascus by Sultan Faraj, the emirs, and the armies of Egypt when they left. A proclamation was made that everyone with whom such property had been deposited should deliver it promptly. He also demanded the money of merchants and other prominent men who had fled from Damascus. In the collection of money on these occasions the inhabitants of the city in distress lodged information against one another. All animals—horses, mules, asses, and camels—in the city and all arms and weapons were demanded also.

According to Ibn Khaldūn's account, the fire which was set on the furnishings and utensils of no value spread to the walls of the houses, which were supported on timbers, and it continued to burn until it reached the Great Omayyād Mosque. The flames mounted to its roof, melting the lead in it, until the ceiling and walls collapsed. Ibn Khaldūn, disgusted with this vandalous act, had only to say, "This was an absolutely dastardly and abominable deed, but the changes in affairs are in the hands of Allāh. He does with His creatures as He wishes and decides in His kingdom as He wills." [16]

Ibn Khaldūn recorded not only the destruction of the city of Damascus and its mosque, but gave also a vivid picture of the preparations of Tamerlane for the siege of the citadel and the techniques applied for that purpose. Ibn Khaldūn was actually in attendance with Tamerlane when he heard the instructions given to the engineers and could, therefore, report, how those in charge of building matters "brought in the foreman of construction, the engineers, and discussed whether by leading off the water which flows round in the moat of the citadel they could by this operation discover its ingress. They discussed this for a long time in his council . . ." [17]

---

[16] Persian historians maintain that Tamerlane actually tried to save the mosque, but that despite all the efforts of his soldiers, the eastern minaret, though built of stone, was reduced utterly, while the "Minaret of the Bride," though of wood, was miraculously saved.

[17] *Ta'rīf*, pp. 373–374. For further details of the Mongol military tactics, see G. Roloff, "Asiatische und Europäische Kriegsführung," in *Der Islam* (1940), XXVI, 110–115.

Ibn Khaldūn's account of the actual siege of the citadel is a very illuminating contribution to the understanding of the Mongol military tactics and warfare. He records how Tamerlane "pressed the siege of the citadel in earnest: he erected against it catapults, naphtha guns, ballistas, and breachers, and within a few days sixty catapults and other similiar engines were set up. The siege pressed ever harder upon those within the citadel, and its structure was destroyed on all sides. Therefore, the men [defending it], among them a number of those who had been in the service of the Sultan, and those whom he had left behind, asked for peace. Tamerlane granted them amnesty, and after they were brought before him the citadel was destroyed and its vestiges completely effaced." [18]

Ibn Khaldūn does not report that the Viceroy of the Citadel, Yazzadār, was put to death after his surrender, nor did he seem to be impressed by the heroic defense of the citadel by the small Mamlūk army against the overwhelming forces of the enemy. He, however, expressed with indignation and loathing the unparalleled atrocities committed by Tamerlane's troops against the inhabitants of the conquered Syrian cities, both in Aleppo and Damascus. He described the acts of barbarous torture, outrage, rapine, and murder, perpetrated on men, women, and children and the unsurpassed and unheard of acts of violence against the whole population.

Ibn Khaldūn conveyed also some details about the numerical strength of Tamerlane's fighting force.[19] While some contemporary sources estimate the strength of the whole army of Tamerlane at 240,000, including 30,000 fighters, some even as high as 800,000, Ibn Khaldūn states only: "The people are of a number which cannot be counted; if you estimate it at one million it would not be too much, nor can you say it is less. If they pitched their tents together in the land they would fill all vacant spaces, and if their armies came into a wide territory the plain would be too narrow for them."

Ibn Khaldūn could not help but write about Tamerlane's army, "that in raiding, robbing and slaughtering settled populations and inflicting upon them all kinds of cruelty, they are an astounding example because of what they attain thereof from the time of their

See also J. Aubin, "Comment Tamerlane prenait les villes," *Studia Islamica* (Paris, 1963), XIX, 82–122, and his article, "Tamerlane à Baghdad," *Arabica* (Leiden, 1962), IX, 306.

[18] For the length of the siege of the citadel the available sources are in disagreement. The siege of the citadel which apparently began on January 14, lasted forty-three days according to Ibn 'Arabshāh, and the actual surrender took place only on February 25 while Maqrīzī, Ibn Taghrī Bīrdī and Ibn Iyās count twenty-one days as the duration of the siege.

[19] See also Ibn al-Furāt, IX, 370.

youth onward, and [in this] follow the custom of the Bedouin Arabs." [20]

Recorder of the Diplomatic Activities of this Period

Ibn Khaldūn, alert to grasp all the ramifications of the Mamlūk-Mongol conflict in his own days, became also the first recorder in Arabic literature of various diplomatic activities and missions, which went on during Tamerlane's stay in Damascus. It is strange that Ibn Khaldūn discussed Tamerlane's diplomatic contact with Barqūq only sketchily and recorded only the dispatch of Tamerlane's messengers to Cairo and their fate. The exchange of letters between Tamerlane and Barqūq have not been registered by Ibn Khaldūn.[21] He concentrated on the diplomatic activities under Sultan Faraj during, and in connection with, the siege and conquest of Damascus.

He registered the dispatch by Faraj of a secret diplomatic mission to the Ottoman Sultan, Bāyazīd (Abū Yazīd), whose assignment it was to reply in person on behalf of Sultan Faraj to the offer made by the Ottoman ruler to conclude an alliance "against the tyrant Tamerlane, so that Islam and the Muslims will not any more be troubled by him." [22] Ibn Khaldūn met, rather accidentally, this ambassador on his return from Damascus along the Mediterranean coast and informs us: "Then one of the ships of Ibn 'Uthmān, Sultan of Asia Minor, passed by us, in which was an ambassador who had travelled to him from the Sultan of Egypt and who was returning with the

[20] *Ta'rīf,* p. 382. Tamerlane is said to have left Damascus on March 19, 1401. The length of his stay there is given variously in the sources ranging from eighty to ninety days.

[21] See *Ta'rīf,* 364–365; *Ibar,* V, 555. In the contemporary Arabic sources, however, the texts of letters exchanged between Tamerlane and Barqūq are preserved in one form or another; see Ibn Ṣaṣrā, *A Chronicle of Damascus,* ed. Wm. Brinner, Vol. I, p. 196, note 1158; Ibn al-Furāt, *Ta'rīkh,* IX, 371–374; Qalqashandī, *Ṣubḥ,* VII, 249, 308; Ibn Taghrī Bīrdī, *Nūjūm,* V, 556–559; Maqrīzī, *Sulūk,* in de Sacy, *Chrestomathie Arabe,* I, transl. pp. 484–489, text, pp. 170–176; Ibn 'Arabshāh, transl. Sanders, pp. 91–94. For a very blurred and illegible transliteration and Latin translation of Tamerlane's letter to Barqūq see B. de Mignanelli, "Ascensus Barcoch," ed. Fischel, *Arabica,* (1959), VI, 168 ff.

[22] *Ta'rīf,* p. 380; see Ibn Khaldūn's remarks on Murād, Bāyazīd, Orkhān and the Ottoman campaigns into "the lands of Christendom" in *'Ibar,* V, 561–563; *Ta'rīf,* p. 315 ff.; *Muq.,* I, 122–123. About the Ottoman-Mamlūk relationship see W. Björkman, "Die Frühesten Türkisch-Ägyptischen Beziehungen im 14. Jahrhundert," *Mélanges Fuad Köprülü* (Istanbul, 1953), pp. 57–63. See also G. Roloff, "Die Schlacht bei Angora (1402)," *Historische Zeitschrift* (Berlin, 1940), CLXI, 244–262; E. D. Ross, "Tamerlane et Bayazid en 1401," *Proceedings of the 20th International Orientalists' Congress* (Louvain, 1940), pp. 323–324.

reply to his message. I sailed with them to Gaza, where I alighted and whence I traveled to Cairo."

Ibn Khaldūn also recorded another diplomatic exchange of letters and envoys between Faraj and Tamerlane, which, too, came rather accidentally to his knowledge. Tamerlane, anxious to have a high Mongol official by the name of Aṭlmish,[23] who was taken prisoner by the Damascus army, released, promised in a letter to Faraj on February 6, 1401, to free his Mamlūk prisoners, including the Shāfi'ite Chief Cadi, Ṣadr ad-Dīn al-Munāwī,[24] in exchange for Aṭlmish. Faraj dispatched to Damascus, therefore, as his personal envoy, one of the "Emirs of the Horse," by the name of Baisaq ash-Shaikhī, informing Tamerlane of Faraj's readiness to comply with the requested exchange. With this mission of Baisaq to Tamerlane, Ibn Khaldūn got acquainted rather accidentally. He did not mention him by name and did not meet this ambassador personally in Damascus because Ibn Khaldūn had left for Cairo prior to the arrival of Baisaq in Damascus; but in Cairo, Baisaq himself got in touch with Ibn Khaldūn, because Tamerlane had entrusted him with a sum of money to be delivered to Ibn Khaldūn as a payment for the mule he had presented to Tamerlane at the latter's request.[25]

Ibn Khaldūn added, himself, a new chapter to the diplomatic activities of that period by sending a letter to the Sultan of the Maghrib at that time. Being throughout his literary activities a passionate letter-writer, as manifested in his Ta'rīf, he entertained with his friends a voluminous correspondence in the Maghrib and in Spain. He continued this practice after his return from Damascus, and sent a letter, which has been preserved in a fragmentary form. In it he informed the Sultan "of all that had taken place between me and the Tatar Sultan Tamerlane and how our meeting with him in Damascus had occurred," and reported: "Last year I went in the Sultan's party to Damascus when the Tatars, marching toward it from Asia Minor and 'Irāq with their king, Tamerlane, had conquered Aleppo, Ḥamā, and Ba'albek and ruined them all and his soldiers had committed there more shameful atrocities then had ever been heard of before. The Sultan [Faraj] with his armies had hastened to the rescue of the

[23] Tamerlane had demanded his release already when he offered a truce to the people of Damascus. See the correspondence in Qalqashandī, *Ṣubḥ,* VII, 320–324.

[24] See above. Ibn Khaldūn mentioned him in connection with his mission on behalf of Sultan Faraj to the rebellious governor of Syria, Tanam, on March, 1400 A.D. and again when he had been taken prisoner by the Mongols pursuing Faraj and his emirs while escaping from Damascus to Egypt.

[25] On this Baisaq, see Ibn 'Arabshāh, trans. Sanders, pp. 155–156.

country and arrived in Damascus first. He remained there facing him [Tamerlane] about a month, then returned to Cairo while many of the emirs and cadis remained behind. I was among those who were thus left." [26]

The Maghribī ruler to whom Ibn Khaldūn addressed himself was probably Abū Sa'īd 'Uthmān b. 'Abdu'l-'Abbās, who had succeeded to the rule in Fez in March, 1393, and ruled until 1420. Ibn Khaldūn could not, of course, have known him personally during his stay in the Maghrib, but the familiar tone of his letter, in which is a statement such as: "If you graciously ask about my welfare it is excellent, thanks be Allāh," may imply some previous communication with him, maybe in his capacity as Maghribī consul in Barqūq's time, or may express just an inherent feeling of kinship with the Maghribī ruler which prompted him to convey to the Sultan of the Maghrib the importance of his adventure with Tamerlane.

Ibn Khaldūn seems to have been motivated in reopening this diplomatic connection with the "Western front" by his desire not only to give an account of his own experiences in Damascus and of the circumstances which brought about his audience with Tamerlane, somehow in an apologetic way, but also by his intention to defend Faraj and to dissipate any doubts in the mind of the ruler of the Maghrib as to Faraj's prestige and courage.

This letter by Ibn Khaldūn most likely precipitated a direct diplomatic exchange between Sultan Faraj and Abū Sa'īd in connection with the affairs of Damascus.[27] In a letter sent by Abū Sa'īd to Faraj dated March, 1401 (as preserved by Qalqashandī), the Maghribī Sultan states expressly that "there had come to him the report of the invasion of Allāh's enemy," but that Tamerlane had departed frustrated and made unnecessary Abū Sa'īd's own contemplated dispatch of armies and a fleet to Faraj's aid. The source of this information may well have been the letter written by Ibn Khaldūn sometime earlier. Faraj's reply to Abū Sa'īd's letter (likewise preserved by Qalqashandī) explained to Abū Sa'īd in great detail the events in connection with his expedition against Tamerlane, the offer of peace by Tamerlane, the news about the rebellion at home, and his return to Cairo, the negotiation for the surrender of Damascus, and the destruction and crimes committed by Tamerlane. He stressed all that had happened was not the result of any bad management, weakness,

[26] *Ta'rīf*, pp. 380–381. Concerning the identity of this Maghrib ruler see Brunschvig, *La Berbérie*, I, 216 and C. E. Bosworth, "Some Historical Gleanings from Qalqashandī's Ṣubḥ al-A'shā," in *Arabica* (1963), pp. 148–153.

[27] For this diplomatic exchange see Qalqashandī, *Ṣubḥ*, VII, 320, 407–411.

or neglect (*taqsīr*) on his part. In this correspondence Faraj also made reference to two copies of a peace treaty with Tamerlane, one of which, bearing his own signature, was to be sent to Tamerlane for his signature.[28]

Portrayer of Tamerlane's Personality

The proximity to the scene of those momentous events in Damascus had enabled Ibn Khaldūn to become not only the first Arab chronicler of the siege and fall of Damascus, the city and its citadel, but the first recorder of the diplomatic activities pertaining to this tense political situation. His direct, and personal contact with Tamerlane and his entourage afforded him also the opportunity to depict Tamerlane as a person and a scholar and to observe some biographical features of the world-conqueror.

Among these biographical details figures the name of Tamerlane's father, Tarāghāi, and his descent from the Banū Jaghaṭāi. Ibn Khaldūn stressed this descent in particular since he saw in the success of the Jaghaṭāis, in their conquests, and in their ascent as the leading power in Central Asia under Sūyūrghatmish and then under Tamerlane, a confirmation of his own theory of *'aṣabīya,* of group loyalty, or solidarity, on which, according to him, the continuity of a dynasty depended. He lauded the Banū Jaghaṭāi because they continued their primitive desert life and refrained from undue luxury and comfort. He credited their great influence and power over vast territories also to their special knowledge of the Yāsā, the tribal law of the Mongols as codified by Jenghiz Khān.

Ibn Khaldūn obtained also a correct understanding of Tamerlane's position within the Mongol hierarchy. Though Ibn Khaldūn referred to Tamerlane invariably with such titles as "Emir," "Sultan," or "King," [29] he was corrected in this by Tamerlane himself, who told him [30] that he actually was not a king but only the guardian or representative of the "sovereign of the throne," (*ṣāḥib at-takht*); that he was but a "relative of kings by marriage," [31] and that the nominal

[28] Details of the peace treaty between Faraj and Tamerlane are given in Qalqashandī, *Ṣubḥ*, XIV, 102–103.

[29] *'Ibar,* V, 506, 532, 540.

[30] That Tamerlane himself was a direct source for Ibn Khaldūn is repeatedly indicated; see *Ta'rīf,* p. 383, where Ibn Khaldūn stated "as Tamerlane has told me."

[31] See *'Ibar,* V, 483, 531, 554, 557, 563; *Ta'rīf,* pp. 363–364. The Persian sources and court historians refer to Tamerlane as *Ṣāḥib Girān,* the "Master of the Happy Constellations," or the "Lord of the Fortunate Conjunction of Planets." Tamerlane's seal bore his signature: Amīr Tīmūr Gūrgān; *gūrgān* or *kūrgān* meant "the

Sultan was Maḥmūd Khān, who succeeded Sūyūrghatmish Khān, one of the descendants of Jaghaṭāi, and the Lord of Samarqand.[32]

Ibn Khaldūn could also describe Tamerlane's physical appearance and approximate his age. He noticed that Tamerlane had a physical defect, that his right knee was lame from an arrow which had struck him while raiding in Sistān in his boyhood, and that Tamerlane therefore "dragged it when he went on short walks, but when he went long distances men carried him on their hands." Ibn Khaldūn did not fail to observe: [33] "He was carried away from before us, because of the trouble with his knee, and was placed on his horse; grasping the reins, he sat upright in his saddle, while the bands played around him until the air shook with them." [34]

He estimated Tamerlane's age at this time—in January, 1401—as being "between sixty and seventy years old." Since Tamerlane's birth date is generally believed to be April 8, 1336, he would have been about sixty-five or sixty-six years old when Ibn Khaldūn met him in Damascus in 1401. According to later Islamic historians, Tamerlane reached the age of eighty years when he died in February, 1405, which, if correct, would change the generally accepted date of his birth.[35]

Ibn Khaldūn also evaluated Tamerlane's intellectual capacity. Based on his discussions with him on a variety of religious and historical topics, he summarized his impression of Tamerlane by stating: "This king Tamerlane is one of the greatest and mightiest of kings. Some attribute to him knowledge, others attribute to him heresy, because they note his preference for members of the House [of 'Alī]; still others attribute to him the employment of magic and sorcery, but in all this there is nothing; it is simply that he is highly intelligent and

---

son-in-law of the kings" or "relative of kings by marriage"; it was also part of the name on coins which were issued in Tamerlane's time.

[32] Maḥmūd Khān was the nominal ruler, though Tamerlane himself administered the government. Maḥmūd Khān was mentioned in the Friday prayers in the Omayyād Mosque after the conquest of Damascus.

[33] *Ta'rīf*, pp. 382–383. Tamerlane is said by all the Muslim sources to have been lamed by an arrow which wounded him in the thigh. According to G. de Clavijo, he was wounded in the right leg when on a raid in Sīstān. Some say he received a wound in his right hand, so that he lost his little finger and the next one to it.

[34] An interesting description of Tamerlane's physical appearance is given by Ibn Taghrī Birdī, *Nujūm*, VI, 281: "Tīmūr was tall in stature with a large brow and great head and very strong; his complexion was white mixed with red; he was broad-shouldered, had thick fingers, a flowing beard, and was paralyzed in one hand and lame in his right leg. He had brilliant eyes and a loud voice and was fearless of death."

[35] According to Ibn Taghrī Birdī, Tamerlane had reached the age of eighty in full enjoyment of his senses and strength.

very perspicacious, addicted to debate and argumentation about what he knows and about what he does not know." [36]

THE HISTORIOGRAPHICAL SIGNIFICANCE OF IBN KHALDŪN'S ACCOUNT OF TAMERLANE

Ibn Khaldūn's account of Tamerlane's siege and destruction of Damascus, his recording of the diplomatic activities of this period, and the glimpses into Tamerlane's personality which Ibn Khaldūn left for posterity constituted a major "Egyptian" contribution to the understanding of the Mamlūk-Mongol conflict of the time. When we put Ibn Khaldūn's account into its proper historiographical perspective by comparing it with other available sources—Persian,, Christian and Arabic—we can gauge its significance and its quality.

In regards to the *Persian* sources [37] on Tamerlane it could be expected that they would give special attention to Tamerlane's victory at Damascus and indeed they did not omit any details concerning their master's life and deeds. Niẓām ad-Dīn Shāmī (d. 1405), commissioned by Tamerlane to write an account of his deeds, incorporated in his *Ẓafar Nāma* (*Book of Victory*), which he presented to Tamerlane, a chapter recording Tamerlane's siege and conquest of Aleppo and Damascus. Sharaf ad-Dīn 'Alī al-Yazdī (d. 1454), the panegyrist of Tamerlane, who completed his *Ẓafar Nāma* in 1424, has given great prominence to the events in Aleppo and in Damascus with all their grim data and facts, seen, however, in the one-sided light of a historian who had to flatter the vanity and pride of his master.

Since the Persian court historians in the service of Tamerlane were expressly charged to put into writing every detail of Tamerlane's words and deeds, whether on the battlefield, at his capital, or in his tent, and were required to describe minutely every phase of Tamerlane's private and public activities, it is surprising that the Persian sources ignored completely Tamerlane's meeting and discussion with Ibn Khaldūn.

A variety of *Christian* sources, though also ignoring Ibn Khaldūn's presence in Damascus, have dealt with Tamerlane, his campaigns in Syria, and his personality in some detail. In fact, the appearance of

---

[36] *Ta'rīf*, p. 382.

[37] Niẓām ad-Dīn Shāmī, *Histoire des Conquêtes de Tamerlan, intitulée Zafarnāma*, ed. F. Tauer (Prague, 1937), pp. 230–237. Maulānā Sharfuddīn 'Ali of Yazd, "The Zafarnāmah," ed. Mawlawī Muḥammad Illāhadād, *Biblioteca Indica*, (Calcutta, 1887–1888) II, 329–345; French translation by Petis de la Croix, *L'histoire du Timur Bec* (Paris, 1722), III, esp. pp. 286–347.

Tamerlane had rekindled the long-held hope that a Christian-Mongol alliance with Tamerlane against the Muslim Mamlūks might lead to the re-conquest of the Holy Land for Christianity.[38] The close relation between Tamerlane and European Christianity found one of its expressions in the dispatch of a Dominican monk, Jean, the Archbishop of Sultānīya, on behalf of Tamerlane to the court of Charles II, the King of France. This Christian envoy of the Mongol-Muslim ruler arrived in Paris on June 15, 1403, and wrote on this occasion his "Mémoire sur Tamerlane et sa cour," which contains many biographical data pertaining to Tamerlane's ancestors, his family, his conquests, his great power, his cruelty and generosity. It refers, however, only briefly to Tamerlane's Syrian campaign and to his siege and conquest of Aleppo and Damascus.[39]

Almost contemporary with the "Mémoire" of the Dominican Jean of Sultānīya, another Westerner wrote a report of Tamerlane's life and personality, namely the Spanish ambassador, Gonzales de Clavijo (d. 1412), who was sent by Henry III, King of Castille and Leon, to Tamerlane's court in Samarqand together with two other Spanish ambassadors, Alfonso Paez and Gomez de Salazar.[40] De Clavijo's account of his "Embassy to the Court of Tamerlane at Samarqand (1403–1406)" is one of the major Western contributions to our knowledge of Tamerlane's personality and life, but not having visited Syria at all, and concentrating on his observations and experiences at Samarqand, he confined himself to but a few short references to Tamerlane's siege and destruction of Damascus.

J. Schiltberger, the Bavarian traveller and adventurer, who served under Bāyazīd from 1396 to 1402, after having become a prisoner of Tamerlane, remained with this conqueror from 1402 to 1405. He, also, made only casual references to the events in Damascus.[41]

The Byzantian chroniclers such as G. Phrantzes, Chalkokondylas,

[38] See J. Delaville le Roulx, "Rapports de Tamerlan avec les Chrétiens," in *La France en Orient au XIVe siècle* (Paris, 1886), I, pp. 384–396; in *Bibliothèque des Ecoles Francaises d'Athenes et de Rome,* XIV and M. Degenhart, "Tamerlan in der Literatur des westlichen Europas," *Archiv für das Studium der Neueren Sprachen* (Braunschweig, 1909), CXXIII, 253–278.

[39] "Mémoire sur Tamerlan et sa Cour par un Dominicain, en 1403," ed. H. Moranvillé, in *Bibl. de l'École des Chartres* (Paris, 1894), LV, 433–464; see also de Sacy, "Mémoire sur une correspondence inédite de Tamerlan avec Charles VI (1403)," *Mémoires de l'Académie des Inscriptions* (Paris, 1882), VI, 470–522.

[40] Published by the Hakluyt Society, trans. by Charles Markham (London, 1859); again trans. by Guy Le Strange (London, 1928), in the *Broadway Travellers Series,* pp. 134, 287–288.

[41] *The Bondage and Travels of Johann Schiltberger in Europe, Asia and Africa, 1396–1427,* published by The Hakluyt Society (London, 1879), pp. 22–23, 128.

J. Ducas and others, concentrated mainly on the recording of the battles of Angora and Smyrna in 1402, and being removed in time and place from the events in Syria have but little to say about the fate of Damascus and Aleppo.[42]

One should have expected authentic reports on the events in Damascus by those Christian residents in the Levant who, as merchants or as consuls of their respective states (Venice, Genoa, Florence, etc.), made Damascus, at that time, their residence. Damascus, in the second part of the fourteenth century was a great commercial center and next to Cairo and Alexandria, the most prominent seat of commercial agents from Europe. The Italian merchants, in particular, dealing with merchandise of all kinds (especially spices) had their storehouses in Damascus and Aleppo as well as in Alexandria and Cairo.

One of the most prominent Italian merchants who resided in the East at the time of Tamerlane's campaign in Syria was Emmanuel Piloti (b. in Crete, 1371; d. 1441?), whose activities brought him through all the commercial centers in the Eastern Mediterranean region. He spent almost twenty-two years in Mamlūk Egypt during which he had various interviews with the Mamlūk Sultan Faraj (1404 and 1408), for whom he went also on a special mission to Naxos. He had visited Damascus several times before and after its destruction by Tamerlane (1401) and he would have been undoubtedly qualified to give a detailed account of what he saw or heard of the events there. His treatise on Egypt has, however, only a very short reference pertaining to Damascus.[43]

Shortly before the arrival of Tamerlane at Damascus, the Venetian consul in the city was Paole Zane. In November, 1400, he together with other Venetian merchants, fled from Damascus to Farmagusta in Cyprus, and he returned to his post in Damascus only after having received instructions from the Senate of Venice, most likely in April, 1401, after the retreat of Tamerlane. Paole Zane, as well as other consuls and officials residing in Damascus, would have been most competent to report about Tamerlane and the events in Damascus to the Venetian Senate.

The only extensive Latin account of Tamerlane's deeds in Damascus stem from the pen of Bertrando de Mignanelli (d. 1455), the

---

[42] About the Turkish sources see Babinger, *Die Geschichtsschreiber*, and "Die altosmanischen anonymen Chroniken," ed. Giese, *Abhdlg. für die Kunde des Morgenlandes* (Leipzig, 1925), XVII, 52–53.

[43] E. Piloti, *L'Égypte au commencement du quinzième siècle d'après le Traité d'Emmanuel Piloti de Crète (Incipit 1420)*, ed. F. H. Dopp (Cairo, 1950), esp. pp. 119–121.

Italian merchant from Siena whose works, "Ascensus Barcoch" and "Vita Tamerlani," also called "Ruina Damasci" constitute the first comprehensive treatment of Barqūq and Tamerlane in Western literature, distinguished by an astoundingly accurate picture of the historical events.[44]

The *Arab* historians of the fifteenth century,[45] as could be expected, have given a detailed description of the events connected with Tamerlane's invasion of Syria. They dealt extensively with the destruction of Damascus and with all the sufferings of the population during this great calamity in Mamlūk Egyptian history. Different from the Persian court historians, their approach was understandably motivated by a deep-seated hatred of Tamerlane, "the tyrant" and "the scourge of the earth." Though these Mamlūk historians offer a more comprehensive and detailed picture, their accounts only echo, and sometimes faintly, those historical events which Ibn Khaldūn was able to witness in person.

In the light of the available Persian, Christian, and Arabic sources, it must therefore be stated that Ibn Khaldūn's account of Tamerlane and the Mamlūk-Mongol conflict is distinguished, as in the case of his biography of Barqūq, by its touch of proximity to the locale of the events and to the main actor of the historical scene, Tamerlane, and by the air of directness which permeates it. Ibn Khaldūn can thus be credited with having introduced the personality of Tamerlane and Tamerlane's conflict with Mamlūk Egypt into Arabic language and literature, first in time and authenticity, and his account can rightly be regarded as one of the most significant contributions made by Ibn Khaldūn to Arabic historiography and scholarship during his Egyptian stay.

---

[44] The author was a Christian merchant from Siena who travelled extensively throughout the Near East and settled in Damascus, where he resided for many years, from 1394 on. He spent the winter of 1400–1401 in Jerusalem, and when he heard of the destruction of Damascus by Tamerlane he fled to Egypt, but he returned to Damascus after Tamerlane's departure. His "Vita Tamerlani," written in Constance, 1416, was published by Stephanus Baluzius, *Miscellanea* (Lucca, 1764), ed. J. D. Mansi, IV, 134–141. For further details see Fischel, in *Oriens,* (1956), IX, 201–203 and *Arabica* (1959), VI, 57–74, 152–172.

[45] About these Muslim historians of the fifteenth century see the works under "External Arabic Sources."

II: Historian of Non-Islamic Monotheistic Religions

1

HISTORIOGRAPHICAL INTRODUCTION

Ibn Khaldûn's contribution to historical research while in Egypt did not, however, confine itself to the history of Mamlûk Egypt in the time of Barqûq and Faraj, nor to the history of Jenghiz Khān and the Tatar tribes and of the Mamlûk-Mongol conflict under Tamerlane. His research had a much wider scope and went beyond the confines of Islam and transcended his own Muslim civilization. It encompassed also part of the non-Islamic world and the history of the non-Arabic and pre-Islamic peoples of the East. However, the civilizations of Asia, the religions of Hinduism and Buddhism remained outside the scope of his interest.

About the world of antiquity, he had a great deal to say. He was acquainted with the cultural and scientific legacy of the classical civilization through the medium of Arabic translations, made in the time of the so-called Golden Age of Baghdād,[1] which gave him a familiarity with, and an appreciation of, Greek thought and Greek concepts of the natural and metaphysical sciences, mathematics, geometry, medicine, philosophy.[2] To the great philosophers of the ancient world, to Socrates, Plato, Aristotle, to the Stoa as well as to the great scientists, Ptolemy, Euclid, Appolonius, Menelaus, Galen,

[1] Ibn Khaldûn spoke repeatedly with great enthusiasm of the Golden Age of Baghdād during the time of the 'Abbāsid Caliph Manṣûr and Ma'mûn through whose initiative and efforts much of the Greek heritage was introduced into the Arabic-speaking world; see *Muq.*, I, 62–63.

[2] All through his writings he expressed the highest admiration for "books of the ancients and of their scientific methods" and thought that they "contain all the useful knowledge which logic could supply." For this aspect see the valuable notes in F. Rosenthal's *Prolegomena* and the literature quoted therein.

Pythagoras, Democrit and others he paid considerable attention.[3]

With the peoples of northern Europe, Ibn Khaldūn showed only a slight acquaintance. He was mainly interested in Europe's geographical configurations which he derived from Arab geographers, in particular from al-Idrīsī,[4] but he did not grasp the essence of the culture of Western or Northern Europe. Only in one passage does he refer to the fact that "the philosophical sciences are greatly cultivated in the 'land of Rome' and along the adjacent northern shore of the countries of the European Christians. They are said to be studied there again and to be taught in numerous classes. . . ."[5] The lands of southern Europe, such as Spain or Sicily, were the objects of his closer attention insofar as they had come, at one time or another, within the orbit of the Islamic civilization[6] and under the Islamic sphere of influence.[7]

Ibn Khaldūn's major interest in dealing with the non-Islamic world seemed to be directed toward the three major monotheistic religions, Judaism, Christianity, and Zoroastrianism.

The widening of Ibn Khaldūn's scope of historical research and his penetration into the history of the non-Arab and pre-Islamic peoples might be surprising when we take cognizance of his expressly stated pronouncement that "my intention is to restrict myself in this work (*Kitāb al-'Ibar*) to the Maghrib, the circumstances of its races and

---

[3] For Ibn Khaldūn's treatment of the dynastic and political history of the Greeks and Romans see mainly *'Ibar,* II, 186–193, 196–210; on the Goths, see *'Ibar,* II, 234–236; see Machado, "La historia de los Godos segun Ibn Jaldûn," *Cuadernos,* I–II, 139–153.

[4] His data on England, Scotland, and other northern countries of Europe, scanty as they are, may have been derived from al-Idrīsī; among other Muslim sources for his geographical knowledge of Europe figure Ibn Khordadhbeh, Ibn Ḥauqal, Sa'īd b. Aḥmad al-Andalusī, and above all al-Bakrī (d. 1094). See A. F. L. Beeston, "Idrisi's Account of the British Isles," *B.S.O.A.S.* (London, 1950), XIII, 265–280; B. Lewis, "The Muslim Discovery of Europe," pp. 409–416 and D. M. Dunlop, "The British Isles according to Medieval Arabic Authors," *The Islamic Quarterly* (1957), pp. 11–28.

[5] *Muq.,* III, 93; *Proleg.,* III, 117–118.

[6] See Machado, "Historia de los Arabes de España por Ibn Jaldûn," *Cuadernos,* IV, 136–147; VI, 146–153; VII, 138–145; VIII, 148–158.

[7] The clashes between the European crusaders (*firanjīs*) and the Islamic states during the Saljūk rule up to the time of Saladin are, of course, treated by him in great detail. He referred frequently to the *akhbār al-firanj.* One of the sources used by Ibn Khaldūn in this connection was 'Imād ad-Dīn al-Iṣfahānī (d. 1183) and his *Barq as-Sāmī;* see *'Ibar,* V, 437–438; on this historian see apart from Brockelmann, *G.A.L.,* Cahen, *La Syrie,* pp. 58 ff., H. A. R. Gibb, "The Arabic Sources for the Life of Saladin," *Speculum* (Cambridge, 1950), pp. 58–72; F. Gabrieli, "The Arab Historiography of the Crusaders," in *Historians of the Middle East* (London, 1962), p. 98–107.

nations, and its subjects and dynasties, to the exclusion of any other regions."[8] He motivated this restriction due to "my lack of knowledge of conditions in the East and among its nations and by the fact that second-hand information would not give the essential facts I am after."[9]

This historiographical attitude of Ibn Khaldūn, the historian of the West, of the Berber and Arab dynasties of North Africa and Spain, however, was changed when he came to Egypt and turned to a thorough and systematic investigation of the Islamic, as well as the non-Islamic, East. This change of mind he indicated quite clearly in remarking: "later on, there was my trip to the East . . . in order to study the systematic works and tomes on [Eastern] history. As a result, I was able to fill the gaps in my historical information. . . ."[10]

Ibn Khaldūn and al-Mas'ūdī

What may have brought about his new approach and the widening of his historiographical scope, his turning to the non-Arab and pre-Islamic civilizations of the East? In the light of a thorough examination, it seems that Ibn Khaldūn's new position was basically due to the inspiration and stimulation he had received from one great Muslim historian who, more than any other of his Muslim predecessors, had a profound impact on his approach to the non-Islamic world of the East. This was al-Mas'ūdī, the great Arab historian of the tenth century.

It may be sufficient to state that al-Mas'ūdī was a prolific and versatile author whose works—more than thirty—included treatises on history, geography, cosmology, meteorology, astronomy, Islamic law and jurisprudence, in which he achieved great competence;[11] and that he was one of the greatest travellers of medieval Islam, a globe-trotter, who visited not only the lands of the Islamic East, but almost the whole of Asia, including China, India, Ceylon and who finally settled down in Fusṭāṭ, Egypt, where he died in 956.[12]

[8] *Muq.* I, 52; *Proleg.*, I, 65.

[9] It was probably due to this early statement that the Egyptian historian Ibn al-Ḥajar, as we have noted above, reproached Ibn Khaldūn for not being familiar with *Akhbār al-Mashriq*. See Sakhāwī, *Ḍau'*, IV, 148.

[10] *Muq.*, I, 7; *Proleg.*, I, 12.

[11] About his life and works see, apart from Brockelmann, *G.A.L.*, I, 143 ff., Suppl. 1, p. 270 and Sarton, *Introduction to the History of Science*, I, 637–639, now the various studies in *Al-Mas'ūdī Millenary Commemoration Volume* (Aligarh, 1960).

[12] About al-Mas'ūdī as geographer, see S. Maqbūl Aḥmad, "al-Mas'ūdī's Contribution to Medieval Arabic Geography," in *I.C.* (1953), XXVII, 61–77; and (1954), XXVIII, 275–286, 509–524.

In Ibn Khaldūn's thoughts and writings, al-Mas'ūdī occupied a privileged and preferential position.[13] This is attested alone by the fact that Ibn Khaldūn has quoted al-Mas'ūdī more often in both his *Muqaddimah* and the other parts of his *'Ibar* than any other Muslim historian of the past, with the possible exception of aṭ-Ṭabarī.

He quoted al-Mas'ūdī hundreds of times by referring mostly to his *Murūj adh-Dhahab* [14] and, though not expressly indicated, to the *Tanbīh*.[15]

Ibn Khaldūn introduced the *Murūj* in different ways; he explicitly refers to it in such forms as "fī kitāb murūj," or "fī Murūj" or in more general terms such as "Kalām al-Mas'ūdī," "Tartīb al-Mas'ūdī" or just "qāla," "dhakara," "za'ama" or "naqala al-Mas'ūdī . . ."

But it is not only the quantitative factor, the frequency of quotation and with it the frequency of critical remarks which indicate Ibn Khaldūn's special relationship to al-Mas'ūdī. Ibn Khaldūn explicitly expresses his positive and qualitative judgment on al-Mas'ūdī by stating that al-Mas'ūdī belongs to those few historians who can almost be counted on the fingers of the hands, "who have become so well-known as to be recognized as authorities and who have replaced the products of their predecessors by their own works . . . who belong to those who are distinct from the general run of historians . . . whose works have been distinguished by universal acceptance of the information they contain and by adoption of their methods and their presentation of material." [16]

Why was Ibn Khaldūn so personal in the case of al-Mas'ūdī and

[13] On his position in Islamic historiography in general, see E. Quatremère, "Notice sur la vie et les ouvrages de Maçoudi," *J.A.* (Paris, 1839), VII, 3rd. sér., 5–31 ff., who stated, "chez les Arabes aucun écrivain ne jamais réuni en même degré que Mas'ūdī une erudition presque universelle"; B. Carra de Vaux, *Les Penseurs de l'Islam,* I, 95–105, calls him "le rivale de gloire de Ṭabarī." A. Sprenger in his preface to *El-Mas'ūdī's Historical Encyclopedia* entitled *Meadows of Gold and Mines of Gems,* Oriental Translation Fund (London, 1841), I, p. v–viii, remarked that "Mas'ūdī has a just claim to be called the Herodotus of the Arabs."

[14] For the *Murūj adh-Dhahab,* see *Les Prairies d'Or* (Meadows of Gold), ed. and transl. by Pavet de Courteille and Barbier de Meynard (Paris, 1861–1877) 9 vols., and the revised French translation by C. Pellat, the first volume of which appeared in Paris, 1962. See also C. Pellat, "Was al-Mas'ūdī a Historian or an Adīb?", *J. of the Pakistan Historical Society* (Karachi, 1961), IX, 231–324.

[15] "Kitāb at-Tanbīh wa l-Ishrāf," ed. de Goeje, *Bibliotheca Geograph. Arab.* (Leiden, 1894), VIII, and the French translation by B. Carra de Vaux, *Le Livre de l'Avertissement et de la Revision* (Paris, 1896). Al-Mas'ūdī's other works, the *Akhbār az-Zamān,* and the *Kitāb al-Awsaṭ,* and other writings remained apparently unknown to Ibn Khaldūn as they have been unknown to most of the earlier generations of historians. See, however the edition of *Akhbār az-Zamān* (Cairo, 1938).

[16] *Muq.,* I, 3; *Proleg.,* I, 7–8.

why did he express such special admiration and praise for him?[17] Why did al-Mas'ūdī occupy a privileged position in the eyes of Ibn Khaldūn?

Ibn Khaldūn's esteem, for al-Mas'ūdī could hardly have been an expression of pure gratitude or an acknowledgment of his indebtedness for so much factual information and so many details for which al-Mas'ūdī served him as a guide and an authority. After all, many other Muslim, Christian, and Jewish sources had supplied him with abundant historical data. There must have been a deeper reason for the fascination al-Mas'ūdī had for Ibn Khaldūn.

This seems to lie in the fact that al-Mas'ūdī impressed him with a new method and outlook which influenced Ibn Khaldūn in the formulation of his own concepts of history and which served him as a source of inspiration. He lauded al-Mas'ūdī's *Murūj adh-Dhahab* because its author "commented upon the conditions of nations and regions in the West and in the East during his period [which was the nine hundred and forties A. D.] He mentioned their sects and customs. He described the various countries, mountains, oceans, provinces and dynasties. He distinguished between Arabic and non-Arabic groups. His book, thus became the basic reference work for historians, their principle source for verifying historical information." [18]

It becomes evident that it was the treatment of non-Islamic peoples and religions as expounded by al-Mas'ūdī which had made a profound impression on Ibn Khaldūn. Indeed, Ibn Khaldūn singled out al-Mas'ūdī expressly as one of the historians who "gave an exhaustive history of pre-Islamic dynasties and nations, and of other [pre-Islamic] affairs in general." [19]

Ibn Khaldūn was so stimulated by al-Mas'ūdī's historiographical approach that he felt it necessary to make the following programmatic statement: "There is need at this time that someone should systematically set down the state of the world among all regions and races, as well as the customs and sectarian beliefs that have changed for their

[17] This high praise for al-Mas'ūdī did not blind Ibn Khaldūn to the weaknesses in al-Mas'ūdī's work and he criticized him for having incorporated stories and fables which have no basis in fact, such as the Statue of the Starling in Rome, or the story about the sea monsters which supposedly prevented Alexander from building Alexandria, or the story about the "copper city" in the desert of Sijilmâsa, all of which Ibn Khaldūn labels as absurd, inconclusive and unproven. He finds fault also with al-Mas'ūdī's statements concerning the Himyarite kings and the Yemenite rulers and regrets al-Mas'ūdī's lack of knowledge of the history of the Berbers.

[18] *Muq.*, I, 51; *Proleg.*, I, 63–64.

[19] *Muq.*, I, 4; *Proleg.*, I, 8.

adherents, doing for this age what al-Mas'ūdī did for his. This should be a model for future historians to follow." [20] This seems clearly to indicate that Ibn Khaldūn intended to emulate al-Mas'ūdī.

Al-Mas'ūdī's universalistic outlook and orientation, his open-mindedness, his wide range of topics, his treatment of non-Islamic religions, the fact that he dealt with the phenomena of history beyond the confines of Islam, that he encompassed the history of the Greeks, the Romans, the Persians, and the Jews, and that he was so keen an observer of cultural, geographical, ethnological, climatic and other conditions—all of which had a special appeal to Ibn Khaldūn.

It was this historiographical approach which can be regarded as the very bond of affinity between these two historians, and though separated in terms of time by over four centuries, al-Mas'ūdī can rightly be credited with having been instrumental in influencing to a large degree Ibn Khaldūn's basic concepts of the historical process, in opening for him that window to the non-Islamic and pre-Islamic world to which Ibn Khaldūn has made so important a contribution of his own.[21]

The Multiplicity of His Sources

While al-Mas'ūdī affected Ibn Khaldūn's methodological and historiographical outlook and directed him towards the investigation of the non-Islamic world and particularly of the monotheistic religions of the East, Ibn Khaldūn needed more specific and first hand information in order to deal adequately with the new topic of his research in all its manifold manifestations. Like any other great historian, Eastern or Western, Ibn Khaldūn was dependent in this research on the written records of the past and on many sources and authorities which

[20] *Muq.*, I, 52; *Proleg.*, I, 65.

[21] Some Western scholars have realized this privileged place of al-Mas'ūdī in the thinking of Ibn Khaldūn. Thus stated de Boer, *The History of Philosophy in Islam*, p. 203, "The historical works of his Oriental forerunners, particularly of Mas'ūdī, have had much influence on the development of his thoughts." Von Gruenebaum observed "Ibn Khaldūn was fully alive to his spiritual kinship with al-Mas'ūdī whom he considered the most respected of Muslim historians"; see *al-Mas'ūdī's Millenary Commemoration Volume*, p. 138; also his *Medieval Islam*, pp. 339–340, note 39, where he stated: "It has been overlooked so far that the basic problems that occupied Ibn Khaldūn's attention were studied by at least one Muslim author more than four centuries before his time—Mas'ūdī." Most pertinent are the remarks by M. Mahdi, who describes al-Mas'ūdī as being "the most important representative of the philosophically oriented tradition in Islamic historiography," and stressed the fact that Mas'ūdī shifted the emphasis from political chronology to world cultural history; see his *Ibn Khaldūn's Philosophy of History*, pp. 152–154.

preceded him. Indeed, Ibn Khaldūn is one of those few Muslim historians who has been most conscientious in mentioning and quoting very scrupulously the sources from which he drew; and his research abounds in countless quotations from many authorities of the past.

According to his own programmatic statement, his research was to include the history of the pre-Islamic Arabs and their genealogy and the history of their contemporaries such as the Syrians, Nabaṭaens, Chaldaens, Persians, Copts, the Children of Israel, the Greeks, Romans, and others. Ibn Khaldūn indicated that he was well aware that all these people whose history he was going to unfold were greatly diversified in respect to language, race, color, and geographical distribution and also in regard to their character and behavior. In regards to the different religious beliefs and laws of these people, he specifically singled out Jews, Christians, Ṣabaeans,[22] and Zoroastrians, and announced his intention to subject them to a thorough historical investigation.

It may well be that Ibn Khaldūn contemplated the realization of this research project while still in the Maghrib and may have even begun it there. That this phase of his research was, however, mainly carried out and brought to fruition during his stay in Egypt can be

[22] Ibn Khaldūn makes frequent references to the *dīn aṣ-Ṣābi'a*. See *'Ibar,* II, 1, 5 ff., 68–72; Ibn Khaldūn does not apply this term to the Mandaeans (the Ṣubbas) of Mesopotamia (mentioned in the Qur'ān, Sūra 2.59; 5.73; 22.17.), the sect residing between Wāsiṭ and Baṣra and practicing the rite of baptism, nor to the Ṣabaeans of Ḥarrān, a pagan sect which had adopted this name in the time of Ma'mūn (830) in order to qualify as "a people of the book" and thus to secure the advantage of a "protected people." He did not use the term "dīn aṣ-Ṣābi'a" in connection with these religious groups, but he denoted with it, in a very general way, a variety of ancient groups as a collective designation for primitive paganism, for those who were devoted to the cult of the stars, planets, suns or idols, to idolatry or astrology in the Ancient East. Thus he applied this term to the original Canaanite population of Palestine, who sacrificed oil and poured it on the rocks of the Roman Temple Venus and the Temple in Jerusalem (*Muq.,* II, 222, 227) or to the Copts of Egypt before Constantine's conversion, to the Nabaṭaens, Himyarites, the Babylonians or Assyrians, or to some Christian heretics and even the Buddhists of China. Following earlier Arab genealogists and authors he indiscriminately included under this term Nimrod and the first kings of Babylonia, the pre-Zoroastrian Persians, the pre-Abrahamic pagans, the pre-Constantine Byzantine rulers, the pre-Islamic Arabs in South Arabia, etc. For further references see Chwolson, *Die Ssabier und der Ssabismus,* I, 266; II, 542; J. Pedersen, "The Sabians" in *A Volume of Oriental Studies,* to E. G. Browne (Cambridge, 1922), pp. 383–393; J. Horovitz, *Koranische Untersuchungen* (Berlin, 1926), pp. 191–192; A. Jefferey, *The Foreign Vocabulary of the Qur'ān,* in Gaekwad's Oriental Series (Baroda, 1938) no. 79, p. 191. Jefferey regarded the identity of the Ṣabaeans as being "still an unsolved puzzle."

substantiated when we examine the kind of sources which he utilized in dealing with Zoroastrianism, Judaism, and Christianity, and realize that many of the major sources he used were of Egyptian provenance. There seems to be no doubt that the availability in Egypt of a great variety of literary treasures and the facilities to establish contacts with representatives of different ethnic and religious affiliation must have greatly encouraged and stimulated him to expound this aspect of his research on a broad basis.

The results of this research are incorporated in the second volume of his *'Ibar* which revealed a new side of Ibn Khaldūn's scholarly personality, namely, the historian of comparative religion. We can discern three major categories of source-material, rather indispensable for his work, which he had constantly and extensively utilized for his presentation of Ancient Israel and early Judaism, of the rise of Christianity and its development and of Ancient Pre-Islamic Iran: 1) Muslim sources, 2) Christian sources, 3) Jewish sources.

1) *Muslim* sources: Ibn Khaldūn had at his disposal in Egypt a great abundance of Muslim sources, some of which undoubtedly were known to him during his stay in the Maghrib. Among these sources frequently quoted by him are, apart from the Qur'ān and the Ḥadīth, the works of aṭ-Ṭabarī and al-Mas'ūdī, and such Muslim authorities as as-Suddā, Suhaylī, Hishām b. al-Kalbī, Ibn Isḥāq, al-Bayhaqī, Ibn Sa'īd al-Maghribī, Ibn 'Asākir, Ḥamza al-Iṣfahānī, Ḥasan al-Baṣrī, al-Jurjānī, Ibn Quṭayba, Ibn Ḥazm, Shahrastānī, Ibn al-Athīr, Abu l-Fidā', and others.[23]

2) *Christian* sources: Among the Christian sources figure not only the Canonical Gospels, but also sources which must have come to his attention only during his stay in Egypt. In his search for a maximum of documentary coverage, Ibn Khaldūn found an unusual Christian source, namely "The Book of Jacob, the Son of Joseph the Carpenter," an apocryphal gospel, or Proto-Evangel of Jacob, of which early Arabic and Coptic translations are known to have existed, and which evidently came into his hands through his contacts with Coptic scholars in Egypt. Ibn Khaldūn made use of this source in his presentation of the origin and growth of Christianity and referred to it in several places, introducing his statements with, "I copied from this Book of Jacob . . . ," "I read in the Book of Jacob . . . ," "it is written in the Book of Jacob. . . ."[24]

---

[23] For all these authors see Brockelmann, *G.A.L.*, and Supplements; F. Rosenthal, *History of Muslim Historiography,* and the respective articles in *Encyclopedia of Islam.*

[24] *'Ibar,* II, 143, 145, 146. See P. Peeters, *Evangiles Apocryphes,* Part I (Paris, 1911); and Emile de Strycker, *La Forme la Plus Ancienne du Protévangile de*

He also made use of Eastern and Western Christian historians of different denominations, Melchites and Coptic. Among these, the most frequently quoted authority was Jirjīs al-Makīn, known as Ibn al-'Amīd (d. 1273), and his Arabic "World History," (*Majmū' al-Mubārak*).[25] Ibn Khaldūn derived an abundance of information from Ibn al-'Amīd concerning the history of the Persians, the Greeks, the Romans, the Byzantines, and post-Biblical Judaism and Christianity and quoted him most extensively and frequently.[26]

Along with Ibn al-'Amīd, Ibn Khaldūn used the Arabic work of a Coptic author, the *Ta'rīkh* of Abū Shākir Buṭrus, known as Ibn ar-Rāhib (d. 1282); [27] he referred steadily also to another Christian author, Ibn Musabbiḥī, or al-Musabbiḥī,[28] all of whom he called collectively the "historians of the Christians."

Apart from these Christian authors, Ibn Khaldūn made use also of the work of Eutychius (d. 940), the Melchite patriarch of Alexandria, known in Arabic as Sa'īd b. Biṭrīq.[29]

The most important Western Christian source for Ibn Khaldūn's history of the non-Arab and pre-Islamic world is the work of the disciple of St. Augustine, Paulus Orosius (fifth century), whom he called the "historian of Rome." His *Historiae Adversus Paganos*, the first continuous history of the world from a Christian point of view, was translated into Arabic in the tenth century,[30] thus enabling Ibn

---

Jacques (Paris, 1961), and especially B. Harris Cowper, *The Apocryphal Gospels* (London, 1897).

[25] For the Arabic text of part of Ibn al-'Amīd's Arabic Chronicle, see G. Elmacini, *Historia Saracenica* (Lugden, 1625), and now C. Cahen, "La Chronique des Ayyoubides d'al-Makīn b. al-'Amīd," in *Bulletin d'Etudes Orientales* (Damascus, 1958), XV, 109–184. For bibliographical details see G. Graf, *Geschichte der christlichen arabischen Literatur, Studi e Testi,* no. 133 (Vatican, 1947), II, 348–351.

[26] It is significant that Ibn Khaldūn quoted Ibn al-'Amīd only once in his *Muqaddimah* in a passage which is obviously a later Egyptian interpolation. Ibn al-'Amīd served also as a source for the Muslim historian Qalqashandī, (d. 1406) and for Maqrīzī, (d. 1442) in matters of Christian history; see E. Tisserant and G. Wiet, in *Revue de l'Orient Chrétien* (Paris, 1922–1923), XXIII, 123–143; and XXVI, 208–211.

[27] Ibn ar-Rāhib (d. 1282): "Chronicon Orientale," (textus Arab. ed. versio latino), ed. L. Cheikho in *Corpus Scriptorum Christianorum Orientalium* (Beirut, 1903), 3rd. Series, I, 42.5 (text); II, 46.8 (transl.); See G. Graf, *Geschichte d. christl., arabischen Literatur,* II, 428–434.

[28] Ibn Khaldūn quotes this author usually from, or in connection with, Ibn al-'Amīd and Ibn ar-Rāhib. I have not been able to identify him; he can hardly be identical with the Fāṭimid historian of the tenth century, who was a Muslim.

[29] See Graf, *Geschichte,* II, 32–38; his historical writings have been widely used by later Christian and Muslim historians. Ibn Khaldūn mentions frequently also a certain Abū Phānīyūs, *'Ibar,* II, 193, 205, 208.

[30] See Paulus Orosius, *Historiae Adversus Paganos, "The Seven Books of History against the Pagans,"* English translation by W. Raymond (New York, 1936); and a

Khaldūn to use it.[31] Ibn Khaldūn attached to this source such great importance that he supplied even details about the name and time of the translator of this Latin work, informing us that it was translated into Arabic in the tenth century, in the time of the Omayyād Caliph al-Ḥakam II al-Mustanṣir (d. 976), by the Christian Cadi of Cordova, Qāsim b. Aṣbagh.[32] The frequency of Ibn Khaldūn's quotation from Orosius (whom he spelled Hurūshiyūsh or Hirūshūsh)[33] indicated how indispensable this Western Christian source[34] was for his investigation of the non-Islamic world.[35]

3) *Jewish* sources: His specific Jewish sources were the "Taurāt" in the widest sense, the five Books of Moses and the prophetic and historical writings in general. He made also extensive use of the "Isra'īliyāt," a source at least of Jewish origin[36] whose bearers and transmitters

---

new translation by Roy J. Deferrari, in *The Fathers of the Church* (Washington, D. C., 1964). For further details on Orosius, see Antonio Truyal y Serra, "The Idea of Man and World History from Seneca to Orosius," *Journal of World History* (1961), VI, 707–713. His work became a kind of Christian textbook for universal history throughout the Middle Ages. See Karl Löwith, *Meaning in History. The Theological Implications of the Philosophy of History* (Chicago, 1949), pp. 174–181.

[31] On all the problems connected with the Arabic translation of Orosius, see G. Levi Della Vida, *La traduzione araba delle Storie di Orosio,* pp. 185–203; and also, with additions, in *al-Andalus,* XIX, 257–293. Levi Della Vida rightly stated "Ibn Ḫaldūn, il solo scrittore arabo che abbia fatto largo e intelligente uso delle Storie de Orosio nella sue compilazione di storia generale," (*Andalus,* p. 261; Miscell. p. 187.) See also the valuable annotations in Ibn Juljul al-Andalusī, *Les Générations des Medicins et des Sages.*

[32] *'Ibar* II, 88, 197. On the translator of Orosius, Qāsim b. Aṣbagh of Cordova, see Ḥājjī Khalīfah, *Lexicon,* V, no. 10626, pp. 172–173.

[33] The first passages in *'Ibar* which mention Orosius, "the historian of Rome," are in vol. II, pp. 10 and 12, preceding Ibn Khaldūn's chapter on the pre-Islamic Arab tribes. Ibn Khaldūn used Orosius subsequently all through *'Ibar,* II, for data pertaining to Persian, Greek, Roman, Jewish and Christian history. He leaned on him also for the genealogy of the "Franks," see *'Ibar,* V, 182, 454.

[34] The absence of any reference to Orosios in Ibn Khaldūn's *Muqaddimah* is of historiographical significance. Whether this would indicate that Orosius remained unknown to him in the Maghrib is still an open question. But even had he become acquainted with Orosius in the West, he apparently could not have made full use of his work without those other Christian authorities which had become available to him in Egypt.

[35] Ibn Khaldūn referred also to a number of other sources, to a certain Bābā aṣ-Ṣābi al-Ḥarrānī and to a Dāhir or Dāhar whom he called "the historian of the Syrians" and, in another context, "the historian of the Persian rule," *'Ibar,* II, 5; 70, who thus far have not been identified. For another bearer of the name Bābā al-Ḥarrānī, see F. Rosenthal, "The Prophesies of Bābā the Ḥarranian," in *A Locust's Leg,* Studies in honor of S. H. Taqizadeh, ed. W. Henning (London, 1960), pp. 220–232.

[36] About Isra'īliyāt, see I. Goldziher, "Mélanges Judeo-Arabes," in *R. E. J.* (Paris, 1902), XLIV, 63–66 and *Z. D. M. G.,* (1934–1935), XLI, 265–268; also S. D. Goitein in

were former Himyarite Jews converted to Islam, such as Ka'b al-Aḥbār,[37] and Wahb b. Munabbih who disseminated among the Arab people a great mass of stories, legends, and traditions based partly on Rabbinic and Midrashic material with the intention of glorifying the past of Israel and its Biblical heroes, and which had molded many beliefs and ideas in early Islam.

Ibn Khaldūn succeeded also in discovering an unusual Jewish source, namely the Hebrew Chronicle of Yūsuf ibn Kuryūn, which, as he stated explicitly, "came into my hands while I was in Egypt." This source, abundantly quoted, as we shall see, served him as a major guide for his outline of the post-Biblical history and for the Roman-Jewish wars until the destruction of the second Temple by Titus.[38]

Ibn Khaldūn's Methodological Approach

For the understanding of Ibn Khaldūn's methodological approach to and his utilization of these many different categories of sources, it should be stated that in no other part of his *'Ibar* has he used such an abundance of evidence from such a variety, diversity, and multiplicity of sources, Muslim, Christian, and Jewish, than in his treatment of the non-Islamic peoples. This may be due to the fact that, while for the history of the Islamic peoples he could take many details for granted, in treading upon new territory he had to establish as broad and reliable a documentary basis as possible.

Particularly characteristic is the integration and combination of all these different sources without regard to their authors' religious or ethnic affiliations, putting them all on an equal footing and correlating them amongst each other. He did not follow any of his sources uncritically, and always compared them with each other, verifying their statements very prudently and carefully, and noticing their divergencies, differences, contradictions and omissions. In comparing genealogical or historical data, he arrived in many cases at the conclusion, "This is far from the truth," "this is not correct," "this is contradictory," "this is impossible." [39]

Tarbitz (Jerusalem, 1934), VI, 89–101, 510–522; and Rosenthal, "The Influence of the Biblical Tradition on Muslim Historiography," in *Historians of the Middle East*, pp. 35–45. While this source was rejected by later historians, especially by as-Sakhāwī, Ibn Khaldūn, following the usage made by Ṭabarī and other earlier Muslim authorities, derived from it many data; see *'Ibar*, II, 10–12 et passim.

[37] See on him the special studies by I. Wolfsensohn, *Ka'b al-Aḥbār und seine Stellung im Ḥadīth* (Frankfurt a. M., 1933); B. Chapira in *R.E.J.* (1919), XLIX, 86 ff., M. Perlmann in *The Joshua Starr Memorial Volume* (New York, 1953), pp. 85–99.

[38] *'Ibar*, II, 116; see later.

[39] *'Ibar*, II, 110, 229 and other places.

In trying to establish the maximum of exactitude and accuracy of the various events and persons of the non-Islamic peoples, Ibn Khaldūn revealed himself as a scrupulous historian of religion who, never satisfied with but one source, tried to place the events of history into their proper time and space.

It is obvious that Ibn Khaldūn did not and could not add any new facts or data pertaining to non-Islamic history. It is, however, the special stress he laid on certain aspects, events and topics, the particular selection of material out of the great mass of information at his disposal, the way in which he deemed it worthwhile to include and to accept or, on the other side, to reject and omit, which gives Ibn Khaldūn's treatment its special methodological color and characteristics.

In all that, we recognize a common denominator which permeates all through his treatment of Ancient Israel and Judaism, the early Church and Christianity, and Ancient Iran. This common denominator, a peculiar "Khaldūnic tinge," as we may call it, indicated that Ibn Khaldūn was particularly attuned not so much to genealogical, dynastic, political, or military aspects—though he gave due attention to all of them—but to the cultural and religious manifestations and highlights in the history of the non-Islamic peoples, to the great religious personalities who made history, to the Holy Books of the monotheistic religions, and to their translation and transmission, to their religious institutions as well as to the heresies, dissentions and sectarian movements and formations of every kind.

How Ibn Khaldūn applied this approach to Ancient Iran, to the early Christian Church and Christianity, and to Ancient Israel and post-biblical Judaism will be demonstrated in the following.

2

IBN KHALDŪN ON THE RELIGIOUS MANIFESTATIONS OF ANCIENT IRAN

It was to be expected that in his general survey of the non-Islamic world and its monotheistic religions Ibn Khaldūn would not neglect to turn his attention to pre-Islamic Iran and its civilization. He shared with many of his Muslim predecessors a high opinion of the ancient civilization of Iran and regarded the ancient Persians, together with the Greeks, as the two great pre-Islamic nations which had most extensively cultivated and advanced the intellectual sciences.[1] The Greeks inherited them from the Persians when Alexander the Great, after the conquest of Achaemenid Persia in the time of Darius, appropriated the books and sciences of the Persians. Ibn Khaldūn recorded regretfully the alleged destruction of the literary treasures, when, in the seventh century, the Muslims conquered Sassanid Persia and Caliph 'Omar decreed their books to be thrown into the water and into the fire.[2] He stressed, however, with satisfaction that "according to our information," science was still flourishing in the non-Arab 'Irāq and farther east in Transoxania because they possessed an abundant civilization and were the ruling nation immediately before Islam.

Ibn Khaldūn's general knowledge of pre-Islamic Iran is attested to in his *Muqaddimah* by many references to some of the rulers and generals of the Achaemenid and Sassanid dynasties, to Kayqāwūs, Yastāsb,

[1] *'Ibar,* II, 153; and see F. Rosenthal, *The Technique and Approach,* p. 73.

[2] *Muq.,* III, pp. 89–90; for a similar report on the destruction of books by Hūlāgū at the time of the conquest of Baghdād, see *Muq.,* II, p. 192 and the parallel version in *'Ibar,* III, 537.

Nebuchadnezzar, Darius, Artaxerxes, Ardashīr, Bahrām, Khosraw I and II, Rustum, Yazdigird, and others [3] and to some aspects of the Persian civilization such as its handicrafts, music, architecture, coinage, flags and banners. But this was rather sketchy and fragmentary. Ibn Khaldūn filled, however, the gap of his knowledge and devoted his time—apparently in Egypt—to studying the history of the various pre-Islamic Persian dynasties such as the Pishdādīyan, the Achaemenids or the Kayyanids, the Parthians, or the Ishkānīya, and the Sassanids.[4]

Hebrew-Iranian Synchronisms

In Khaldūn's treatment of the Iranian and other pre-Islamic civilizations, a special feature prevails which is characterized by the stress he laid on what is being called Hebrew-Iranian synchronisms. Following the custom of the early Persian and Arab genealogists and chroniclers,[5] Ibn Khaldūn tried to bring biblical genealogy and chronology into harmony with the ancient Iranian tradition and their legendary heroes, and to synchronize the legendary and traditional past of the ancient world with biblical events and personalities. Ibn Khaldūn seemed to favor these ancient traditions as recorded by genealogists and selected those aspects which were in accord with the biblical genealogy or could be correlated with the "Taurāt" as a major guide and yardstick for the verification of these stories and legends.[6]

According to this Hebrew-Iranian synchronism, Adam is identified with Kumerat, Noah with Afrīdūn, and Manūshihr, whose power was challenged by Afrāsiyāb, is placed in the time of Moses and Joshua, and other legendary heroes of the Persian past are steadily correlated to persons and events of biblical times. It is rather surprising that Ibn Khaldūn, the critical empiric historian, would not free himself from this trend of earlier Muslim writers and accepted this method rather uncritically.

---

[3] It is strange that Cyrus is not mentioned by name in the *Muqaddimah,* though he must have been meant when Ibn Khaldūn referred in *Muq*., I, 417 to "One of the Persian Kayyanīd rulers [who] brought the Jews back to Jerusalem. . . ." In *'Ibar,* II, however, he dealt extensively with Cyrus.

[4] Ibn Khaldūn's account of the four pre-Islamic dynasties of Iran is covered in *'Ibar,* II, 153–182.

[5] See the works of Ṭabarī, al-Mas'ūdī, Suhaylī, Ibn-Qutayba, Ya'qūbī, Dīnawārī, Ḥamzah al-Iṣfahānī and others.

[6] See J. Horowitz, "Hebrew-Iranian Synchronism," in *Oriental Studies in Honor of C.E. Pavry* (Oxford, 1933), pp. 151–155; A. Christensen, *Recherches sur l'histoire légendaire des Iraniens* (Stockholm, 1917); and Th. Noeldeke, *Geschichte der Perser und Araber zur Zeit d. Sassaniden* (Leiden, 1879).

This synchronization of events is carried on by Ibn Khaldūn also beyond the legendary history of Iran and he does not miss any opportunity to interconnect biblical, Achaemenid and Sassanid history. Thus, speaking about Cyrus the Great, he mentions that it was he who had restored the Temple in Jerusalem and that he allowed the exiled of Babylon, who had been brought there by Nebuchadnezzar, to return. Darius is mentioned in connection with the renewal of the decree of Cyrus and Artaxerxes is duly brought into relation to the events connected with Esther, Mordecai and Haman. When he deals with Cambyses, he refers to him as one of those three kings to whom the biblical Book of Daniel must have referred.[7]

Even in dealing with the Sassanid rulers, he shows this Bible-centered feature, mentioning among others that in the time of Shāpūr, Titus, the Roman general, destroyed Jerusalem and expelled the Jews and that Shāpūr's rule coincided with Jesus' appearance in Jerusalem.[8]

Apart from the tendency toward Hebrew-Iranian synchronisms, there can be discerned in Ibn Khaldūn's presentation of ancient Iran also a Greek-Iranian synchronistic approach. He tries to correlate the date of Persian rulers with contemporary cultural events in Greece, in particular with the activities of great scholars and philosophers. Thus he points out that at the time of Artaxerxes and Darius there appeared great philosophers in Greece, among whom he mentions specifically Socrates, Pythagoras and Euclid. He also recorded that in the time of the first Sassanid ruler, Ardashīr b. Babak, lived Galen,[9] the famous physician, who came from Greece to Persia and added that in his very days also appeared Democritus, the philosopher.

Zoroaster and the "Dīn al-Majūsīya"

In his survey of pre-Islamic Iran, Ibn Khaldūn recorded not only the dynastic, political and military events of the various dynasties, but stressed also the religious movements which emerged on Iranian

[7] Ibn Khaldūn's synchronistic details are all scattered throughout his chapters on Iran and other parts of *'Ibar,* II.

[8] *'Ibar,* II, 146 ff.

[9] Ibn Khaldūn referred frequently to Galen and made many contradictory statements about him. See *Muq.,* I, 70, 157, 188; III, 118; and *'Ibar,* II, 148, 188, 205 et passim; and *Proleg.,* III, 149, note 723. On the problem of Galen in Arabic literature see R. Walzer, *Galen on Jews and Christians* (Oxford, 1949); Levi Della Vida, "Fragments of Galen in Arabic translation," *J.O.A.S.* (1950), LXX, 182–187; and the study by G. Vajda, "Galien-Gamaliel," in *l'Annuaire de l'Institut de Philologie et d'histoire Orientales et Slaves, Mélanges Isidore Levy* (Bruxelles, 1953), XIII, 641–652.

soil, especially the religion of Zoroastrianism (Dīn al-Majūsīya).

Strangely enough, Ibn Khaldūn did not discuss in his *Muqaddimah* the religious manifestations of ancient Iran apart from a few references to the Mōbedhān, the priest of the fire temples. In one instance he refers to the "Magian," quoting an Islamic tradition that "every infant is born in the natural state, it is his parents who make him a Jew or a Christian or Magian." [10] The names of Zoroaster and the Holy Book, the Avesta, are conspicuously absent in his *Muqaddimah.*

It should be stated that Ibn Khaldūn attached, in the early stage of his research, to the term "Majūs" a great variety of meanings; for him the "Magians" are the inhabitants of the first zone "who had no divinely revealed book, no scripture, and had not been reached by a prophetic mission," thus remaining pagans and unbelievers. They constituted, according to him, a majority of the world's inhabitants.[11]

He mentioned the appearance of the Magi at the time of Jesus as reported by the Gospels, without explaining this term. He referred to Constantine, the Byzantine Emperor, as a "Magian" (Majūs) before his conversion to Christianity; he regarded Jenghiz Khān and his ancestors as well as Hūlāgū Khān, as being adherents of the "religion of the Magians." [12] Ibn Khaldūn applied also the term "Magian," following uncritically the custom of earlier Arabic chroniclers of the Maghrib and Muslim Spain, to the Norsemen, the Normans of the Franks and Scandinavian peoples in general, and to the pirates who arrived in Spain with their fleet in the middle of the eighth century.[13]

The term "Dīn al-Majūsīya" as the customary designation of Zoroaster's religion and all its ramifications, in its strictly historical connotation,[14] became the object of his investigation, however, in his *'Ibar,* II. For the examination of the life and activities of Zoroaster, of the Avesta and of the various sectarian movements following Zoroaster, Ibn Khaldūn made use of many Muslim and Christian authori-

---

[10] *Muq.,* I, 225, 247; II, 229.

[11] For these references, see *Muq.,* I, 72–73, 100, 116, and 346.

[12] See the chapter on Jenghiz Khān and the Tatars.

[13] Ibn Khaldūn devoted a special chapter to the Norsemen; see *'Ibar,* IV, 130 and *'Ibar,* VI, 212 (de Slane transl., II, 139). About the Norsemen, see Dozy in *Recherches,* II, 250 ff., Appendix XXXIV; V. F. Minorsky, "Ḥudūd al-'Ālam" (The Regions of the World), E. J. Gibb Memorial Series (London, 1937), XI, 158, 328; Lévi-Provençal in *E.I.*

[14] For the Qur'ānic meaning of "Majūs," see A. Jeffery, *Foreign Vocabulary of the Qur'ān* (Baroda, 1938), p. 259; J. Horowitz, *Koranische Untersuchungen* (Berlin, 1926), p. 127; H. S. Nyberg, *Die Religionen des alten Iran* (Leipzig, 1938), pp. 430–443.

ties and of "Persian scholars," but in particular of al-Mas'ūdī[15] and Ṭabarī.[16] Since these latter historians derived their information to a large degree from the ancient Pehlevi chronicle, known as "Khwatāi Namek" (*Khodāi Nāma*, The Book of the Kings), fragments of which had been translated into Arabic by Ibn al-Muqaffā' in the time of the Caliph Manṣūr (760), Ibn Khaldūn was indeed carrying on the chain of transmission of early Iranian sources into the Muslim historiography of the fifteenth century.[17]

In collecting the various traditions on Zoroaster's life and activities Ibn Khaldūn must have felt quite confused to find in his sources so wide a divergency of opinion and so many conflicting and contradictory statements.[18] He did not attempt to harmonize these conflicting views and recorded them according to the sources he had used, thus becoming almost the depository of the various prevailing concepts. He recorded that Zoroaster was regarded as the son of Spitamar,[19] a descendant of Manūshihr, the legendary King of Iran, and as the original scene of Zoroaster's activities he mentioned Azerbaijān but also Palestine as a starting point of his mission. He referred also to the alleged association of Zoroaster with a Hebrew prophet as reported by aṭ-Ṭabarī, al-Mas'ūdī and others and stated: "The view was held by some of the 'Ahl al-Kitāb' of the people of Palestine

---

15 For the passages on Zoroaster in al-Mas'ūdī's writings see J. J. Modi, "Zarathustra and Zoroastrianism in Maçoudi's Kitāb Murūj al-Zahab," in *J. of the K.R. Cama Oriental Institute* (Bombay, 1933), XXV, 148–158; also M. Mo'in, "Mas'ūdī on Zaraouštra," in *Al-Mas'ūdī Millenary Commemoration Volume*, pp. 60–68.

16 Ṭabarī, *Ta'rikh*, I, 648, 675 ff. and 681–683.

17 See *Muq.*, III, 346 on Ibn al-Muqaffā', see F. Gabrieli, "L'Opera di Ibn al-Muqaffa'" in *R.S.O.*, XIII, 197–247; Th. Noeldeke, "The Iranian National Epic," *K.R. Cama Oriental Institute* (Bombay, 1930), Publication no. 7. H. S. Nyberg, "Sassanid Mazdaism According to Moslem Sources" in *J. of the K.R. Cama Oriental Institute* (Bombay, 1958), no. 39, pp. 1–63 shows how the "Khwaitāi Nāmeh" was utilized by Muslim historians, especially by Tha'ālibī, whom he regarded as "the richest collection of Muslim material concerning Zoroastrianism." See also Gerard Lecomte, *Ibn Qutayba (889), l'homme, son œuvre, ses idées* (Damascus, 1965), pp. 180–189; N. Pigulevskaja, *Les villes de l'état iranien* (The Hague, 1963), pp. 195–230, with an excellent survey of the relevant Pehlevi sources, pp. 93–118.

18 For the passages on Zoroaster by Ibn Khaldūn see *'Ibar*, II, 161–163, 166–172. Since our purpose here cannot be to discuss the substance of the problems involved, stressing only Ibn Khaldūn's methodological approach to the sources on Zoroaster, it might be sufficient to refer, from among the vast literature on Zoroaster's life and activities, to the works of A. V. William Jackson; A. Christensen, G. H. Sadighi, E. Herzfeld, W. B. Henning, O. Klima and M. N. Dhalla.

19 Ibn Khaldūn's actually calls him according to Ṭabarī (II, 676–682), Asbimān; the reading in the Bulāq edition is corrupt.

[Jews, Christians], that Zoroaster was a servant to some of the disciples of the Prophet Jeremiah,[20] with whom he was a favorite; he proved, however, to be perfidious in some of his affairs and false to him and Allāh cursed him and afflicted him with leprosy."

This disciple of the Hebrew prophet who allegedly had influenced Zoroaster's teachings was, according to Ṭabarī, Barūkh, the son of Neriah, the scribe of Jeremiah.[21] Ṭabarī also refers to a prophet whom he calls SMY, whom, however, Ibn Khaldūn did not mention by name.[22]

Following an account derived from the "scholars of Persia" Ibn Khaldūn incorporated the view that "a prophet of the Children of Israel was sent to Kaystāsp in Balkh, where Zoroaster and Jamāsp, the wise man, also of the descent of Manūshihr, stayed. Both wrote down in Persian what this prophet told them in Hebrew. Jamāsp knew the Hebrew language and translated it to Zoroaster. This was in the thirtieth year of Kaystāsp's rule." [23]

Ibn Khaldūn, always fascinated by the Holy Books of the monotheistic religions, conveyed also an account of the book attributed to Zoroaster, the Avesta.[24] On the authority of "the scholars of Persia," he stated that Zoroaster brought down a book which he claimed to be divinely inspired, "which was written in golden letters upon the hides of 12,000 oxen. Kaystāsp placed it in a temple in Iṣṭakhr and entrusted it to fire priests and forbade them to instruct in it to the common people."

Ibn Khaldūn gathered from the available sources details about the nature of this Holy Book and stated, "This book was called 'Bistā' ["Nisnā" (?)] which is the book 'Zamzama'; it revolves around sixty let-

[20] This association of Zoroaster with the Prophet Jeremiah is regarded by de Sacy (*Notices et Extraits,* II, 319) as being the result of a confusion with Urmia, the city in Azerbaijān.

[21] For the latest discussion concerning Barūkh, see Jacob Neusner, "Note on Barukh ben Neriah and Zoroaster," in *Numen, International Review for the History of Religions* (Leiden, 1965), XII, 66–69.

[22] See Ṭabarī, I, 681 and about SMY in *E.I.*

[23] J. Darmesteter, "Textes pehlevis rélatifs au judaisme," *R.E.J.* (Paris, 1889), XVIII, 1–15; and 1890, XIX, 41–56; L. H. Gray, "The Jews in Pahlavi Literature," *Actes du XIV Congrès International des Orientalists* (Paris, 1906), pp. 161–192. See also *Jewish Encyclopaedia,* XI, 462–465.

[24] *'Ibar,* II, 161 ff. The spelling of the word Avesta is faulty and corrupt in all the available texts of *'Ibar,* II. Ibn Khaldūn shares with earlier Muslim sources such as Ṭabarī, al-Mas'ūdī, and Ibn al-Athīr, spellings such as "nasnā," "nasya," "bisna," and "bista." For all the details on the Avesta see the literature quoted above and F. Nau, "Etude historique sur la transmission de l'Avesta," in *Revue de l'histoire des religions* (Paris, 1927), XCV, 149–199.

ters of the alphabet. It was explained by Zarādusht, his interpretation was called 'Zend.' Then he interpreted it a second time, and he called it 'Zendīya,' and in Arabic, Zindīq. This book, in their opinion, has three sections: the first section dealing with the history of the ancient nations, another section dealt with prediction of the future, and a third section dealt with their laws [*nomos*] and statutes, for example, that the sun is a Niblah, that the prayers are said at sunrise, and at noon and sunset, and that it prescribes prostrations and prayers." [25]

Conversions and Dissensions

Ibn Khaldūn, always attuned to cases of conversions by individual rulers from one religion to another, never missed an opportunity in his writings to stress such events. Repeatedly he referred to the conversion of the South Arabian Himyarite king, Dhū Nuvās,[26] to Judaism, to the conversion of the Ethiopians to Christianity, and to the conversion of the Byzantine emperor, Constantine, and his mother, Helen, to Christianity,[27] and he took, therefore, due cognizance of the conversion of the Iranian king, Kaystāsp, to the new religion of Zoroaster.

He recounted in detail Zoroaster's dramatic meeting with this king and excerpted from al-Mas'ūdī how "Zoroaster turned to Kaystāsp and presented him with his teaching. The king was awed by it, and led his people to accept this belief and killed those who refused . . ." and that "Kaystāsp accepted the 'Dīn al-Majūsīya' from Zoroaster in the thirty-fifth year of his prophetic mission . . ."

Ibn Khaldūn dealt also with Kaystāsp's conflict with the King of the Turks, quoting as the reason for the conflict, according to Ṭabarī, the legendary beast which was to stand at the gates of the king's palace.

Ibn Khaldūn omitted many of the legendary aspects of Zoroaster's revelation, mythology and cosmology, his visions of the angels, his preachings and teachings, and concentrated on some of the innovations which were brought about by Zoroaster. He recorded that he gave his people two feasts, the "Naurūz," [28] during the spring season, and the "Mahrajān," [29] during the autumn season, and some similar

[25] *'Ibar,* II, 161–162.

[26] *'Ibar,* II, 82 ff., 86, 90.

[27] See next chapter on Christianity.

[28] See J. Markwart, "Das Naurōz, seine Geschichte und Bedeutung" in *Modi Memorial Volume* (Bombay, 1930), pp. 709–765.

[29] S. H. Taqizadeh, "Persian Eras and Calendars used in Islam," *B.S.O.A.S.* (1939), pp. 107–133; pp. 904–922; see also his *Old Iranian Calendar, R.A.S.* (London, 1958).

laws, and that Jamāsp, the wise man, the counselor of Kaystāsp, was appointed in Zoroaster's place as the first in a series of Zoroastrian priests, Mobedhān.

Ibn Khaldūn sifted carefully from the many sources at his disposal those facts which would allow him to present Zoroaster as the founder of a great religious movement and as the author of the Holy Book, the Avesta.

He recorded, also, the two sectarian movements which emerged on Persian soil as an offshoot of Zoroastrianism, namely, Mānī and Mazdak.

In his account on Shāpūr he treated the appearance and teachings of Mānī (d. 271), the dualist (*thanawī*), the author of "Light and Darkness." [30] He reported that Shāpūr at first accepted the teachings of Mānī but returned later to the Zoroastrian religion of his forefathers. Ibn Khaldūn applied to Mānī the term "Zindīq" [31] which, as he explained by following the terminology of earlier Muslim authors, denoted one who professed Islam openly but hides infidelity. He reported that when Bahrām b. Hormuz (273–276) became the ruler, he gathered the leading men and scholars to examine Mānī's teachings and they proclaimed them as blasphemous and killed Māni and persecuted his adherents.

Ibn Khaldūn did not record the development of the religion of Zoroastrianism and its spread after the appearance of Mānī but concerned himself with another "Zindīq," with Mazdak,[32] who appeared on the scene in the time of the Sassānid ruler, Kawādh b. Peroz (d. 531). Ibn Khaldūn characterized Mazdak as one "who would justify anything and everything who permitted the people's wealth to be taken and who proclaimed that no one has the right to keep anything for himself." Ibn Khaldūn conveyed a picture of the confused religious and social situation of Iran as a result of Kawādh's acceptance

---

[30] *'Ibar* II, 172. On Mānī and Mānichaism see G. Fluegel, *Mani und seine Lehren und seine Schriften* (Leipzig, 1862); A. V. Williams Jackson, *Researches in Manichaeism* (New York, 1932); Geo. Widengren, *Mani und der Manichäismus* (Stuttgart, 1961); and J. P. Asmussen, *Xuāstvānīft, Studies in Manichaeism* (Copenhagen, 1965).

[31] For the term "Zindīq", see H. H. Schaeder, *Iranische Beitraege* (Koenigsberg, 1930), pp. 274–291; P. Krauss, "Beiträge zur islamischen Ketzergeschichte," *R.S.O.* (1933, 1934) XIV; G. Vajda, "Les Zindiqs en pays d'Islam au debut de la période Abbaside," in *R.S.O.* (Rome, 1937), XVII, 173–229; B. Lewis, "Some Observations on the Significance of Heresy in the History of Islam," in *S.I.* (1953), I, 42–63; see also P. J. de Menasce, *Une Apologétique Mazdéenne du IXᵉ Siècle: Škand-Gumānīk Vičār, La Solution Décisive des Doutes* (Fribourg, 1945); and Jacob Neusner, "A Zoroastrian Critique of Judaism," *J.A.O.S.* (1963), LXXXIII, 283–294.

[32] *'Ibar,* II, 176 ff.

of Mazdak, his subsequent deposition, and the enthronement of his brother Gamasāp.

Ibn Khaldūn's discussion of the religious manifestations on Iranian soil has been noted only by one Western scholar, R. Gottheil. He was acquainted with the fact that Ibn Khaldūn had dealt with Zoroaster and stated, "There is also a long account of Zoroaster in the 'Kitāb al-'Ibar' of Ibn Ḥaldūn, the most philosophical of all the Mohammedan historians." Gottheil, however, dismissed it with the remark, "It contains nothing new and I omit it." [33]

It is to be regretted that by thus discarding Ibn Khaldūn's account of Zoroastrianism, many of the Iranists failed to take notice of Ibn Khaldūn's investigation which, though not original and culled from earlier sources, constitutes an important contribution for the understanding of Ibn Khaldūn's historiographical outlook and approach to his sources.

[33] See Richard Gottheil, "References to Zoroaster in Syriac and Arabic Literature," pp. 35 ff.

3

HISTORIAN OF EARLY CHRISTIANITY

From Jesus to the Apostles

In traversing the spiritual frontiers of Islam and penetrating into the field of non-Islamic monotheistic religions, Ibn Khaldūn made also Christianity, in many of its manifestations, the object of his historical investigation.

At an early stage in his research, Ibn Khaldūn seemed to have been reluctant to deal with Christianity and its doctrines, as can be deduced from a passage in his *Muqaddimah,* where he stated: "We do not think that we should blacken the pages of this book with discussion of their [Christian] dogmas of unbelief. In general, they are well known; all of them are unbelief. This is clearly stated in the noble Qur'ān. It is not for us to discuss or argue those things with them. It is for them to choose between conversion to Islam, payment of the poll tax, or death." [1] This attitude, however, was abandoned by him, or at least it did not prevent him from embarking on a thorough survey of the life of Jesus and his disciples, the Christian Canon, the spread of Christianity in the Byzantine Empire, the hierarchy of the church, and its sectarian movements.

Ibn Khaldūn is by no means the first or only Muslim author who dealt with the origin and development of Christianity. He was preceded by other Muslim scholars such as Ya'qūbī,[2] al-Mas'ūdī, aṭ-Ṭabarī, al-Birūnī, Ibn Ḥazm, and ash-Shahrastānī; [3] but Ibn Khaldūn's

[1] *Muq.*, I, 421–422; *Proleg.*, I, 480.

[2] See *Ta'rīkh,* ed. Houtsma (Leiden, 1883).

[3] Though Ibn Khaldūn quoted both Ibn Ḥazm (d. 1064) and Shahrastānī (d. 1153) in many passages of his *'Ibar,* he seemed not to have utilized their information for this topic.

account is characterized by a much greater factual knowledge and by the usage of a great variety of sources. In his search for the maximum documentary coverage for his outline of the rise and development of early Christianity in all its ramifications, Ibn Khaldūn relied on the Canonical Gospels, on an apocryphal gospel, and on those many Christian and Muslim authorities which became accessible to him during his stay in Egypt.[4]

The result of his intensive research is embodied in a special chapter, entitled "The Story of Jesus, the Son of Mary, and the Apostles after him and the Writing of the Four Gospels of Christianity and the Council of the Priests," and is greatly supplemented by lengthy discourses in his chapters on Roman (Latin) and Byzantine (Greek) history.[5] Based on all his sources, Ibn Khaldūn gives the traditional genealogy and history of Joseph, Mary and their family, (inserting many legends and stories about them), their journey to Egypt, their return to Bethlehem, the miraculous birth of Jesus, their sojourn in Jerusalem,[6] and the coming of the Māgis in connection with Herod's decree to kill all two-year-old sons.

Ibn Khaldūn is most eager to establish the exact date of the birth of Jesus and to relate it to other happenings and events in history. Thus he quotes that Jesus was born in the forty-second year of the rule of Emperor Augustus, in the thirty-second year after Herod's rule over Jerusalem, or 363 years after Alexander's visit to Babylon. He even tried to synchronize the birth of Jesus with historical events which happened after the rise of Christianity and stated that Jesus appeared in the forty-first year of the Sassanid ruler, Shāpūr, that 313 years passed from Alexander to Jesus, or that the period between Muḥammad and Jesus was 600 years.[7]

Ibn Khaldūn refers to Jesus' baptism, at the age of thirty, in the Jordan by John or Yaḥyā, the son of Zakarīyā' the Baptist,[8] who as he stated was born in the days of Herod, the King of the Jews, lived in the wilderness and led the life of an ascetic, ate only locusts and wore only wool and camel skins. Ibn Khaldūn relates the many mir-

---

[4] See above on "The Multiplicity of Sources."

[5] *'Ibar*, II, 143–153 ff.

[6] Ibn Khaldūn gives the genealogy of Jesus according to the Gospel of Matthew and the Proto-Evangel of Jacob.

[7] For his synchronistic approach see above.

[8] See Asin y Palacios, "John the Baptist in Muslim Writings" in *M.W.* (Hartford, 1955); and A. A. Neuman, "A Note on John the Baptist and Jesus in Josippon," *Hebrew Union College Annual* (Cincinnati, 1950–1951), XXIII, Pt. II, 137–149.

acles which are ascribed to Jesus—the revival of the dead and the cure of the sick—and the crowd who joined him and believed in him.

He dwells on the story of the betrayal of Jesus by Judas Iscariot, on the intervention of the Jewish high priest before Pontius Pilate and Jesus' death. He places these events in the days of Augustus, the first of the Roman emperors, and "in the time of Herod, the King of the Jews, who had taken away the royal authority from the Hasmoneans—his relatives by marriage . . ." and recounts that the Jews, envying Jesus and declaring him a liar, got the permission of the Roman emperor to put an end to Jesus' activities "and the story of Jesus as recited in the Qur'ān occurred."

In conformity with the Qur'ān, he stresses that the crucifixion of Jesus did not actually occur and was prevented by placing his likeness upon another person who was crucified in Jesus' stead.[9] As a Muslim, he, of course, refuted the divinity of Jesus and the fact of his redemptive power through his crucifixion, but accepted the Qur'ānic story of the ascension of Jesus.

Ibn Khaldūn lists the names of Jesus' twelve apostles, and their respective missions and assignments to various countries. "He sent some of them as messengers [apostles] to all parts of the world and they made propaganda for his religious group." They spread the "religion of Jesus" which was called "Dīn an-Naṣranīya" after the village of Nazareth where Jesus lived with his mother after their return from Egypt.[10]

The Christian Canon

Ibn Khaldūn, profoundly interested in the Holy Scriptures of the monotheistic religions, in the "Taurāt" of Judaism, and in the Avesta of Zoroastrianism, culled from the works of the "historians of the Christians," as he called Ibn al-'Amīd, Ibn al-Rāhib, al-Musabbiḥī

[9] For the Qur'ānic passages on Jesus, John the Baptist and other aspects of early Christianity, see Giuseppe Gabrieli, "Gesù Cristo nel Qorano," in *Bessarione*, IX (1901), 32–60; Wilhelm Rudolph, *Die Abhängigkeit des Qorans von Judentum und Christentum* (Stuttgart, 1922); Karl H. Becker, *Islamstudien* (Leipzig, 1924); Richard Bell, *The Origin of Islam in its Christian Environment* (London, 1926); Tor Andrae, *Der Ursprung des Islams und das Christentum* (Uppsala, 1926); Karl Ahrens, "Christliches im Qoran," *Z.D.M.G.* (1930), Vol. LXXXIV pp. 15–68; J. W. Sweetman, *Islam and Christian Theology* (London, 1945–1947), 2 vols; and James Kritzeck, "Jews, Christians, and Moslems," in *The Bridge*, ed. J. M. Oestereicher (New York, 1958–1959), III, 84–121.

[10] *'Ibar*, II, 143.

and others, many details on the Christian Canon, its composition, and on the early Church and its hierarchy.

In listing all the Christian writings which made up their Canon, Ibn Khaldūn mentioned that "Matthew wrote his Gospel in Jerusalem in Hebrew. It was translated into Latin by John, the son of Zebedee, one of the apostles. The Apostle Luke wrote his Gospel in Latin for a Roman dignitary. . . . Peter wrote his Gospel in Latin, and ascribed it to his pupil Mark. These four recensions of the Gospels differ from each other. Not all of it is pure revelation, but the Gospels have an admixture of the words of Jesus and of the apostles. Most of their contents consist of sermons and stories. There are very few laws in them." [11]

He conveyed the structure of the Canon of the New Testament in the form in which it was handed down by Clement, a pupil of Peter, which consisted of forty-three books, including the Old Testament.

"The Books of the religious law of Jesus as received by the apostles, are in addition to the Hebrew Canon which belongs to the old religious law of the Jews: the four recensions of the Gospel; the Book of Paul, which consists of fourteen epistles; the Katholika [General Epistles], which consists of seven epistles, the eighth being the Praxis [Acts], stories of the Apostles; the Book of Clement, which contains the laws; the Book of the Apocalypse [Revelation] which contains the vision of John, the son of Zebedee." [12]

The Ecclesiastical History of Eastern Christianity

Ibn Khaldūn did not limit himself to the beginnings of Christianity, but he surveyed also the development of Christianity and its spread into the Byzantine Empire, and gave a condensed ecclesiastical history of Eastern Christianity from Constantine on. He dealt with the attitude of the various Byzantine emperors towards early Christianity, originally adherents of the "religion of the Magians" and who, only after many vacillations, did adopt Christianity and made it the state religion through the conversion of Constantine and his mother, Helen.

He reported the building of the Church of the Holy Sepulchre in

[11] The data on the Gospels and their authors are given by Ibn Khaldūn twice in parallel versions; see *Muq.*, I, 418 ff.; from *Proleg.*, I, 476–477; *'Ibar*, II, 201–203.

[12] See *Muq.*, I, 419; *'Ibar*, II, 197, 200, 218; Rothstein, "Der Kanon der biblischen Bücher bei den babylonischen Nestorianern im 9/10 Jhdt.," *Z.D.M.G.*, LVIII, 634–663; and A. Baumstark, "Der Bibelkanon," pp. 393–398.

Jerusalem by Helen, which is considered to stand upon the grave of Jesus and which, in Christian usage, is called the "Church of the Resurrection" (*"al-Qiyāma"*). Ibn Khaldūn, however, following the custom of earlier Muslim writers, called it—in a derogatory way—*"al-Qumāma,"* the "Church of the Dung Hill," referring to the report that Helen had "ordered dung and excrements to be thrown upon the Rock until it was entirely covered and its site obscured. That she considered the proper reward for what the Jews had done to the grave of the Messiah." [13]

The conversion to Christianity of Constantine and his mother, Helen, was regarded by Ibn Khaldūn as one of those great turning points and milestones in the history of the transmission of ideas, and he stressed this history-making event repeatedly in his writings.[14]

Ibn Khaldūn surveyed, also, the major Ecumenical Councils of the Church at Nicea, Constantinople, Ephesus, and Chalcedon and their results, resolutions and formulations, the writing of a "tract," the "creed," which is known as the authoritative confession of faith (*amānat ahl-majma'*). He reported, "They assembled in Nicea in the days of Constantine, in order to lay down [the doctrine of] true Christianity. Three hundred and eighteen bishops agreed upon one and the same doctrine of Christianity. They wrote it down and called it 'the Creed.' They made it the fundamental principle to which they would all have reference . . ." [15]

He acquainted himself thoroughly with the religious institutions and the leadership in Christianity and dealt in a special chapter entitled "On the Meaning of the Names of Pope, Patriarch, etc.," with the bearers of ecclesiastical offices and the various terms of those in charge of the Christian community. He defines the terms "monk," "priest," *"Baṭrīk,"* (the Patriarch), and above all, *"Bābā"* ("Pope"), the title of the Patriarch of Rome, the most important see in Christendom. The Pope is, as he stated, "the successor of Peter, the greatest

---

[13] See *Ta'rīf*, pp. 349–50; *'Ibar*, II, 149, 212, 225; *Muq.*, I, 478, and *Muq.*, II, 225–226. About the usage of this term "al-Qumāma" by Muslim geographers, see G. Le Strange, *Palestine under the Moslems* (London, 1890), p. 202; and *E.I.*, s.v. al-Ḳuds.

[14] The conversion of Constantine and Helen is repeatedly mentioned by him in various contexts.

[15] *Muq.*, I, 420 ff.; *Proleg.*, I, 478–479; *'Ibar*, II, 210 ff., 329–331. Ibn Khaldūn shows an astounding acquaintance with the various Councils in Constantinople, Ephesos, and Chalcedon and their theological differences. It is quite significant that in his *Muqaddimah* Ibn Khaldūn referred only to the Council at Nicea while in his *'Ibar*, II, which mirrors the result of his research in Egypt, he offers a much broader investigation.

of the disciples of Jesus and his Apostle, who until the present day, is called al-Bābā [Pope], 'the father of the fathers.' "[16]

Ibn Khaldūn listed the names of the patriarchs of the early centuries in the various sees of the Orient, Jerusalem, Alexandria, Antioch, and gathered a great amount of detail trying to establish the exact dates of the appointment and ordination of each of the various patriarchs in their respective sees.[17]

The relationship of the ecclesiastical Christian authorities to the secular powers, and particularly to the emperors, on whose heads the Pope personally placed the crown were discussed by Ibn Khaldūn. He compared the hierarchy of the church with the religious leadership in the Muslim community and stressed that for the Muslim community "the Holy War is a religious duty, because of the universalism of the [Muslim] mission and [the obligation to] convert everybody to Islam either by persuasion or by force. Therefore, caliphate and royal authority are united in [Islam], so that the person in charge can devote all the available strengths to both of them at the same time."[18]

Sectarian movements

Interested in every sort of deviation from established patterns in religious matters, in sectarian formations and dissensions, schisms, and heresies, Ibn Khaldūn recorded the doctrinal disputes and controversies on the nature of Jesus, the question of the resurrection of body and soul, the Trinity, the heresy (*kufr*) of Nestorius, Patriarch of Antioch, and all the rivalries and disagreements of the patriarchs which gave rise to the sectarian movements within Oriental Christianity.

He refers in his outline of the history of the Romans and the Byzantines, to individual heretical figures such as Marcion and Bar Dayṣān,[19] but also paid special attention to the split of the early Oriental Church into the Melchites, Jacobites, and Nestorians.

[16] On all these titles and terms, see *Muq.*, I, 420–422; *'Ibar*, II, 148 ff., 218–219.

[17] For a detailed list of the patriarchs in Alexandria, probably based on Ibn al-'Amīd, as his source of information in Qalqashandī see E. Tisserant et G. Wiet, "La Liste des Patriarches d'Alexandrie dans Qalqashandī," *Revue de l'Orient Chrétien*, (Paris, 1922–1923), XXIII–XXIV 123–243; and J. Maspero, *Histoire des Patriarches d'Alexandrie* (Paris, 1923).

[18] See *Muq.*, I, 415; *Proleg.*, I, 473.

[19] See *'Ibar*, II, 205 and other passages. Ibn Daysān from Edessa (d. 222), the last of the Gnostics who wrote against the polytheism of the heathens and the dualism of Marcion, occupies a considerable place in the discussions of Muslim theologians and historians. The Church excommunicated him as a dangerous infidel. See H. H. Schaeder in *Z. f. Kirchengeschichte* (Stuttgart, 1932), LI, 21–74.

Formidable efforts to collect data on these heresies were made by Ibn Khaldūn, and he described in detail the theological dissensions which broke out within the Christians with regard to the basic principles and articles of their faith. "They split into groups and sects, which secured the support of various Christian rulers against each other . . . Finally these sects crystallized into three groups, which constitute the [Christian] sects, the Melchites, the Jacobites, and the Nestorians. Others have no significance." [20]

The spectacle of a "Christianity divided," of Christians persecuting Christians, each securing the support of various Christian rulers against one another, with all their bitter internal strifes, might have had a comforting effect for a Muslim historian in view of a similar situation in the early Muslim community with its internal conflicts among the "Believers," the Khārijites, Shi'ites, and others.

Ibn Khaldūn's interest in the history of Christianity, apart from scholarly motivations, might have been stimulated also by the fact that he, himself had travelled in May, 1401, to the Holy Land, Palestine, where he visited the Christian holy sites in Jerusalem, and stood before the Church of the Holy Sepulchre, refraining however from entering into it.[21]

He visited also Hebron, (*al-Khalīl*), the tomb of Abraham and the other patriarchs, and passed on his way through Bethlehem, where he was much impressed at the great building erected on the place, which he—erroneously—designated as the birthplace of the Messiah (Jesus). He mentioned the images of Roman emperors on top of the building with the dates of their rule inscribed, testifying to the greatness of their empire.[22]

Though Ibn Khaldūn paid little attention to the contemporary scene in regards to the non-Muslim minorities in Egypt, in surveying the patriarchs of Alexandria he incorporated an interesting remark about the situation of the Church in Egypt in his time, stating, "that the Patriarch of the [Christian] subjects in Egypt is of the Jacobite persuasion. He resides among them. The Abyssinians follow the religion of the Egyptian Christians."

With the Coptic community, he dealt only from an historical point of view, stressing their role during the Islamic conquest of Egypt and

[20] Based on Ibn al-'Amīd, *'Ibar,* II, 152–153; 219 ff.

[21] He has indicated his interest in places of worship, holy sites and sanctuaries in a detailed survey dealing with Jerusalem, Bethlehem, Nazareth, Mount Gerizim, Mecca, Medina, etc., see *Muq.,* II, 215–229.

[22] *Ta'rīf,* p. 350 ff. While in Bethlehem, Ibn Khaldūn suggested (to his readers) that "whoever desired to study these monuments and their Latin inscriptions should address himself to professional guides and interpreters."

their services in the government as skilled officials, tax collectors, bookkeepers, craftsmen, and farmers.[23]

Ibn Khaldūn's detailed knowledge of early Church history shows how and to what a degree he, the orthodox Muslim, could detach himself from the fetters of his own faith and penetrate into the theological and doctrinal differences of another religion. Indeed, among the Arab-Muslim scholars who attempted such a study, it was Ibn Khaldūn, the great Muslim thinker of the fourteenth century, who achieved astounding scholarly objectivity in regards to the various non-Islamic religions.

---

[23] On the Copts, see *'Ibar,* II, 74–78; and the scattered references in *Muq*.

4

HISTORIAN OF BIBLICAL AND POST-BIBLICAL JUDAISM

Biblical History

Since, according to the Muslim view, history begins not with Muḥammad's appearance but with the biblical story of creation, of Abraham and the Patriarchs, biblical history has become an integral part of the religious history of Islam. The heroes of the biblical era were regarded as a prelude to Muḥammad's historical mission to the Arabs and occupy, therefore, a prominent position in the Islamic-Koranic concept of revelation and prophecy.[1] It should, therefore, not be surprising that Ibn Khaldūn directed his attention, as some of his Muslim predecessors did, to Israel's past as part of his "Universal History."

Based on the biblical account of the "Taurāt," the Qur'ānic story, and the material from his Muslim and Christian sources, Ibn Khaldūn investigated the history of ancient Israel, and dealt very extensively with all the major biblical events and heroes, with Noah, the Patriarchs Abraham, Isaac and Jacob, Joseph in Egypt and the sojourn of the Israelites in Egypt, the life-story of Moses, up to the Exodus from Egypt.[2]

He continued his account of the march of the Children of Israel through the desert, the crossing of the sea, the "great song" on the sea,

[1] See N. Abbott, "Early Islamic Historiography," in *Studies in Arabic Literary Papyri*, Vol. I (Chicago, 1957), LXXV, 1–31; and the study by F. Rosenthal mentioned in note 36, chapter 1, this section.

[2] His account of the biblical period is mainly covered in *'Ibar*, II, 81–115, apart from many references and passages all through his *'Ibar* and *Muqaddimah*.

the giving of the Law, the Ten Commandments (*aḥkām at-Taurāt,* or *al-Kalimāt al-'Ashr*), the story of the golden calf, the rebellion under Koraḥ, the various encounters and battles with the Amalikites, Moabites, and other Canaanite tribes, the emergence of the class of the Levites, the death of Moses and the final conquest of Canaan under the leadership of Joshua.

After his survey of events from the Exodus to Joshua, he discussed the period of the Judges and inserted a very typical methodological remark: "The period from Joshua to Saul is called the Judges and Elders. I shall here mention those judges in their successive order, depending on the correctness of it as recorded in the Books of aṭ-Ṭabarī and al-Mas'ūdī but checking them with the accounts of Abu l-Fidā' in his 'History' about the Judges and Kings of Israel and also comparing them with Orosius, the Roman historian." [3]

He dealt with the advent of the Kingdom under Saul, his battles with the various Canaanite tribes, with the Philistines, the story of David and Goliath, the friendship of David with Jonathan until the crowning of David as King of Judea. In special chapters he unfolded "the rule of Solomon and his sons," "the separation of Israel from the tribes of Judah and Benjamin" and "the history of the ten tribes." In the course of his account, he mentioned all the kings of Israel and Judea and many of the Hebrew prophets and leaders who appeared under the various rulers.

Ibn Khaldūn dealt also with the return of the exiles as a result of the decree of Cyrus, the beginning of the restoration of the Temple in Jerusalem, the difficulties the Samaritans put in the way of its building, the renewal of the permission for the building of the Temple by Darius, the restoration of the Torah by Ezra and the role played by Nehemiah, Zerubabel, Mordecai, Esther, Haman, Daniel, and others.

Post-Biblical History: Ibn Khaldūn and Yosiphon

Ibn Khaldūn is one of the few Islamic historians, if not the only one, who was not satisfied to present merely the biblical history. He made every effort to outline also the post-biblical history from the restoration of the first Temple on until the destruction of the second Temple by Titus. While, however, for the biblical period Ibn Khaldūn had at his disposal a broad documentary basis to lean on, for

[3] *'Ibar,* II, 88.

the post-biblical period he could not draw on a similar abundance of source material.

Apparently after a thorough search, he must have realized that there were no Arabic sources available for the period and regretfully expressed, "This period was not reported by any of the leaders, nor did I find any reference in the books of history, despite their great numbers and extent." Ibn Khaldūn might have refrained from dealing with this period, as his Muslim predecessors had done, had he not unexpectedly found during his stay in Egypt, an Arabic-written Jewish source which provided him with precisely the kind of information he desired.

Ibn Khaldūn must have been greatly elated to have succeeded in finding a source for the post-biblical period in Jewish history, up to the destruction of the Temple in 70 A. D. It was probably this joy at having discovered such a unique chronicle that prompted him to give an unusually elaborate description of the author and his work. Thus he writes: "There came into my hands while I was in Egypt a book by one of the learned men of the Jews, one of the contemporaries of that period, dealing with the history of the Holy Temple and of the two kingdoms during the period between the first destruction by Nebuchadnezzar and the second destruction by Titus when the great expatriation [*al-Jalwā al-Kubrā*] took place . . . It contained the entire history of this period in great detail. The book contained the whole history of the two dynasties which existed then, that of the House of the Hasmoneans and that of the House of Herod . . . Thus I have summarized here its contents as I found it in the book, for I did not find anything about it anywhere else . . ." [4]

Ibn Khaldūn attributes the authorship of this book to a Yūsuf b. Kuryūn, one of the contemporaries of that very period and described him as "one of the most important of the Jews and one of their generals when the Romans marched against them . . . Vespasian, the father of Titus, besieged him . . . Yūsuf fled to one of the mountain passes and hid himself there. He [Vespasian] succeeded then in capturing him, but pardoned him, showed him favor, and he remained among his followers; . . . he had the same connection with his son,

[4] See *'Ibar,* II, 116 ff. While Ibn Khaldūn confines himself in his method of quoting geographical and historical sources mainly to the mention of the name of the author and the title of his work, in referring to this chronicle he elaborates in great detail on the author, his work, his time, and other aspects. He has applied this elaborate way of defining his sources in some other cases particularly in regard to the works of at-Ṭabarī, al-Mas'ūdī, al-Idrīsī, al-Bakrī, Ibn Baṭṭūta, Orosius, Ibn Sa'īd al-Gharnātī al-Maghribī and others.

Titus, under whose rule the children of Israel were exiled from Jerusalem . . ."

In calling Yūsuf b. Kuryūn "one of the leaders of the Jews and one of their generals . . . one of the priests of the Jews . . . friend of Vespasian and Titus" and above all, "the historian of the second restoration of the Temple in Jerusalem before the great expatriation," Ibn Khaldūn simply identified the author of this Chronicle with Josephus Flavius, the Jewish general and historian, the author of *The Jewish Wars* (*de Bellum Judaicum*) and *The Jewish Antiquities.*

There are, however, two basic objections to this identification. First, Josephus Flavius' name in Hebrew was not Joseph ben Gurion, but Joseph b. Matityāhū; and second, Ibn Khaldūn could not have used Josephus Flavius' work, of which there existed until his time only the original Greek version and the Latin translation called *Hegesippus,*[5] compiled in the early fourth century. Ibn Khaldūn did not read either Latin or Greek, but since he expressly stated, "I have read in it," and "I have seen it in the book," it must have been an Arabic-written book—and this was undoubtedly the Arabic translation of the Hebrew chronicle of Yūsuf b. Kuryūn.

It is quite evident that Ibn Khaldūn here fell victim to a confusion which was very common among medieval scholars, Jewish and non-Jewish, by not realizing that the work he was referring to and using so extensively was not written by Josephus Flavius, but was a Hebrew chronicle of the Middle Ages, generally known as the *Chronicle of Yosiphon.*[6]

[5] The Latin *Hegesippus* is a free translation from the Greek "Josephus," with the purpose of giving a Christian version; see E. Schürer, *Geschichte des jüdischen Volkes im Zeitalter Jesu* (Leipzig, 1901), I, 159–161. About the Slavonic version of "Josephus," see S. Zeitlin, "The Slavonic Josephus and its Relation to Josiphon and Hegesippus," *J. Q. R.*, XX (1929), 1–50.

[6] How confused Ibn Khaldūn was himself about the author of this source is evident from the fact that in his chapter on the Roman-Jewish wars, he referred to Yūsuf b. Kuryūn as the Jewish General and the Jewish Priest of Tiberias, while at the same time he regarded him as the author of the Chronicle from which he so continuously quoted; *'Ibar,* II, 42, 137, and other passages. De Slane, the French translator of the *Prolegomena,* has rightly recognized (*Notices et Extraits,* XIX, 473) that here Ibn Khaldūn has confused the author of the Jewish Antiquities, "avec le faux Josèphe dont l'ouvrage en hébreu fut composé dans le VIIe ou le VIIIe siècle de notre ère." De Slane was, however, not aware of Ibn Khaldūn's much more extensive usage of this "faux Josèphe" in *'Ibar,* II. The editor of *'Ibar,* II (Cairo, 1934), notwithstanding de Slane's remarks, still maintained that Yūsuf b. Kuryūn in the usage of Ibn Khaldūn was identical with Josephus Flavius. The spelling of the name Ibn Kuryūn is corrupt in all the printed texts of *'Ibar,* II, ed. Bulāq, Cairo, and Beirut. The name is printed sometimes Ibn Karbūn or even Ibn Karmūn and thus copied also by some Western scholars.

This Hebrew chronicle contained, apart from legendary accounts and stories pertaining to early Greek and Roman history, and its major and central portion, a history of the Hasmonaean dynasty, of the House of Herod, and the Jewish wars with Rome, based on Josephus Flavius, the books of the Maccabees and other apocryphal books, on Nicholaus of Damascus,[7] on the Latin version of *Hegesippus* and on other Latin and classical sources.

The time and the date of the original composition of *Yosiphon* has been a controversial issue among the historians, but the consensus tends to be now that this chronicle must have been written in the middle of the tenth century in Latin Christian Europe, or, more specifically, in Southern Italy.[8] This chronicle soon became one of the most popular books of medieval Jewry, and the degree of its popularity is indicated not only by many editions and prints[9] but also by the many translations during the centuries, from Hebrew into European languages such as German, Latin, English, French, Yiddish, Ladino,

[7] See Ben Zion Wacholder, *Nicholaus of Damascus*, U. C. Publication in History, (Berkeley-Los Angeles, 1962), LXXV, especially 94–97 and the Notes.

[8] About the date of the original composition of *Yosiphon* many rather contradictory views have been expressed. For the earlier views see A. Neubauer, "Pseudo-Josephus: Joseph ben Goryon," *J. Q. R.* (1899), XI, o.s., 355–364 and the references there to Chwolson, Rappoport, Graetz, Zunz, Weiss, and Fraenkel; also *Jewish Encyclopaedia,* VII, 259–260. For more recent discussions on this point see F. Y. Baer, "Sefer Josefun ha-Ibri" in *Sefer Dinaburg* (Jerusalem, 1949–1950), pp. 178–205, who places its composition into the tenth century. S. Zeitlin, *The First Book of the Maccabees* (New York, 1950), pp. 58 ff., and his "Josippon," in *J. Q.R.* (1963), LIII, 277–297 puts its date into the fourth century; Abraham A. Neuman, "Josippon: History and Pietism" in *Alexander Marx Jubilee Volume* (New York, 1950), I, 637–667, and his "Josippon and the Apocrypha" in *J. Q. R.* (1952), XLVIII, n.s. 1–26, fixes the time of its composition before the completion of the Talmud. See P. E. Schramm, *Kaiser, Rom und Renovatio* (Berlin, 1929), II, 112 ff., who suggests the first half of the twelfth century in his chapter on "Schilderung der Kroenung eines römischen Kaisers aus dem Hebräichen Geschichtswerk Josippon." See also K. Trieber, "Zur Kritik des Gorionides," *Nachrichten von der Koenigl. Gesellschaft der Wissenschaften zu Goettingen, Phil-histor. Klasse* (1895), pp. 381–401; D. Flusser, "The Author of the Book of Josiphon: His Personality and His Age," (in Hebrew) in *Zion* (Jerusalem, 1953), XVIII, 109–112; M. Sanders and H. Nahmad, "A Judeo-Arabic Epitome of the Yosippon," in *Essays in Honor of Solomon B. Freehof* (Pittsburg, 1964), pp. 275–299.

[9] The Hebrew text of *Yosiphon* was printed at various times: Mantua, 1476–1479; Constantinople, 1510; Muenster, 1541; Berditshev, 1896–1913 (by A. Kahana and d. Guenzburg); and Jerusalem, 1956 (Hominer). A new critical edition of the Hebrew *Yosiphon* is in preparation by D. Flusser of the Hebrew University, Jerusalem. For a survey of the editions and translations of *Yosiphon,* see U. Cassuto in *Encyclopedia Judaica* (Berlin), IX, 419–425; and S. Baron, *A Social and Religious History of the Jews* (New York, 1952 ff.), VI, 191 ff.

and into Oriental languages such as Ethiopic,[10] Judeo-Persian,[11] and above all, into Arabic.[12]

The Arabic translation of *Yosiphon* was carried out by a certain Zakarīyā' b. Sa'īd al-Isrā'īlī, a Jew from Yemen,[13] and it was this Arabic translation which Ibn Khaldūn had "discovered" in Egypt and which became his guide for the outline of the post-biblical history of the Jews.

In a series of chapters he deals with "The History of the Restoration of the Temple after its first destruction and what happened to the Children of Israel in the period between the two dynasties, the Hasmoneans and the House of Herod, until the Destruction of the Second Temple." [14] He gives a survey of the events from the appearance of Alexander the Great in Jerusalem, the division of his empire amongst the Ptolemaeans and Seleucides, the war of Antiochus in Syria against the Jews, the rise of the house of the Hasmonaean, the role of Mattatias and his sons, Juda, Jonathan, and Simon until the ascent of the Hasmonaean king, Hyrcanus the First. He continued to outline the history of Antipater, the father of Herod, the rise of the house of Herod, the intervention of the Romans, the outbreak of the Jewish-

[10] The Ethiopic translation is the only one that has been critically investigated and edited by Murād Kāmil, in *Des Joseph b. Gorion Geschichte der Juden* (New York, 1938); see the comprehensive review by J. Simon in *Orientalia* (Rome, 1940), IX, 378–387.

[11] Excerpts from the Hebrew *Yosiphon* are found in Judeo-Persian literature, see W. Bacher, *Ein Hebräisch-Persisches Wörterbuch aus dem vierzehnten Jahrhundert* (Budapest, 1900), p. 41. *Yosiphon* seems to have penetrated even to the Jewish diaspora in India; see for a fragment from *Yosiphon* in the Malabārī or the Malayālam dialect of the Cochin Jews in D. S. Sassoon's Catalogue *Ohel David* (London, 1932), I, 349.

[12] For the various Arabic manuscripts of *Yosiphon* thus far known in the libraries of Europe (Paris, London, Oxford), see Murād Kāmil, *Des Joseph b. Gorion*, pp. X–XII. The oldest Arabic manuscripts are preserved in Paris; see de Slane, *Catalogue des Manuscrits Arabes*, p. 342, n. 1906, completed in 1342. It is this manuscript which has served J. Wellhausen as a basis for his "Der Arabische Josippus" in *Abhandl d. kgl. Ges. d. Wiss. zu Göttingen, Phil-Hist. Klasse*, N. F., (Berlin, 1897), I, pp. 1–50. Wellhausen did not edit or translate the Arabic text of this manuscript; he gives but a "Referat über den Inhalt" (p. 4). For the Arabic manuscripts in London, see Ch. Rieu, *Suppl. to the Cat. of the Arabic Mss.*, in the Brit. Museum (London, 1894), p. 22b; for Oxford, see *Bibliothecae Bodleianae, Codicum Manuscriptorum Orientalum Catalogus*, (Oxford, 1787), p. 180b. Another Arabic manuscript is extant in Istanbul in *Collection Ahmat III*, no. 3009, to which my colleague, Professor Bernard Lewis, London, has kindly drawn my attention. A critical edition of the Arabic text of Yūsuf b. Kuryūn, based on all the available manuscripts, long overdue, is being prepared by me.

[13] See Ḥājjī Khalīfah, "Kashf aẓ-Ẓunūn," *Lexicon*, II, 121.

[14] See *'Ibar*, II, 116–141.

Roman wars and the final collapse of the Jewish state with the destruction of the second Temple under Titus in 70 A. D.[15]

In unfolding the post-biblical history of the Jews as derived from *Yosiphon*, Ibn Khaldūn quoted his source not only more than sixty times, but incorporated from the Arabic version a large part of its contents, sometimes almost verbatim, into his own "History."

In the light of so abundant a documentation it can be stated that Ibn Khaldūn is the first medieval Muslim historian[16] who made the most extensive use—not only of Orosius "the historian of Rome," and of Ibn al-'Amīd, Ibn ar-Rāhib[17] and others[18] of "the historians of the Christians,"—but also of Yūsuf b. Kuryūn, "the historian of the Jews," the chronicler of the post-biblical period and "the historian of the second restoration of the Holy Temple in Jerusalem."

Ibn Khaldūn and the Hebrew Scriptures

The utilization of the *Chronicle of Yosiphon* enabled Ibn Khaldūn to present, not only the historical aspects of post-biblical Judaism, but supplied him, together with biblical sources, with some understanding of the fundamental structure of the religion and the law of Judaism. He derived from *Yosiphon* many details about the "Taurāt," the

[15] It should be noted that Ibn Khaldūn used the *Chronicle of Yūsuf b. Kuryūn* not only for post-biblical Jewish history but also for matters of general relevance. The earliest quotation given by Ibn Khaldūn from this source pertains, indeed, to aspects of Roman legendary history and to the foundation of Rome. Typically for his approach, Ibn Khaldūn compared the data derived from Yūsuf b. Kuryūn with Orosius, realizing a discrepancy in their respective views.

[16] The assumption that the Spanish Muslim scholar, Ibn Ḥazm (d. 1064), the author of "Book of Religions and Sects" (*Kitāb al-Milal wa-n-niḥal*), was the earliest scholar who has quoted from the Arabic version of Yūsuf b. Kuryūn cannot be maintained any longer. It seems that Ibn Ḥazm could not have used the Arabic version of Yūsuf b. Kuryūn so early at all and he must have obtained the passage he quoted from the original in Hebrew with the help of one of his Jewish friends with whom he collaborated. The passage in question has been translated by A. Neubauer in *J. Q. R.* (1899), XI, o.s., 356, and J. Graf in *Oriens Christianus* (1938), XXXV, 177. See Ibn Ḥazm's *Kitāb al-milal wa-n-niḥal*, ed. Yūsuf Mankūrūnī (Cairo, 1908), I.

[17] Some quotations from *Yosiphon* in the works of Ibn al-'Amīd and of Abū Shākir Buṭrus b. ar-Rāhib indicate that these Christian historians were acquainted with either the Arabic or Ethiopic translation of *Yosiphon*. Ibn ar-Rāhib does not present a narrative history but synchronized tables. His quotation from Yūsuf b. Kuryūn refers to the number of casualties inflicted upon the Jews by the Romans during the Roman-Jewish war in Jerusalem.

[18] Al-Maqrīzī (d. 1442) was also acquainted with Yūsuf b. Kuryūn and derived, apparently from him, his information on the Jewish sects in the first century, the Pharisees, Sadducees, and Ḥassidim. See de Sacy, *Chrestomathie Arabe*.

Holy Book of the Jewish religion, its composition and transmission. Of all the great religious books of non-Islamic peoples, none is more highly regarded by Ibn Khaldūn than the Hebrew scriptures, the "Taurāt," which is "the oldest book of the revealed writings that came down to us" and which represents the very essence of the religious foundation of Judaism. Few Muslim historians have given the "Taurāt" such a central place as has Ibn Khaldūn. All through his writings he introduced quotations from it with "it is mentioned in the "Taurāt" or "as I have read in the 'Taurāt' " or "all this is explained in the 'Taurāt.' "[19]

Despite these statements it is evident that Ibn Khaldūn could not have derived his information from a direct acquaintance with the Hebrew Bible. He undoubtedly had used an Arabic translation of the Old Testament[20]—probably based on a Syriac version—and may have received additional oral information from Jewish scholars. Ibn Khaldūn did not, however, mention any cooperation or personal contact with Jewish scholars unlike earlier Muslim scholars such as Ibn Quṭaybah, al-Mas'ūdī, Ibn Ḥazm, al-Birūnī, Abu' l-Fidā' and others who, when quoting biblical passages in their writings, would usually indicate that their knowledge was derived from persons who knew Hebrew and Arabic and who had read the Bible with them and would explicitly give the names of their informants.[21]

Interested in the composition and the structure of the Holy Books, Ibn Khaldūn excerpted from *Yosiphon* details about the Hebrew Canon. Based on this author, he recorded the twenty-four books of the Bible but presented also a different concept of the Hebrew Bible of forty-three or even forty-six books which, as stated, was fixed by the Apostles who met in Rome and then was put into writing by Clement, a disciple of Peter.[22]

As the books "which belong to the old religious law of the Jews" he listed "the Pentateuch in five volumes; the Book of Joshua bin

---

[19] *Ta'rīf*, pp. 354–355; 'Ibar, II, 5 ff., 27 and other places.

[20] *Muq.*, I, 249–250; II, 233; about the first Arabic translation of the Torah, see M. Zucker, *Rav Saadya Gaon's Translation of the Torah* (New York, 1959). It is noteworthy that Ibn Khaldūn refers to Sa'adya as "the Fayyūmī of the Jewish scholars" in *"Ibar*, V, 561; he may have derived this name from al-Mas'ūdī's *Tanbīh*, ed. de Goeje, pp. 113–114.

[21] See I. Goldziher, "Über Bibelzitate im Muhammedanischen Schriftum," pp. 315–321; and W. Bacher, *Bibel und biblische Geschichte in der Muhammedanischen Literatur.* Despite some preliminary attempts to investigate the many instances of biblical quotations by Muslim authors, a thorough investigation of this whole aspect is still to be carried out.

[22] *'Ibar*, II, 148 and a parallel version in *Muq.*, I, 419; see *Prolegomena*, I, 477 n.

Nūn; the Book of Judges; the Book of Ruth (Rā'ūth); the Book of Judith (Yahūdhā); the four Books of Kings; the Book of Chronicles in one volume; the three Books of Maccabees by Ibn Kuryūn; the Book of Ezra, the religious leader (*imām*); the Book of Esther and the story of Hāmān; the Book of Job, the Righteous One; the Psalms of David the Prophet; the five Books of David's son, Solomon; the sixteen Prophecies of the major and minor prophets; the Book of Jesus, the son of Sīraḥ, the minister (vizier) of Solomon."

This peculiar concept of the biblical Canon, so different from the traditional one with all the variations in the order and the names of the books and the inclusion of apocryphal books, poses many questions, and one would like to know what specific books Ibn Khaldūn meant to include among his "four Books of the Kings" or among the "five Books of Solomon," where the Book of Daniel belonged and why other apocryphal books such as the books of Tobit, Baruch, Bel and the Dragon have not been given the same status as the Book of Judith and the Book of Jesus, the son of Sīraḥ.[23]

A particularly revealing feature in this concept is Ibn Khaldūn's attribution of the authorship of "the three Books of Maccabees" to Ibn Kuryūn. Indeed it was as "Book of the History of the Hebrews, entitled the Book of the Maccabees," that the whole *Chronicle of Yosiphon* became known, as listed by Ḥājjī Khalīfah. This may well indicate Ibn Khaldūn's close contact with the Coptic circles in Egypt, among whom the work of Yūsuf Ibn Kuryūn was so popular that they elevated it to the rank of a "Holy Book," although the official Coptic Church did not recognize it as such.[24]

The Septuagint Translation

Translation as means of an intellectual contact between peoples and civilizations, as the transmission of ideas, was greatly appreciated by Ibn Khaldūn, who himself was so deeply indebted to the translation and transmission of great books of the ancient world into his native

[23] See A. Baumstark, "Der Bibelkanon bei Ibn Chaldūn," *Oriens Christianus*, pp. 393–398, who stresses the West-Syrian-Palestinian character of Ibn Khaldūn's Canon; I. Goldziher in *Z.D.M.G.* (1878), XXXII, 31, note 4, regards Ibn Khaldūn's Canon as closest to that of the Abyssinian Church.

[24] For this aspect see M. Chaine, "Le Canon des Livres saints dans l'Eglise Ethiopienne," *Recherches de Science Religieux* (Paris, 1914), V, 22–39; A. Baumstark, "Der äthiopische Bibelkanon," *Oriens Christianus* (Rome, 1905), V–VI, 162–173; and I. Guidi, "Il canone biblico della Chiese copta," *Revue Biblique* (Paris, 1901), X, 161–174.

language, Arabic, during the period of the Golden Age of Baghdād. The translation of Holy Books of the monotheistic religions, the Avesta, the Gospels, or the "Taurāt" into other languages had, therefore, a great appeal to him. In regards to the Gospels, he referred apparently to the Vulgate when he stated "the Romans, a people which speaks Latin, have translated into their language the Pentateuch and the books of the Hebrew Prophets in order to understand more clearly the decisions of God." [25]

Ibn Khaldūn's main attention centered, however, around the Greek translation of the Hebrew Bible, the Septuagint. The story of the Septuagint translation has been a favorite topic of Muslim and Christian scholars, such as Ibn Qutayba, al-Mas'ūdī, Ibn Ḥazm, Abu' l-Ma'ālī, al-Birūnī, Abu' l-Fidā', and such Christian authors as Eutychius and Maḥbūb Agapius, and has been recorded by them with various degrees of exactitude and discrepancies in details.[26]

Ibn Khaldūn, not familiar with either the letter of Aristeas [27] or with Philo's work or with the Rabbinic or Midrashic sources pertaining to the Septuagint translation, relied mainly on Muslim sources, on Ibn al-'Amīd, and in particular, on the Hebrew *Chronicle of Yosiphon*. From the latter source, Ibn Khaldūn copied various statements concerning the circumstances which led to the Greek translation of the "Taurāt." He quoted from *Yosiphon* how Ptolemy of the Macedonian dynasty, the King of Egypt, a lover of the sciences, had summoned seventy of the Jewish sages (*akhbār*) and ordered them to translate for him the "Taurāt" and the Books of the Prophets.

In another connection he inserted a more detailed description of the Septuagint translation, also following *Yosiphon*, describing in great detail how anxious Ptolemy of Egypt was to know the content of the Books of the Jews and that he wrote to the High Priest of Jerusalem, who chose for him seventy of the great scholars of the Jews. They were cordially received in Alexandria where they arrived with their books, and the king "appointed for each of them a scribe to dictate to him the interpretation until all the books were translated from Hebrew to Greek. He gave the priests presents and for their sake he granted the Jews in Egypt—some 100,000 in number—freedom

[25] *Muq.*, III, 245; *Proleg.*, III, 284.

[26] Most of the Muslim sources dealing with the Septuagint translation are studied by G. Vajda, "La Version des Septante dans la littérature Musulmane," *R. E. J.* (1931), XCI, 65–70.

[27] See *Letter of Aristeas*, ed. and trans. by M. Hadas, Dropsie College Edition (New York, 1951).

of worship. He made a table and engraved on it a map of Egypt and the Nile and decorated it with jewels and precious stones. He sent it to Jerusalem and it was placed in the temple.[28]

The frequency with which Ibn Khaldūn mentioned the Septuagint translation may well indicate that he was aware of its effect on the pagan Hellenistic world, as a turning point in the history of religious thought before Christianity, preparing the pagan world spiritually for the ultimate acceptance and spread of monotheism.

His Critical Approach to the Bible

Ibn Khaldūn has incorporated in his presentation of the biblical and post-biblical history of the Jews and in his discussions of the "Taurāt" many names and terms which he rendered in Arabic transliteration, explaining in each case "this is a Hebrew word," or "its meaning in Hebrew is . . ." [29] Among those Hebrew terms are the names of Jewish holidays such as Ḥanukkah, Purim, Passover, Sukkoth; institutions such as Ohel Mo'ed, the Mishkan, Tabernacle, and Cherubim. He was particularly interested in the title and position of the "Kōhen," [30] whom he called the chief of the Jews and whom he compared with the Imām who watched over the conservation of the religion and who directed the prayers and sacrifices. As a requirement for a "Kōhen" he mentioned his descent from the house of Aaron and referred also to the fact that the "Kōhen" selected seventy of the Elders (Shaikh). He referred also to the "Riyāsat al-Jālūt" (Headship of the Diaspora).[31] Repeatedly he used the term "al-jalwā al-Kubrā," derived from Yūsuf b. Kuryūn, with which the Jews designated the epoch after the destruction of the second Temple.[32]

Ibn Khaldūn also draws from Yūsuf b. Kuryūn the Hebrew names of the various Jewish groups and sects in the time of the Hasmonaean ruler, Hyrcanus, in Jerusalem and mentioned the Rabbanim, Karaites,

[28] For the passages dealing with the Septuagint, see *'Ibar*, II, 119, 177, 189, 191, and 212, based on Ibn al-'Amīd and Yūsuf b. Kuryūn. The discrepancies in the numbers of scholars involved in the translation, seventy or seventy-two, and other differences do not concern us here.

[29] In innumerable places of Ibn Khaldūn's writings.

[30] About "Kōhen," see *Muq.*, I, 415–418.

[31] *'Ibar*, II, 163. For further explanation of this term, "Riyāsat al-Jālūt," see W. J. Fischel on "The Resh Galūta in Arabic Literature," in *J. L. Magnes Anniversary Book* (Jerusalem, 1938), pp. 181–187.

[32] This term, rendered by de Slane in "Les Prolégomènes," XIX, 476, with "la grande expatriation" and by F. Rosenthal in *Prolegomena*, I, 475 with "the great exile" occurs many times and is derived from the *Chronicle of Yosiphon*.

Ḥasīdim, Sadūqim, Perūshim, 'Ibādites, and Samaritans.[33] Despite these frequent references to Hebrew words and terms, Ibn Khaldūn did evidently not know Hebrew, yet there seemed to have existed some cooperation between him and some Jewish scholars, whether in the Maghrib or in Egypt, which is indicated in the care he took to transliterate correctly the Hebrew words into the Arabic script.[34] He had acquired a sound understanding of the basic structure of the Hebrew alphabet and script in which the "Taurāt" was revealed. He referred to the fact that the Hebrew language has consonants which do not exist in Arabic and that, on the other side, there are characters in Arabic which are strange to Hebrew.

He criticized the prevailing neglect of the proper transliteration of Hebrew names and terms into Arabic; and he tried to rectify that method for himself by adding meticulously and conscientiously dots or vowels to each transliterated name or term so as to avoid any wrong spelling and to ensure its correct reading.[35] He makes some pertinent remarks about the transliteration of Hebrew and Arabic and stated: "If one of these consonants in their pronunciation stands between two Arabic consonants, the Arabs used to assimilate them to the pronunciation of one of the two consonants so that those differ greatly from the original [Hebrew] pronunciations." [36]

In approaching the Bible and Judaism as a historian, Ibn Khaldūn expressed a number of critical views about some of the biblical statements. He directed his criticism, among others, against those Muslim historians, in particular, al-Mas'ūdī[37] who had uncritically accepted the figures given in the biblical account as to the numerical strength —over 600,000 warriors—of the Children of Israel in the time of the Exodus under Moses.[38]

Ibn Khaldūn expressed his serious doubts that from a military as

[33] Concerning the Jewish sects, see *'Ibar,* II, 122, and 192; there are scattered references to the Samaritans, whose history and peculiarities he had listed.

[34] See M. Schreiner, "Zur Geschichte der Aussprache des Hebräischen," pp. 243–255; I. Goldziher, "Linguistisches aus der Literatur der Muhammedanischen Mystik," pp. 764–785, esp. 774–776.

[35] See *'Ibar,* II, 5, 33; *Muq.,* I, 53–54; and de Sacy, *Chrestomathie Arabe,* III, 343–346.

[36] He mentions also the peculiarities of other scripts such as the Syrian used by the Chaldeans and Nabaṭaeans, the Arabic, the Latin of the Byzantines, the Turkish, etc., *Muq.,* I, 53–54; *Muq.,* III, 244–245.

[37] See *Murūj adh-Dhahab,* I, 92–94; IV, 20 ff.

[38] *'Ibar,* II, 82; *Muq.,* I, 9 ff.; see Exodus 12:37; Numbers 1:46, 11:21. The biblical account speaks actually of 603,550 men on foot, in agreement with the number given in Exodus 38:26. See the pertinent remarks by J. H. Greenstone in *Numbers, with commentary* (Philadelphia, 1948), pp. 12–14 and p. 288.

well as an economic point of view, such a large number was at all feasible. He commented: "al-Mas'ūdī forgets to take into consideration whether Egypt and Syria could possibly have held such a number of soldiers. Every realm may have as large a militia as it can hold and support, but no more. This fact is attested to by well-known customs and familiar conditions. Moreover, an army of this size cannot march or fight as a unit. The whole available territory would be too small for it. If it were in battle formation, it would extend two, three, or more times beyond the field of vision . . ." [39]

Ibn Khaldūn wondered how the desert could support such a large number; how such an army could maneuver and fight and be able to engage the enemy in battle; how the family of the Israelites, in the course of such a limited number of years could have multiplied from seventy individuals who went down to Egypt to such a huge number. While such an increase of the Children of Israel could not be explained rationally, it could be regarded as a miracle fulfilling the promise God gave to Abraham, Isaac and Jacob "to multiply them until they were more numerous than stars of heaven and pebbles of the earth." [40]

In subjecting other biblical passages to a critical analysis, he expressed astonishment about the absence in the "Taurāt" of the names of individuals expressly mentioned in the Qur'ān: 'Ād, Thamūd, Hūd and Ṣāliḥ. He also repudiated the statements of certain Muslim genealogists who ascribed the darkness of the skin of the descendants of Ham, the son of Noah, to the curse of Noah against him. Ibn Khaldūn objected to this reasoning since there is no mention in the "Taurāt" of the dark color of Ham. On the other side, he found no reason to reject the statements in the "Isra'īliyāt" that the guard of Solomon was composed of 12,000 foot soldiers and that his cavalry consisted of 1,400 horses standing on guard at the gates of his palace.[41]

Though Ibn Khaldūn tried to refrain from polemics and theological discussions, he could not free himself from the prevailing traditional polemics of Muslim scholars concerning the genuineness of the text of the Holy Scriptures.[42] Some Islamic theologians accused the "Ahl al-

[39] *Muq.*, I, 9–10; *Proleg.*, I, 16; *'Ibar*, II, 82–85. For similar critical remarks in regards to the geographical impossibility of so large a number of Israelites at the time of the Exodus, see M. Perlmann, "Eleventh-Century Andalusian Authors on the Jews of Granada," *Proceedings of the American Academy for Jewish Research* (New York, 1949), XVIII, 273 ff.

[40] *Muq.*, I, 12.

[41] *Muq.*, I, 11; see also, I, 151, 306; II, 340.

[42] See, for all these aspects, I. W. Sweetman, *Islam and Christian Theology* (London, 1945–1947), 2 vols.; E. Fritsch, *Islam und Christentum im Mittelalter*

Kitāb," "the people of the book," Jews and Christians, of having corrupted the text of their divine books (Tabdīl, or Taḥrīf) or having charged them with misinterpretations (*ta'wīl*) of certain passages of the Holy Scriptures.[43] Though Ibn Khaldūn maintained that the Scriptures had once contained the name of "Our Lord and Master Muḥammad, the Arab Prophet," he did not accept that sweeping critical view that the "Taurāt" was corrupted by the Jews or Christians and stated "this is unacceptable to thorough scholars and cannot be understood in its plain meaning, since custom prevents people who have a revealed religion from dealing with their divine scriptures in such a manner." [44]

Ibn Khaldūn is thus a representative of that school of thought which charged the "Ahl al-Kitāb" not with textual falsification but only with a wrong interpretation.

His Approach to Ancient Chronology

When Ibn Khaldūn undertook to delve into the history of pre-Islamic civilizations, he was confronted with the problem of chronology and the need of correlating the dates of important events in pre-Islamic history to the calendar of the Hejira era. Ibn Khaldūn did not offer a systematic treatise on chronology nor did he indulge in any theoretical discussion of time, mathematical or astronomical calculations along the lines of an al-Birūnī.

Whenever convenient to him, he referred to events of pre-Islamic history in their relation to various eras, either the era of the creation, the era of the deluge, the era of Alexander, the Seleucid calendar. In conformity with the practice of his sources, he used also as his chronological starting point the building or destruction of cities such as Rome, Troy, Carthage, Alexandria, Jerusalem, or the era according to the birth or death of great historical figures such as David, Nebuchadnezzar, Alexander, Caesar, Cleopatra, Augustine, Diocletian or Yazdigird.

Ibn Khaldūn did not give priority to any of the calendaric systems of pre-Islamic history and retained the variety and multiplicity of the

(Breslau, 1930); and W. M. Watt, "The Early Development of the Muslim Attitude to the Bible," *Transactions, Glasgow Oriental Society* (Glasgow, 1957), XVI, 50–62.

[43] See Ignazio di Matteo, "Il taḥrīf od alterazione della Bibbia secondo i musulmani," pp. 64–111, 223–260; see also, the passages in *Livre de la création et de l'histoire de Moṭahhar b. Ṭahir al-Maqdisī*, ed. and transl. by C. Huart (Paris, 1916), pp. 32–34.

[44] *Muq.*, I, 12–13; *Proleg.*, I, 20–21.

calendaric reckoning of the eras of the pre-Islamic and non-Islamic peoples as he found them in the sources, from which he drew, without putting them in a continual sequence and without attempting to correlate them with the Islamic calendar and chronology.

Thus, to illustrate his chronological approach, he stated that Alexander the Great appeared 400 years after the building of Rome, that Caesar died 750 years after the building of Rome, that Cleopatra died 700 years after the building of Rome, that the building of Rome took place in the time of David, and that the destruction of Troy took place 400 years after the building of Rome.

The era most often used by Ibn Khaldūn in regard to the history of the Jews was the era "before" and "after" the destruction of the Temple by Nebuchadnezzar or Titus, and he fixed these events as a calendaric beginning, entirely in the spirit of the Jewish calendar, derived from his Jewish source, *Yosiphon*. He referred to the epoch of the "great expatriation" (*al-jalwā al-kubrā*) of the Jews, the destruction of the Temple by Titus and mentions that it took place 5,230 years after the creation, 1,100 years after the building of Jerusalem, 830 years after the building of Rome, or in the fifty-third year of Titus.

Application of His Socio-Philosophical Views to Jewish History

The *Chronicle of Yūsuf b. Kuryūn,* together with the "Taurāt" and his other sources, provided Ibn Khaldūn not only with the basis for an understanding of the history of biblical and post-biblical Judaism and its fundamental tenets and views; they had also, as it seemed, a decisive influence on the formulation of some of his major philosophical and historiographical concepts. It appears that various highlights in the development of the Jewish people had supplied Ibn Khaldūn with some dramatic illustrations in support of, and confirmation for, some of his fundamental concepts in regard to the rise and fall of states and dynasties.

One of Ibn Khaldūn's basic views on the processes of history was his "generation-theory." [45] In distinguishing four stages in the development of a dynasty, its foundation, its conservation, its imitation, and its destruction, Ibn Khaldūn postulated that the duration of the life of a dynasty does, as a rule, not extend beyond three or four generations. As proof and confirmation for this theory, Ibn Khaldūn referred explicitly to some biblical events, in particular to the forty years of

[45] For his generation-theory see *Muq.*, I, 247–250 and other chapters of his *Muq.*

wandering of the Children of Israel in the desert. He stated that these forty years were intended "to bring about the disappearance of the generation then alive and the growth of another generation [one] that had not witnessed and felt the humiliation [in Egypt]. This is proof of the assumption that [a period of] forty years, which is identical with the [average] life of a single individual, must be considered the duration of a generation." [46]

As further support for this point, he quoted the passage from Exodus 20:5 (probably from the Vulgate), "God your Lord, is powerful and jealous, visiting the sins of the fathers upon the children unto the third and fourth [generations]." [47] This shows, he continues, "that four generations in one lineage are the limit in this extent of ancestral prestige," and he reiterates "that forty years is the shortest period in which one generation can disappear and a new generation can arise." [48]

Another fundamental concept in Ibn Khaldūn's philosophical scheme is that of *'aṣabīya,* the "esprit de corps," the "group feeling," the most powerful force in the creation and development, rise, duration and fall of a religion, society or nation.[49] Even for this theory, Ibn Khaldūn found certain events and phases in Jewish history as a confirmation and stated explicitly that in this respect "the Israelites are a good example." [50] He regards the Jews as those who "originally had one of the greatest 'houses' in the world because of the great number of prophets and messengers born among their ancestors, extending from Abraham to Moses, the founder of their religious group and law; and next because of their group feeling, *'aṣabīya,* and the royal authority that God had promised and granted them by means of that group feeling." [51]

In demonstrating the influence of *'aṣabīya* on the emergence of nations or their disappearance, he presents Jewish history in terms of his own philosophy of history as a proof of its validity. He singled out a number of stages in the development of Jewish history, showing the loss of *'aṣabīya,* or the assertion of it at various critical moments in the nation's rise. He pointed out that it was imperative to create a

---

[46] *Muq.,* I, 306; *Proleg.,* I, 344.

[47] *Muq.,* I, 250; *Proleg.,* I, 281.

[48] *Muq.,* I, 257; *Proleg.,* I, 289.

[49] This is the most central concept in Ibn Khaldūn's socio-philosophical system. This term occurs more than 500 times in his *Muqaddimah;* for detailed discussion see the studies by F. Gabrieli, 'Ayād, E. Rosenthal, Khemiri, Bouthoul, Gibb, Mahdi, Ritter, F. Rosenthal, listed in the "Ibn Khaldūniana" bibliography.

[50] *Muq.,* I, 256; *Proleg.,* I, 287.

[51] *Muq.,* I, 244; *Proleg.,* I, 275.

new generation in the desert which did not know humiliation, oppression, or domination by a foreign dynasty and was thus instilled with a new *'aṣabīya*.[52]

This rise of the Hasmonaean dynasty and its success over their oppressors, the Greeks, as described in the *Chronicle of Yūsuf b. Kuryūn,* brought about the rebirth of *'aṣabīya,* of their national group feeling amongst them which enabled them to throw off their yoke and to establish their own rule; but they lost their group feeling again when the Romans defeated the Jews and conquered Jerusalem and when they were exiled and remained under the domination of foreigners, while only their religious affairs were taken care of by their head, called the "Kōhen." [53]

Ibn Khaldūn used the historical experience of the Jews to prove also his views in regards to the sedentary culture in cities. He stated, "The rule of the Jews in Syria lasted about 1400 years. Sedentary culture thus became established among them . . . customary ways and means of making a living and in the manifold crafts belonging to it as regards food, clothing, and all the other parts of [domestic] economy, so much so that these things, as a rule, can still be learned from them to this day. Sedentary culture and its customs became firmly rooted in Syria through them and through the Roman dynasties which succeeded them for 600 years. Thus, they had the most developed sedentary culture possible." [54]

Ibn Khaldūn applied his views on *'aṣabīya* also to the medieval Jew and tried to explain, almost to justify, their state of degradation, which he regarded as the result of their political defeat, their exile, their mode of living and the oppression, harshness and slavery under which they suffered throughout the centuries. He stated that "slavery and bondage can break the spirit of a tribe and destroy its *'aṣabīya,"* and he warns therefore "the master should not treat his people harshly." [55]

It should be stated that Ibn Khaldūn's outline of biblical and post-biblical Jewish history, as incorporated in his *Muqaddimah* seemed to be in many instances but a condensation of his much more detailed account in volume II of his *'Ibar.* Since this latter account is based on the *Chronicle of Yosiphon* which "came into my hands while in

[52] *Muq.,* I, 256–257; *Proleg.,* I, 288–289.

[53] *Muq.,* I, 417–418; *Proleg.,* I, 475–476.

[54] *Muq.,* II, 251–252; *Proleg.,* II, 287–288.

[55] *Muq.,* III, 265; *Proleg.,* III, 306. See Dover, "The Racial Philosophy of Ibn Khaldūn," *Phylon,* pp. 114–115.

Egypt,"[56] those portions concerning post-biblical Jewish history in his *Muqaddimah* must be regarded as an "Egyptian" contribution, an "Egyptian" interpolation and addition to his earlier "Maghribī" draft of his *Muqaddimah*.[57]

[56] *'Ibar*, II, p. 116.

[57] For further possible allusions to biblical concepts in Ibn Khaldūn's theory, see Flint, *History of the Philosophy of History*, I, 151–171; and Cook in *Cambridge Ancient History*, I, 223.

PART THREE:

Ibn Khaldūn and His "Autobiography"

HIS TA'RĪF AND ITS EVALUATION

It was during his stay in Egypt that Ibn Khaldūn could add to his biographical treatment of such great figures in history as Jenghiz Khān, Hūlāgū, Barqūq, and Tamerlane, and also produce a biography of his own life. This autobiography, known as *Ta'rīf,* which has guided us in the preceding deliberations as a major source of information, constitutes one of the most original accomplishments of his Egyptian phase.

Autobiography as a literary category was not at all new in Arabic literature; many an Arab scholar before and after Ibn Khaldūn has written his own life story, such as Yāqūt (d. 1229), Abū Shāma (d. 1268), Ibn al-Khaṭīb (d. 1374), Suyyūṭī (d. 1505), and others. But Ibn Khaldūn's "Autobiography" is one of "the most detailed biographical accounts in Medieval Muslim literature." [1]

As all authors of an autobiography, Ibn Khaldūn must have been conscious of the singular experiences which were his. During his colorful and exciting career in the Maghrib and in the Mashriq, in North Africa and in Egypt, he must have regarded these experiences as significant and meaningful enough to be handed down to future generations.

There can be no doubt that his "Autobiography" in its present form is a product of his stay in Egypt even though the chapters dealing with his early life in his native Maghrib could well have been written already in the Maghrib. But it is improbable that he could have found the leisure in the Maghrib to concentrate on such a task, nor is it likely that he would have started to write his "Autobiography" amidst the stream of life, which was, in the Maghrib, far from having reached its fruition and climax.

[1] See F. Rosenthal's "Die arabische Autobiographie," esp. pp. 33–34.

Ibn Khaldūn's Arabic text of his "Autobiography" as it was known until recently, consisted of several long chapters dealing with his life story in the Maghrib and in Egypt up to the year 1394.[2] It was attached to the very end of the seventh volume of the *'Ibar*, entitled "Ta'rīf bi Ibn Khaldūn—Mu'allif hadha al-Kitāb" (the "Autobiography of the Author of this Book").[3]

These chapters which until now have constituted the "Autobiography" were clearly intended to be merely a part of, or an appendix to, his great work, attached to the last volume of the *'Ibar*.[4] Even where, as in a Paris manuscript,[5] the "Autobiography" stands at the beginning of Volume III, or as in a Leiden manuscript,[6] where it stands at the end of Volume V, or as in a Tunis manuscript,[7] where it is at the beginning of the *Muqaddimah*, it still remained, though differently placed by copyists, attached to his *'Ibar* as an integral part and not an independent work.

That it was thus regarded is furthermore confirmed by the historian, al-Maqqarī (d. 1632), who stated[8] that he saw in Fez a manuscript bearing Ibn Khaldūn's signature—a manuscript in eight (!) large volumes—at the end of which Ibn Khaldūn had recounted his own life (*'arrafa binafsihi*) at length.

Since Ibn Khaldūn lived in Cairo until 1406, the hitherto available text of his *Ta'rīf* could rightly be regarded as incomplete and fragmentary. Had Ibn Khaldūn failed to record the remaining twelve years of his activities in Egypt from 1394 to 1406?

This question can now be answered thanks to the discovery of various new manuscripts of Ibn Khaldūn's "Autobiography" in the libraries of Istanbul, Cairo, Tunis, and Morocco, which gave us a full picture of his life and activities in Mamlūk Egypt under Sultan

[2] For the text of this incomplete *Ta'rīf*, see 'Ibar (ed. Būlāq, 1868), VII, 379–462; republished by 'Abdul Jawād Khalaf, on the margins of his Cairo edition of the *Muqaddimah* (Cairo, 1904). For a condensed and abridged French translation of the "Autobiography" see de Slane in *J.A.* (1844), pp. 5–60, 187–210, 291–308, 325–353; reprinted with corrections in his "Prolégomènes," *Notices et Extraits* (1863), XIX, vi–lxxxiii, 2nd ed. (Paris, 1934).

[3] This term "at-Ta'rīf bi" has been used by Ibn Khaldūn for biographies of other historical personalities such as Jenghiz Khān (*'Ibar,* V, 525) and Yūsuf b. Kuryūn (*'Ibar,* II, 116); see also *'Ibar,* IV, 92, 431; *Ta'rīf,* p. 41, 79, 278, 297.

[4] It is noteworthy that nowhere in Ibn Khaldūn's writings is there any indication that he intended to write a separate work on his own life.

[5] Paris Ms. no. 1528. See de Slane, *Catalogue,* p. 289.

[6] *Catalogus Codicum arabicorum,* ed. de Goeje and T. Houtsma (Leiden, 1888), I, no. 1350.5.

[7] B. Roy, *Extrait du catalogue des manuscrits* . . . , no. 6216.

[8] Maqqarī, *Nafḥ aṭ-Ṭīb,* IV, 425.

Barqūq (1382–1399) and the early years of Sultan Faraj (1399–1406) until about nine months prior to his death in 1406.

The newly-discovered *complete* text of his "Autobiography" is a separate and independent composition—a book of its own.[9]

It may be assumed that Ibn Khaldūn, as he continued during his stay in Egypt to add steadily new chapters to his draft and at the same time to revise the earlier installments of his "Autobiography," regarded it as inexpedient to attach this autobiographical material any longer as a mere annex or appendix to his last volume of the *Kitāb al-'Ibar* and made it a separate work, which necessitated a new and distinctive title.[10]

While the only title for his incomplete "Autobiography" was simply "at-Ta'rīf bi Ibn Khaldūn" ("Autobiography of Ibn Khaldūn" or "Acquainting [the reader] with Ibn Khaldūn"), using it merely as a section-title (*faṣl*), the newly-found manuscripts of his complete "Autobiography" have different titles. Some manuscripts of his complete "Autobiography" are carrying the title "ar-Riḥla" or "Riḥlat Ibn Khaldūn" while others have "at-Ta'rīf bi Ibn Khaldūn" ("mu'allif al-kitāb), to which are added, perhaps by a later scribe or copyist, the words "wa-riḥlatuhu gharban wa sharqan," ("His journey in the West and in the East.") [11]

It must, however, be stated, that none of these titles do full justice to its content. First of all, it does not actually deserve the title "Riḥla" in the accepted sense of the Arabic term. If we understand under "Riḥla" that well-known type of Arabic travel literature which is mainly and basically a description in a geographical sense and usually a journey in fulfillment of the Ḥājj, the pilgrimage to Mecca, with visits to other religious and cultural centers in the Islamic world, Ibn Khaldūn's "Riḥla" does not qualify at all as belonging to that category of "Riḥla" literature.[12]

Unlike those Muslim authors from the Maghrib and Spain, such as

[9] Ed. Muḥammad b. Tāwīt aṭ-Ṭanjī, entitled *at-Ta'rīf bi Ibn Khaldūn wa-riḥlatuhu gharban wa-sharqan*. For a detailed description of the various manuscripts of the *Ta'rīf*, their interrelationship and interdependence, see Ṭanjī's Preface; Fischel, *Ibn Khaldūn and Tamerlane;* and also Badawī, *Mu'allafāt Ibn Khaldūn*.

[10] 'Alī Merad "L'Autobiographie d'Ibn Khaldūn," pp. 531–564.

[11] See *Catalogue of the Arabic books in the Khedivial Library* (Cairo, 1308 H., 1888–1891 A.D.), V, 36; *Catalogue of the Ayā Sūfia Library* (Istanbul, 1304 H., 1886–1887 A.D.), no. 3200, p. 192; *Catalogue of the As'ad Effendi Library* (Istanbul, 1262 H., 1846 A.D.), no. 2268, p. 132; see also Ḥājjī Khalīfah in his *Lexicon,* III, no. 5881, p. 350; Wüstenfeld, *Geschichte,* No. 456, p. 31; *G.A.L., Suppl. II,* p. 342.

[12] See Hadj Sadok, "Le Genre 'Rih'la'," in *Bulletin des études arabes* (Algiers, 1948), pp. 195–206.

Ibn al-Jubayr (c. 1185), or Ibn Baṭṭūṭah (d. 1377), who, after having widely travelled, have written down the impressions of their journeys into far lands, Ibn Khaldūn did not deal with physical or cultural geography at all, but with his personal history, the history of his own life and activities. True, he speaks of his travels within North Africa and to Spain, his trip to Egypt, and from there his journeys to Mecca, Jerusalem, and Damascus. But all this is intended to convey not primarily information about land and people, about distances and stations, or any other specific geographical data, but to convey only the "stations" in his own life.

Even the title "Ta'rīf" (followed by the preposition "bi") is not an adequate coverage of its contents. His autobiographical account differs greatly from similarly entitled biographical sketches of other Muslim authors. It contains long historical excursuses and surveys,[13] which in most cases have only slim or no relationship to his personal life, and serve at best in some parts as background for a better understanding of the contemporary scene.

In many a chapter of his *Ta'rīf,* he deals with purely objective and factual matters, with the history of various dynasties in the Maghrib and in Egypt before the ascent of the Circassian Mamlūks and other historical factors which could just as well have been parts of his "Universal History," the *'Ibar.* In some cases, as a matter of fact, these chapters are actually nothing but a slightly different and condensed version of events which he had already surveyed in much greater detail in one of the seven volumes of his *'Ibar.*

Even the biographical data in his *Ta'rīf,* invaluable and informative as they are, offer at a closer examination only a partial biographical picture of the author. The *Ta'rīf* is by far not conveying the whole, complete, and comprehensive story of his private life and his public activities. Rewarding as the data of his life story are, it seems to be rather a "selective" account, written by Ibn Khaldūn as he wanted to be seen and judged by posterity.

How selective and incomplete Ibn Khaldūn's "Autobiography" actually is became evident when we combed thoroughly the totality of his writings in search of data of biographical relevance. Then it is realized that such important data are scattered all through his *Muqaddimah* as well as the six other parts of his *'Ibar,* usually introduced by him in the first person, such as "I found," "I met," "I studied," "I con-

[13] It contains also over 750 verses of poetry and about 140 pages of letters in rhymed prose, particularly his correspondence with his friend Lisān ad-Dīn b. al-Khāṭib, in which a great deal of current history is expounded.

sulted," "I have heard," "I was told," etc., all of which one should have expected to find in his "Autobiography." [14]

That his *Taʿrīf* is far from mirroring all the essential facts of his life story and that it must be regarded as being by no means the exclusive source of information about him, becomes even more convincing when we are confronted with important biographical data concerning his activities in Egypt derived from external Arabic sources.[15]

Among those aspects which he had omitted and left unrecorded in his *Taʿrīf,* but which one should have expected to find in an autobiographical account of any person are details about his personal life, his wife, his children, his students, friends and colleagues in Cairo, to whom only passing, casual references are made.[16] It is from external sources that we learn that he had five daughters and two sons and that the two sons, by the names of Muḥammad and ʿAlī, arrived safely in Cairo after the shipwreck which caused the tragic death of his wife and daughters. No indication is given as to the later fate of these two sons, nor does he refer to his later private life, although it is stated by an external source that he had married again.[17]

We search, also in vain, in his *Taʿrīf* for any references to his own literary accomplishments, his works written before or after the *Muqaddimah,* with the one exception in regards to the treatise on the Maghrib which he wrote for Tamerlane. For his smaller studies which he composed before he embarked to Egypt, we are again dependent on external Arabic studies, in particular on Ibn al-Khaṭīb.[18] Whether Ibn

[14] Those biographical references in his *Muqaddimah* and *ʿIbar* are mostly of Egyptian provenance and relate to his Egyptian stay, to scholars whom he had met in Egypt and who supplied him with new information, and to books which became accessible to him only while in Egypt, during his pilgrimage or during his travels to Damascus. All of these references show clearly the impact of his Egyptian stay on his work, and, in addition, supply us with biographical details not recorded in his *Taʿrīf*. Special reference ought to be made to *Muq.*, I, 326; *Muq.*, II, 195–200; *Muq.*, III, 92–93, 274; *ʿIbar,* II, 116; *ʿIbar,* IV, 113.

[15] Among those external Arabic sources figure all those Arabic authors mentioned in the list of "External Arabic Sources."

[16] References to his wife and children are scattered throughout his *ʿIbar* and *Taʿrīf.*

[17] See Sakhāwī, *Ḍau'*, IV, 146 ff.

[18] See *Taʿrīf,* p. 374. For information on his smaller treatises written at an early stage, see Ibn al-Khaṭīb, as quoted by Maqqarī in *Nafḥ aṭ-Ṭīb,* IV. They comprise a commentary of the *Burda,* abridgements of some of the works of Ibn Rushd, of ar-Rāzī, a treatise on elementary arithmetic, a commentary on the principles of jurisprudence by Ibn al-Khaṭīb and other smaller treatises.

Khaldūn omitted the mention of these studies because of his own low regard for them, since he seemed to have felt an aversion towards "brief handbooks" which, in his eyes were detrimental to scholarship, can only be surmised.[19]

In regards to his relationship to some emirs during his Cairo stay, especially towards Emir al-Jūbānī, he again remained quite silent. He seemed to have been very restrained in expressing in his *Ta'rīf* the many acts of kindness which this emir accorded him after his arrival in Cairo without whom he would never have reached this pinnacle of success. It was through al-Jūbānī's mediation that he was introduced to Sultan Barqūq, and that he received many appointments in the educational and judicial fields. It is again from external Arabic sources that we can piece together Ibn Khaldūn's relationship with al-Jūbānī and other emirs.[20]

From these sources we learn also about his involvement with the Majordomo Jamāl ad-Dīn Maḥmūd al-Ustādār and about certain financial transactions in which he took part.[21]

These and other omissions might have been caused by the fact that his "Autobiography" was evidently written at intervals and in installments at various times, and that he anticipated perhaps a more comprehensive, complete, and revised account of his original draft at a later date.

Despite all these shortcomings and limitations, it cannot be emphasized too strongly that his *Ta'rīf,* written and completed in Egypt, constitutes a historical, literary and human document of the first order, a guide of immeasurable value, without which we would have been deprived of the major source for the understanding of the time, the life, and activities of one of the greatest and most remarkable personalities Islam has ever produced.

On the last page of a complete manuscript of the *Ta'rīf,* obtained from Cairo, are to be found, written by the owner or copyist, some Arabic passages, given here in translation:

> This excellent book has been corrected with zeal, with desire for exactitude,
> Watch being kept in doubtful places against committing errors during its writing;

[19] See *Proleg.,* I, Introduction, xliii–xliv.

[20] On Emir al-Jūbānī see above, p. 38.

[21] *Muq.* I, p. 326. For these transactions see Ibn al-Furāt, IX, 435–436; Ibn Iyās, I, 305; Gaudefroy-Demombynes, "Notes sur l'histoire de l'organisation judiciaire," pp. 143–144.

It has been compared with the original text, in which is the handwriting of the author, hoping for Allāh's reward.
This is the composition of Ibn Khaldūn, who has obtained the scepter of victory in the field of discourse.
May Allāh give him reward in the high places of Paradise on the Day of Judgment!
May whoever possesses this book obtain the greatest good; may Allāh bless him!

CHRONOLOGICAL TABLE OF MAJOR EVENTS IN IBN KHALDŪN'S "EGYPTIAN PHASE"

Year A. D.	Month and Day	Event
1382	October 24	Ibn Khaldūn's departure from Tunis for Egypt.
	November 26	Enthronement of Barqūq as Sultan.
	December 8	Ibn Khaldūn's arrival in Alexandria.
1383	January 6	Ibn Khaldūn's arrival in Cairo.
		His first meeting with Sultan Barqūq.
1384		Lecturer at al-Azhar Mosque.
		Appointment as teacher at the Qamḥīya Madrasah in Cairo.
		Appointment as lecturer at the Ẓāhirīya Madrasah in Cairo.
	August 11	Ibn Khaldūn's first appointment as Mālikite Chief Cadi in Cairo.
		Loss of his family and daughters by shipwreck on their way from Tunis to Egypt.
1385	June 17	Dismissal from his first cadiship.
1387	September 29	Departure for the pilgrimage to Mecca.
	December 14	Arrival in Mecca.
1388	May	His return to Cairo.
1389	January	Appointment as teacher at the Ṣarghitmishīya Madrasah.
	April	Appointment to the Baybarsīya Khānqā in Cairo.
		Revolt of Yalbughā an-Nāṣirī against Barqūq.
		Deposition of Sultan Barqūq.
		Removal of Ibn Khaldūn from the Baybarsīya Khānqā.

1390	February	Return of Barqūq to the throne.
1390–1399		Ibn Khaldūn "out of office."
1399	May 22	Ibn Khaldūn's second appointment as Mālikite Chief Cadi in Cairo.
	June 20	Death of Sultan Barqūq. Sultan Faraj succeeds Barqūq.
1400	March	Revolt of Tanam against Faraj. First journey of Ibn Khaldūn with Faraj to Damascus.
	May	Ibn Khaldūn visits Jerusalem, Bethlehem, and Hebron.
	September 3	Ibn Khaldūn's dismissal from his second cadiship.
	October 30	Conquest of Aleppo by Tamerlane.
	November 19	Faraj prepares military expedition against Tamerlane.
	November 28	Ibn Khaldūn leaves with Faraj for Damascus.
	December 20	Tamerlane leaves Baalbek for Damascus.
	December 23	Arrival of Faraj's army in Damascus.
	December 24	Ibn Khaldūn takes residence in the 'Ādilīya Madrasah.
	December 25	First clashes of the advance forces of the two opposing armies.
	December 29	Tamerlane arrives before Damascus.
1401	January 3–4	Tamerlane offers peace to the people of Damascus.
	January 6	Reports of a seditious plot against Sultan Faraj.
	January 7	Sultan Faraj and Yashbak and other emirs return to Cairo.
	January 10	Ibn Khaldūn is let down the wall of Damascus to meet with Tamerlane. First meeting of Ibn Khaldūn with Tamerlane.
	January 10–February 26	Further audiences with Tamerlane.
	February 26	Last meeting of Ibn Khaldūn with Tamerlane.
	February 27	Ibn Khaldūn leaves Tamerlane and returns to Cairo.
	March 17	Ibn Khaldūn arrives in Cairo.
	March 19	Tamerlane and his army leave Damascus.
	March, end	Ibn Khaldūn receives Tamerlane's payment for his mule.
	April	Ibn Khaldūn's third appointment as Mālikite Chief Cadi in Cairo.
	August	Ibn Khaldūn's letter to the ruler of the Maghrib.
1402	March	Dismissal from his third cadiship.
	July 4	Ibn Khaldūn's fourth appointment as Mālikite Chief Cadi in Cairo.

1403	September 23	Ibn Khaldūn's dismissal from his fourth cadiship.
1405	February 11	Ibn Khaldūn's fifth appointment as Mālikite Chief Cadi in Cairo.
	February 18	Death of Tamerlane.
	May 27	Ibn Khaldūn's dismissal from his fifth cadiship.
1406	February	Ibn Khaldūn's sixth appointment as Mālikite Chief Cadi in Cairo.
	March 17	Death of Ibn Khaldūn in Cairo.

IBN KHALDŪNIANA:

A BIBLIOGRAPHY OF WRITINGS ON AND PERTAINING TO IBN KHALDŪN

Since the European discovery of Ibn Khaldūn in the early decades of the nineteenth century, an ever-increasing number of publications, books, studies and smaller articles have appeared—and continue to appear—in European, Semitic and Oriental languages, dealing with a wide range of topics and problems emanating from Ibn Khaldūn's legacy.

The following "Ibn Khaldūniana" bibliography mirrors and reflects this world-wide scholarly interest and is intended to serve as a guide and help for the furtherance of Ibn Khaldūn studies. It includes the most essential publications on and pertaining to Ibn Khaldūn, although absolute completeness has been precluded by the very diffusion of the material in innumerable journals and periodicals, scattered all over the globe, not easily accessible and available.

This bibliography is based on the "Selected Bibliography" which I published a decade ago in Franz Rosenthal's English translation of *The Muqaddimah* (Volume III, pp. 485–512, New York, 1958), but has here been re-arranged and considerably supplemented and updated.

I am most grateful to the Bollingen Foundation for having given me the permission to use my previous material.

'Abādī, 'Abdul-Ḥamid
"If Ibn Khaldun would live in this age"
Hilāl (Cairo, 1939), pp. 132–133.

'Abbās, Aḥmad
"Vie et œuvre d'Ibn Ḥaldūn"
Falāsifat al-Islām fi l-ġarb al-'arabī. Tetouan, 1961, I.

'Abdal-Wahhāb, H. H.
Khulāṣat ta'rīkh Tūnis
Tunis, 1953.

Al-Muntaḥabāt at-tūnusīya li' n-nāši'a al-madrasīya
Cairo, 1944, pp. 111–115.

'Abd el-Jalīl, J. M.
Brève histoire de la littérature arabe
Paris, 1947, pp. 215–216, 284–285.

Adams, Charles C.
Islam and Modernism in Egypt
London, 1933.

Adivar, Abdülhak Adnan
"Ibn Ḥaldūn"
Islâm Ansiklopedisi (Istanbul, 1943), fasc. 47, pp. 738–743.

Afshār, Irāj
Index Iranicus (Fehrest maqālāt-e Farsī) Repertoire methodique des articles persans (1910–1958)
Teheran, 1961, nos. 235, 236, 763, 1091, 1095, 3172.

Aḥmad Bābā b. Aḥmad at-Tinbuktī
Nayl al-ibtihāj bi taṭrīz ad-dībāj
Fez, 1903, pp. 143–145.

Aḥmad, Z. A.
Politik dan hukum negara (in Indonesian)
Djakarta, 1951.

'Alām, Manzoor
"Ibn Khaldūn's Concept of the Origin, Growth and Decay of Cities"
Islamic Culture (Hyderabad, 1960), XXXIV, 90–106.

Alatas, Ḥusain
"Objectivity and the Writing of History (The conceptions of History by al-Ghazālī, Ibn Khaldūn . . .)"
The Islamic Review (Woking, 1954), XLII, 11–14.

'Alī Pāshā Mubārak
al-Khiṭaṭ al-jadīdah at-tawfīqīyah
Bulāq, 1887–1888, XIV, 5–6.

Altamira, y Crevea, R.
"Notas sobre la doctrina histórica de Abenjaldūn"
Homenaje à D. Francisco Codera. Saragossa, 1904, pp. 357–374.

Amari, Michele
Bibliotheca Arabo-Sicula
Lipsia, 1857 ff., I, 460–508; Turin-Rome, 1880–1881, II, 163–243, 719–720; and Appendices.

"Altri frammenti arabi relativi alla Storia d'Italia (di Ibn Ḥaldūn)"
Atti della R. Accademia dei Lincei. Rome, 1889, VI, 5–31.

Amīn, A.
"Tīmūr-Lank wa' l-'ulamā'"
Revue ath-Thaqāfa (Cairo, 1939), no. 13, pp. 7–9.

Anawati, Georges C.
"'Abd al-Raḥmān ibn Khaldoun—un Montesquieu Arabe"
La Revue du Caire (Cairo, 1959), XXII, 175–191, and 303–319.

"Ibn H̱aldūn et sa philosophie de l'histoire"
Analecta de l'Inst. d'Et. Or de la Bibl. Patr. d'Alexandrie, XI, 163–186.

Anesī, 'Alī Nūreddīn al-
"Il pensiero economico di Ibn Ḥaldūn"
Rivista della Colonie italiane (Rome, 1932), VI, 112–127.

Arendonk, C., van
"Ibn Khaldūn"
Encyclopedia of Islam (Leiden-London, 1938), Supplement, pp. 90–91.

Arnold, Thomas W.
The Caliphate
Oxford, 1924.

Arnold, Thomas W. and A. Guillaume, editors
The Legacy of Islam
Oxford, 1931.

Arri, G. di Asti
Ebn Khaldoun da Tunisi: Storia generale degli Arabi e di alcuni celebri popoli loro contemporanei dalla loro origine fino al Kalifato di Moavia
Paris, 1840.

'Āshūr, Muḥammad al-Fāḍil
"Ibn Khaldūn"
al-Fikr, Revue Culturelle Mensuelle (Tunis, 1958), III, 702–707.

Astre, G. A.
"Un précurseur de la sociologie au XIVe siècle: Ibn Khaldoun l'Islam et l'Occident"
Les Cahiers du Sud. Paris, 1947, pp. 131–150.

Ayache, G.
"Ibn Khaldoun et les Arabes"
Mahrajān. Rabāṭ, 1962, pp. 19–32.

'Ayād, Kāmil M.
"Die Anfaenge der islamischen Geschichtsforschung"
Geist und Gesellschaft, Kurt Breysig zu seinem 60. Geburtstag. Vom Denken über Geschichte. Breslau, 1928, III, 35–48.

Die Geschichts- und Gesellschaftslehre Ibn Ḫaldūns
Stuttgart-Berlin, 1930.

"Ibni Haldūn's Kadar Islāmda Tarih"
Iş Meçmuasi (Istanbul, 1938), no. 14, pp. 24–36, 76–79.

Ayalon, David
"The Circassians in the Mamlūk Kingdom"
Journal of the American Oriental Society (London, 1949), p. 136 ff.

"The System of Payment in Mamlūk Military Society"
Journal of the Economic and Social History of the Orient (Leiden, 1957), I, 37–65, 257–296.

"Studies on the Transfer of the 'Abbāsid Caliphate from Baghdād to Cairo"
Arabica (Leiden, 1960), VII, 41–59.

"Ibn Khaldūn's View of the Mamelukes" (in Hebrew)
L. A. Mayer's Memorial Volume. Jerusalem, 1964, pp. 142–144 (English summary, p. 175).

Babinger, F.
Die Geschichtsschreiber der Osmanen und ihre Werke
Leipzig, 1927.

Bacher, W.
"Bibel und Biblische Geschichte in der Muhammedanischen Literatur"
Jeschurun, edited by Kobak. Bamberg, 1872, IX, 18–47.

Badawī, 'Abd ar-Raḥmān
Mu'allafāt Ibn Khaldūn
Cairo, 1962.

Bammate, Haidar
Visages de l'Islam
Lausanne, 1946, pp. 175–179.

Bargès, J. J.
"Lettre sur un ouvrage inédit attribué à Ibn Khaldoun"
Journal Asiatique (Paris, 1841), 3. sér., XII, 483–491.

Barnes, H. E.
"Sociology before Comte"
American Journal of Sociology (Chicago, 1917–1918), XXIII, 197–198.

A History of Historical Writing
Norman, 1937, pp. 94–96. 2nd rev. ed., New York, 1963.

Barnes, H. E. and H. Becker
Social Thought from Lore to Science
2nd ed., Washington, 1952, I, 266–279, 706–708.

Barthold, V. V.
Mussulman Culture
Calcutta, 1934, pp. 66–68.

"Uluġ Beg und seine Zeit"
Abhandl. für die Kunde des Morgenlandes. Leipzig, 1935, XXI.

"12 Vorlesungen über die Geschichte der Türken Mittelasiens"
Die Welt des Islams. Berlin 1935, XVII.

La découverte de l'Asie
Paris, 1947, pp. 29–31.

Turkestan Down to the Mongol Invasion
E. J. W. Gibb Memorial Series. 2nd. ed., London, 1958, n.s., V.

Batsieva, S. M.
The Social Foundations of Ibn Khaldūn's Historical-Philosophical Doctrine (in Russian)
Pamiati Akademika, Ignatiia Ilianovich Krachkovskogo. Leningrad, 1958, pp. 192–205.

The Historical-Philosophical Doctrine of Ibn Khaldūn (in Russian with English summary)
Akademiia nauk SSSR Sovetskoe vostokovedenie. Moscow, 1958, pp. 75–86.

A Historical-Sociological Treatise of Ibn Khaldūn's "Muqaddima" (in Russian)
Academy of Science, Institute of the Peoples of Asia. Moscow, 1965.

Baumstark, A.
"Der Bibelkanon bei Ibn Chaldūn"
Oriens Christianus (Rome, 1904), IV, 393–398.

Becker, C. H.
"Aeltester geschichtlicher Beleg fuer die afrikanische Schlafkrankheit"
Der Islam (Strassburg, 1910), I, 197–198. (See *Islamstudien,* Leipzig, 1932, II, 149–150.)

Bel, A.
"Ibn Khaldūn"
Encyclopaedia of Islam (Leiden-London, 1927), II, 395–396.

Catalogue de la Mosquée d'El-Qarouiyine à Fès
Fez, 1918.

Belyaev, V. I.
"Istoriko-sociologicheskaia istorija Ibn Chalduna"
Istorik Marksist (Moscow, 1940), no. 4–5, pp. 78–84.

Ben Cheneb, Moḥammed
"Etude sur les personnages mentionnés dans l'Idjāza du Cheikh 'Abd El Qādir El Fāsy"
Actes du XIVe Congrès International des Orientalistes (Algiers, Paris, 1908), Part III, no. 335, pp. 512–515.

Bercher, L.
Initiation à la Tunisie
Paris, 1950, pp. 191–192.

Bergh, Simon, van den
Umriss der muhammedanischen Wissenschaften nach Ibn Ḫaldūn
Leiden, 1912.

Bielawski, Józef
"Ibn Khaldūn—Arab historian, philosopher and sociologist of the 14th century" (in Polish)
Pryzglad Orientalistyczny (Warsaw, 1957), no. 2, pp. 127–146.

"Twórca socjologii w świecie Islamu . . ."
Kultura i Spoleczénstwo (Warsaw, 1959), III, 4–34.

Björkman, W.
Beiträge zur Geschichte der Staatskanzlei im islamischen Ägypten
Hamburg, 1928.

Blachère, Régis
"Ibn Khaldoun"
Les Ecrivains célèbres. Paris-Geneve, 1955, I, 192–193.

Boer, T. J. de
The History of Philosophy in Islam
London, 1903, pp. 200–208. (Arabic translation, Cairo, 1938.)

Bombaci, Alessio
"La dottrina storiografica di Ibn Ḫaldūn"
Annali della Scuola Normale Superiore di Pisa (1946), XV, 159–185.

"Postille alla Traduzione De Slane della 'Muqaddimah' di Ibn Ḫaldūn"
Annali dell'Istituto Universitario Orientale di Napoli (Rome, 1949), n.s., III, 439–472.

Bosch, Kheirallah, G.
"Ibn Khaldūn on Evolution"
Islamic Review (Woking, 1950), p. 26.

Bousquet, Georges-Henri
Le droit musulman par les textes
Algiers, 1947, pp. 93–95.

L'Islam Maghrebin
4th ed., Algiers, 1954.

Les Textes économiques de la Mouqaddima (1375–1379)
Paris, 1961.

"La Caqāliba chez Ibn Khaldoun"
Rivista degli Studi Orientali (Rome, 1965), pp. 139–141.

Bouthoul, Gaston
Ibn Khaldoun: Sa Philosophie Sociale
Paris, 1930.

"L'esprit de corps selon Ibn Khaldoun"
Revue Internationale de Sociologie (Paris, 1932), XL, 217–221.

"Preface to 'Les Prolégomènes d'Ibn Khaldoun' "
Second reproduction of *Notices et Extraits,* Vol. XIX (Paris, 1934–1938), I, vii–xxiv.

Traité de Sociologie: Les Guerres
Paris, 1951, pp. 388–391.

Bouvat, L.
L'Empire Mongol
Paris, 1927, pp. 6–7.

Brockelmann, Carl
Geschichte der arabischen Litteratur
Berlin, 1902, II, 242–245. 2nd ed., Leiden, 1949, II, 314–317.
Zweiter Supplementband, Leiden, 1938, II, 342–344.

History of the Islamic Peoples
New York, 1947.

Browne, Edward Granville
A Literary History of Persia
London and Cambridge, 1902–1924, 4 vols.; see II, 86–89; III, 412; IV, passim.

Brunschvig, Robert
La Berbérie orientale sous les Ḥafṣides des origines à la fin du XVe Siècle
Paris, 1947, 2 vols.; II, 385–394.

Brunschvig, Robert and G. E. von Grunebaum, editors
Symposium on Classicisme et déclin culturel dans l'histoire de l'Islam
Paris, 1957.

Bukhsh, S. Khuda
"Ibn Khaldūn and his History of Islamic Civilization"
Islamic Culture (Hyderabad, 1927), I, 567–607.

Contributions to the History of Islamic Civilization
Calcutta, 1929–1930, II, 201–260. (English translation of A. von Kremer.)

Buret, L.
"Notes marginales sur les 'Prolégomènes': Un pédagogue arabe du XIVe siècle: Ibn Khaldoun"
Revue Tunisienne (Tunis, 1934), V, 23–32.

Busṭānī, Buṭrus al-
Dā'irat al-ma 'ārif
Beirut, 1876 ff., I, 460–468.

Bustānī, Fu'ād Ifrām al-
"Ibn Khaldūn: Extracts from the Prolegomena"
Ar-Rawā'i' (Beirut, 1927), no. 13.

Cahen, Claude
La Syrie du nord à l'époque des croisades
Paris, 1940, pp. 84–85.

Cahun, Léon
L'Introduction à l'histoire de l'Asie: Turcs et Mongols
Paris, 1896, pp. 495–497.

Cairns, Grace E.
Philosophies of History. Meeting of East and West in Cycle-Pattern Theories of History
New York, 1962, pp. 322–336.

Canard, M.
"Les relations entre les Merinides et les Mamelouks au XVIe siècle"
Annales de l'Institut d'Etudes Orientales. Algiers, 1939–1941, V, 41–81.

Caro Baroja, Julio
"El Poder Real, según Aben Jaldûn"
Africa (Madrid, 1955), XII, 212–14.

"Aben Jaldûn y la ciudad musulmána"
Africa, XII, 484–88.

"Aben Jaldûn: Antropólogo Social"
Estudios Mogrebies. Madrid, 1957, pp. 11–58.

Carra de Vaux, B. Baron
Les penseurs de l'Islam
Paris, 1921, I, 278–293.

Casanova, P.
"La Malḥamat dans l'Islam primitif"
Revue de l'histoire des religions (Paris, 1910), LXI, 151–161.

Mohammed et la fin du monde
Paris, 1911, pp. 45 ff. and pp. 133 ff.

Chaix-Ruy, J.
"Sociología Psicología de la Vida Social en la Obra de Ibn Jaldūn"
Revista Mexicana de Sociología (Mexico, 1954), XXI, 7–22.

Chambliss, Rolin
Social Thought from Hammurabi to Comte
New York, 1954, pp. 283–312.

Chwolson, David
Die Ssabier und der Ssabismus
St. Petersburg-Leipzig, 1856, 2 vols.

Cohen, Gerson D.
"Ibn Khaldūn—Rediscovered Arab Philosopher"
Midstream (New York, 1959), V, pp. 77–90.

Colosia, Stefano
"Contribution à l'étude d'Ibn Khaldoun"
Revue du Monde Musulman (Paris, 1914), XXVI, 318–338.

The Columbia Encyclopedia
S.v. Ibn Khaldūn.
3rd. ed., New York, 1963.

Cook, St. A.
"The Semites: The Writing of History"
The Cambridge Ancient History. New York, 1923, I, 223–225.

Coquebert de Montbret fils, E.
"Extraits des Prolégomènes historiques d'Ibn Khaldoun"
Journal Asiatique (Paris, 1824), 1. sér., V, 148–156; (1825) VI, 106–113; (1827) X, 3–19.

Corcos, David
"The Jews of Morocco under the Marinides"
Jewish Quarterly Review (Philadelphia, 1964), LIV, 271–288; LV, 53–81, 137–150.

Crozat, Charles, editor
Āmme Hukuku Dersleri
Istanbul, 1944–1946, II, pt. 2, 794–812.

Dā'irat al-Ma'ārif al-Islamīyah
(Arabic translation of *Encyclopaedia of Islam*)
Cairo, 1934, L, fasc. 3, pp. 152–155.

Dāghir, Yūsuf A.
Maṣādir ad-dirāsah al-adabīyah
Saïda, 1950–1956, 2 vols.

Darbishire, Robert S.
"The philosophical rapprochement of Christendom and Islam in accordance with Ibn Khaldūn's scientific criticism"
Muslim World (Hartford, 1940), XXX, 226–235.

Demeerseman, A.
"Ce qu'Ibn Khaldoun pense d'al-Ghazzālī"
Institut des belles lettres arabes (Tunis, 1958), no. 82, pp. 161–193.

Dermenghem, E.
Les plus beaux Textes Arabes (en traduction)
Paris, 1951, pp. 209–215, 225–230.

Dodge, B.
Muslim Education in Medieval Times
Washington, 1962.

Donaldson, Dwight
"The Shia doctrine of the Imamate"
Muslim World (Hartford, 1931), XXI, 14–23.

Dover, Cedric
"The Racial Philosophy of Ibn Khaldūn"
Phylon, The Atlanta University (Atlanta, 1952), XIII, 107–119.

Dozy, R.
Scriptorum Arabum loci de Abbadidis
Leiden, 1846–1863, II, 206–216; III, 235–236.

"Compte-rendue critique des 'Prolégomènes d'Ibn Khaldoun,' texte Arabe par E. Quatremère, traduit par de Slane"
Journal Asiatique (Paris, 1869), 6. sér., XIV, 133–218.

Recherches sur l'histoire et la littérature de l'Espagne pendant le Moyen âge
3rd ed. Leiden, 1881. 2 vols. I, 89–116 and Appendices.

Dubler, C. E.
"Fuentes árabes y bizantinas en la Primera Crónica General, Intercambios cristiano-islámicos"
Vox Romanica (Bern, 1951), XII, 120–122.

Dyck, Edward A., van
Iktifā' al-qanū' bimā huwa maṭbū'
Cairo, 1896–1897, pp. 76–77.

'Enān, Muḥammad, 'Abdullāh
Falsafat Ibn Khaldūn al-ijtimā'īya (Arabic translation of Ṭāhā Ḥusain)
Cairo, 1925.

Ibn Khaldūn: Ḥayātuhū wa-turāthuhu al-fikrī
Cairo, 1933.

Ibn Khaldūn
Cairo, 1939.

Ibn Khaldūn: His Life and Work
2nd ed., Lahore, 1946.

Encyclopaedia of Islam
(See Arendonk, Bel and Macdonald.)

Encyclopedia Americana
S. v. Ibn Khaldūn.
New York-Chicago, 1950, XIV, 617.

Encyclopaedia Britannica
S.v. Ibn Khaldūn.
Chicago, 1950, XII, 34.

Enciclopedia Italiana
S.v. Ibn Khaldūn.
Milano, 1933, XVIII, 682.

Entsiklopediia Bolshaia Sovetskaia
S.v. Ibn Khaldūn.
Moscow, 1950, XVII, 259.

'Ezzat, Abdu'l 'Azīz
Ibn Khaldoun et sa science sociale
Cairo, 1947.

The Philosophy of History and Sociology
Cairo, 1960.

Fahmi, Muṣṭafā
Kitāb 'ilm al-ijtimā'
Cairo, 1938.

Farrūkh, 'Umar
Ibn Khaldūn wa-muqaddimatihi
Beirut, 1943; 2nd ed., 1951.

"Dirāsāt 'an Muqaddimat Ibn Khaldūn"
Revue de l'Académie Arabe (Damascus, 1954), XXIX, 67–76, 203–214.

The Arab Genius in Science and Philosophy
The American Council of Learned Societies. Washington, 1954, X, 131–154.

Farûkī, Kamal A.
Islamic Jurisprudence
Karachi, 1962.

Fāsī, Muḥammad al-
"Ibn Ḥaldūn et la politique"
Falāsifat al-Islām fī l-ġarb al-'arabī. Tetouan, 1961, I.

Faure, Adolphe
"Grandeur et Solitude d'Ibn Khaldoun"
Mahrajān. Rabāṭ, 1962, pp. 5–12.

Ferrand, Gabriel
Relations de Voyages et Textes géographiques relatifs à l'Extrême-Orient
Paris, 1914, II, 459–461.

Ferrero, G.
"Un sociologo arabo del secolo XIV: Ibn Khaldoun"
La Riforma sociale (Torino, 1896), VII, 221–235.

Fikr, al-
Revue culturelle mensuelle
Special Ibn Khaldūn Issue (Tunis, 1961), VI, no. 6.

Findikoğlu, Ziyaeddin Fahri
"Ibni Haldun ve Felsefesi"
Iş Meçmuasi (Istanbul, 1934), no. 8.

"Ibn Haldun un hayati ve fikirleri"
Iş Meçmuasi (Istanbul, 1938–1940), no. 14–22.

"Les Théories de la connaissance et de l'histoire chez Ibn Ḥaldūn"
Proceedings of the 10th International Congress of Philosophy. Amsterdam, 1948, I, 274–276.

"La conception de l'histoire et la théorie méthodologique chez Ibn Khaldoun"
Üçler Basimeve, Gençlik Kitabevi neşriyati. Içtimaī eserler serisi, nr. 9. Istanbul, 1951.

"Türkiyede Ibn Haldunizm"
Fuad Köprülü Armağani. Istanbul, 1953, pp. 153–163.

"Istanbul kütüphanelerindeki yazma Ibn Ḥaldûn nushalarından biri hakkinda"
Zeki Velidi Togan a Armağan. 1950–1955, pp. 360–364.

"L'Ecole Ibn-Khaldounienne en Turquie"
Proceedings of the 22nd International Congress of Orientalists in Istanbul. Leiden, 1957, II, 269–273.

Fischel, Walter J.
"Ibn Khaldūn and Tīmūr"
Actes du XXIe Congrès International des Orientalistes
Paris, 1949, pp. 286–287; also *Bulletin des Etudes Arabes* (Algiers, 1950), no. 47, p. 61.

"Ibn Khaldūn's Activities in Mamlūk Egypt (1382–1406)"
Semitic and Oriental Studies, presented to William Popper, edited. Berkeley-Los Angeles, 1951, pp. 102–124.

Ibn Khaldūn and Tamerlane: Their historic meeting in Damascus, 1401 A.D. (803 A.H.): A study based on Arabic Manuscripts of Ibn Khaldūn's "Autobiography," with a translation into English and a commentary
Berkeley-Los Angeles, 1952.
Translated into Persian by Sa'īd Nafīsī. Teheran, 1957.
Translated into Arabic by Muḥammad Tawfīq. Edited by Muṣṭafā Jawād. Beirut-Baghdad, 1963.
Translated into Urdu. Academy of Sind. Lahore, 1967.

"The Biography of Ibn Khaldūn"
Yearbook, The American Philosophical Society, 1953. Philadelphia, 1954, pp. 240–241.

"Ibn Khaldūn's Use of Jewish and Christian Sources"
Proceedings of the 23rd International Congress of Orientalists. Cambridge, 1954, pp. 332–333.

"Ibn Khaldūn and Josippon"
Homenaje Millás-Vallicrósa. Barcelona, 1954, I, 587–598.

"Ibn Khaldūn's 'Autobiography' in the Light of External Arabic Sources"
Studi Orientalistici in onore di G. Levi Della Vida. Rome, 1956, I, 287–308.

"Ibn Khaldūn's Sources for the History of Jenghiz Khan and the Tatars"
Journal of the American Oriental Society (1956), LXXVI, 91–99.

"Ibn Khaldūn: On the Bible, Judaism and Jews"
Ignace Goldziher Memorial Volume, Part 2. Jerusalem, 1956, pp. 147–171.

"Vita Tamerlani. A New Latin Source on Tamerlane's Conquest of Damascus (1400–1401)," by B. de Mignanelli, translated into English with an introduction and a commentary
Oriens (Leiden, 1956), IX, 201–232.

"Selected Bibliography of Ibn Khaldūn," in *The Muqaddimah,* translated into English by Franz Rosenthal.
New York, 1958, III, 485–512.

"Ascensus Barcoch: A Latin Biography of the Mamlūk Sultan Barqūq of Egypt (d. 1399)," by B. de Mignanelli, translated and annotated.
Arabica (Leiden, 1959), VI, 57–74 and 152–172.

"Ibn Khaldūn's Contribution to Comparative Religion"
Proceedings of the 24th International Congress of Orientalists. Wiesbaden, 1959, pp. 334–335.

"Nashāṭ Ibn Khaldūn fī Miṣr al-Mamlūkīya (1382–1406)" (in Arabic)
Dirāsāt Islāmīya, Anthology of writings by Americans on Islam, edited by N. Ziyāda. Beirut, 1960, pp. 177–212.

"Ibn Khaldūn and al-Mas'ūdī"
Al-Mas'ūdī Millenary Commemoration Volume, published by the Indian Society for the History of Science. Aligarh, 1961, pp. 51–59.

"Ibn Khaldūn's Use of Historical Sources"
Studia Islamica. Paris, 1961, XIV, 109–119; see also, *Proceedings of the 25th International Congress of Orientalists.* Moscow, 1962, II, 71.

"Ibn Khaldūn on Pre-Islamic Iran"
Proceedings of the 26th International Congress of Orientalists. New Delhi, in press.

Ibn Khaldūn in Egypt, His Public Functions and his Historical Research (1382–1406), A Study in Islamic Historiography
Berkeley-Los Angeles, 1967.

Flint, R.
History of the Philosophy of History in France, Belgium, and Switzerland
Edinburgh, 1893, I, 157–170.

Fluegel, G.
"Ibn Chaldūn"
Allgemeine Encyclopädie der Wissenschaften und Kuenste, edited by Ersch und Gruber. Leipzig, 1838, 2. sect., 15 Teil, pp. 26–28.

Frank, H.
Beitrag zur Erkenntniss des Sufismus nach Ibn Ḫaldūn
Leipzig, 1884.

Freytag, G. W. F.
Chrestomathia Arabica grammatica historica
Bonn, 1834, pp. 150–182.

Gabrieli, Francesco
"Il concetto della 'aṣabiyya nel pensiero storico di Ibn Ḫaldūn"
Atti della Reale Accademia delle Science di Torino. Torino, 1930, LXV, 473–512.

Storia della letteratura araba
Milano, 1951, pp. 263–265.

Gabrieli, Giuseppe
"Saggio di bibliografia e concordanza della storia di Ibn Ḫaldūn"
Rivista degli Studi Orientali (Rome, 1924), X, 169–211.

Garcin de Tassy, J.
"Supplément à la notice de M. de Hammer sur l'introduction a la connaissance de l'histoire, célèbre ouvrage d'Ibn Khaledoun"
Journal Asiatique (Paris, 1824), 1. sér., IV, 158–161.

Gardet, L.
La Cité Musulmane: Vie sociale et politique
Paris, 1954.

Gardet, L. and M. M. Anawati
"La place du Kalām d'après Ibn Khaldūn"
L'Introduction à la théologie musulmane. Paris, 1948, pp. 121–124.

Gaudefroy-Demombynes, M.
"Ibn Khaldoun, Histoire des Benou l-Ahmar, rois de Grenade"
Journal Asiatique (Paris, 1898), 9. sér., XII, 309–340, 407–462.

"Notes sur l'histoire de l'organisation judiciaire en pays d'Islam"
Revue des Etudes Islamiques (Paris, 1939), pp. 109–147.

Gautier, E. F.
"Un passage d'Ibn Khaldoun et du Bayān"
Hespéris (Paris, 1924), XLI, 305–312.

L'Islamisation de l'Afrique du Nord: Les siècles obscurs du Maghreb
Paris, 1927; 2nd ed., 1937.

Mœurs et coutumes des Musulmans
Paris, 1931.

Gautier-Dalché, J.
"Ibn Khaldoun et son temps"
Mahrajān. Rabāṭ, 1962, pp. 33–38.

Gibb, Hamilton A. R.
Arabic Literature
Oxford, 1926, pp. 112–113.

Modern Trends in Islam
Chicago, 1947.

"The Islamic Background of Ibn Khaldūn's Political Theory"
Bulletin of the School of Oriental and African Studies (London, 1933–1935), VII, 23–31. Republished in *Studies in the Civilization of Islam*, edited by Stanford J. Shaw and William R. Polk. Boston, 1962, pp. 166–175.

Giesecke, H. H.
Das Werk des 'Azīz b. 'Ārdašīr Āstarābāḏī
Leipzig, 1940, pp. 114–115.

Goitein, S. D.
Extracts from Ibn Khaldūn's Muqaddimah: On the Method of History (in Hebrew), edited with introduction, notes and vocabulary
Jerusalem, 1943.

"An Arab on Arabs: Ibn Khaldūn's Views on the Arab Nation" (in Hebrew)
The New East, Quarterly of the Israel Oriental Society (Jerusalem, 1950), I, 115–121, 198–201.

Goldziher, I.
"Linguistisches aus der Literatur der muhammedanischen Mystik"
Zeitschrift der Deutschen Morgenländischen Gesellschaft (Leipzig, 1872), XXVI, 766–767.

"Ueber muhammedanische Polemik gegen Ahl al-Kitāb"
Zeitschrift der Deutschen Morgenländischen Gesellschaft (Leipzig, 1878), XXXII, 345, 361, 368.

"Materialien zur Kenntnis der Almohadenbewegung in Nord-Afrika"
Zeitschrift der Deutschen Morgenländischen Gesellschaft (Leipzig, 1887), XLI, 30–140.

Muhammedanische Studien,
Halle, 1889–1890, 2 vols.

A Short History of Arabic Literature, Translated from Croatian into Hebrew by P. Shinar
Jerusalem, 1952, pp. 140–141.

"Über Bibelzitate im muhammedanischen Schrifttum"
Zeitschrift für die Alttestamentl. Wissenschaft (Giessen, 1893), XIII, 315–321.

Gonzalez-Palencia, A.
Historia de la Literatura Arábigo-Española
2nd ed., Barcelona, 1945, pp. 183–185.

Gottheil, Richard
"References to Zoroaster in Syriac and Arabic Literature"
Classical Studies in Honor of Henry Drisler. New York, 1894, p. 35.

Gräberg, af Hemsö, J.
Notizia intorna alla famosa opera istorica di Ibnu Khaldoun, filosofo affricano del sec. XIV
Florence, 1834, pp. 1–58.

"An account of the great historical work of the African philosopher Ibn Khaldoun"
Transactions of the Royal Asiatic Society of Great Britain and Ireland.
London, 1835, III, 387–404.

Grande Encyclopedia Portuguesa e Brasileira
S.v. Caldune.
Lisbon-Rio de Janeiro, V, 488.

Grande Encyclopédie
S.v. Ibn Khaldoun.
Paris, XX, 515–516.

Greef, Guillaume de
Le transformisme sociale; essai sur le progrès et le regrès des sociétés
Paris, 1901, pp. 115–118.

Grunebaum, G. E. von
"As-Sakkākī: on Milieu and Thought"
Journal of the American Oriental Society (Baltimore, 1945), LXV, 62.

"Islam: Essays in the Nature and Growth of a Cultural Tradition"
The American Anthropologist (Chicago, 1955), LVII.

Unity and Variety in Muslim Civilization, edited
Chicago, 1955.

Medieval Islam, a study in Cultural Orientation
3rd. ed., Chicago, 1956.

Modern Islam: Search for Cultural Identity
Berkeley-Los Angeles, 1962.

Guernier, E.
Le Berbérie, l'Islam et la France; le destin de l'Afrique du Nord
Paris, 1950, I, 226–235, 396–402.

Guillaume, A.
The Traditions of Islam
Oxford, 1924. Cf. pp. 89–93, 159–68.

"Arabian Views on Prophecy (Ibn Khaldūn), Prophecy and Divination among the Hebrews and other Semites"
The Bampton Lectures. New York, 1938, pp. 197–213.

Gumplowicz, Ludwig
"Ibn Chaldūn, ein arabischer Sociologe des 14 Jahrhunderts"
Sociologische Essays. Innsbruck, 1899.

"Un Sociologue arabe du XIVe siècle"
Aperçus sociologiques. Lyon-Paris, 1900, pp. 201–226.

Ḥadīth, Majallat al-
Special Issue on the Occasion of Ibn Khaldūn's Six Hundredth Anniversary (1332–1932)
Aleppo, September, 1932.

Ḥājjī Khalīfah, Muṣṭafā b. 'Abdallāh
Kashf aẓ-Ẓunūn: Lexicon Bibliographicum et Encyclopaedicum, edited by G. Flügel
Leipzig-London, 1835–1858, II, no. 2085, p. 101 et passim.

Hammer-Purgstall, J. von
Ueber den Verfall des Islam nach den ersten drei Jahrhunderten der Hidschra
Vienna, 1812.

"Extraits d'Ibn Khaledoun"
Fundgruben des Orients. Vienna, 1816, V, 389 ff.; 1818, VI, 301–307, 362–364.

"Notice sur l'introduction à la connaissance de l'histoire, célèbre ouvrage arabe d'Ibn Khaldoun"
Journal Asiatique (Paris, 1822), 1. sér., I, 267–278; IV, 158–161.

Geschichte des Osmanischen Reiches
Pest, 1825 ff., I, 301; III, 489, 765; VIII, 253.

Über die Laenderverwaltung under dem Chalifate
Berlin, 1835.

Ḥarakāt, Ibrāhīm
"Ibn Khaldūn's 'Kitāb al-'Ibar' as a Historical Source"
Āfāq, Revue des Ecrivains du Maghreb Arab (Rabāṭ, 1963), I, 123–132.

Hartmann, R.
"Zur Vorgeschichte des Abbāsidischen Schein-Chalifates von Cairo"
Abhandlungen der Deutschen Akademie d. Wissenschaften zu Berlin. Berlin, 1950.

Ḥawfī, A. M. al-
Ma' Ibn Khaldūn
Cairo, 1952.

Herbelot, Barthélemy d'
Bibliothèque Orientale, s.v. Khaledoun
Paris, 1697, II, 418.

Heyworth-Dunne, Gamal-Eddine
A Basic Bibliography on Islam
The Muslim World Series. Cairo, 1955, IV, 28–30.

Hirschberg, H. Z.
"The Berber Heroine known as the 'Kahena' " (in Hebrew)
Tarbitz. Jerusalem, 1957, XXVI, 370–383.

"History of the Jews in North Africa from Antiquity to Our Times" (in Hebrew)
Mosad Bialik. Jerusalem, 1965, 2 vols.

Hitti, Ph. H.
History of the Arabs
London-New York, 1951.

Hoogvliet, Marinus
Specimen e litteris orientalibus exhibens diversorum scriptorum locos de regia Aphtasidarum familia . . .
Leiden, 1839.

Hookham, Hilda
Tamburlaine the Conqueror
London, 1962.

Horten, Max
Die Philosophie des Islam
Muenchen, 1924.

Hostelet, G.
"Ibn Khaldoun, un précurseur arabe de la sociologie au XIVe siècle"
Revue de l'Institut de Sociologie (Bruxelles, 1926), XI, 151–156.

Hourani, Albert H.
Arabic Thought in the Liberal Age, 1798–1939
London-New York, 1962.

Huart, Cl.
Littérature Arabe
Paris, 1923, pp. 345–349.

Ḥusain, Ṭāhā
Etude analytique et critique de la philosophie sociale d'Ibn Khaldoun
Paris, 1917. See Arabic translation by M. 'Enān, Cairo, 1925.

Ḥuṣarī, Sāṭī' al
Dirāsāt 'an Muqaddimat Ibn Khaldūn
Beirut, 1943–1944, 2 vols.; 2nd ed., Cairo-Baghdad, 1961.

"al-'Arab fi muqaddimat Ibn Khaldūn"
al-Amālī (Beirut, 1939), no. 51.

"La sociologie d'Ibn Khaldoun"
Actes du XVe Congrès International de Sociologie. Istanbul, 1952.

Ibn 'Arabshāh, Aḥmad b. Muḥammad
The Life of Timur
Translated into Latin by Jacob Golius, Lugduni (Batavorun) 1638. Oxford, 1703–1704.
Translated into French by Pierre Vattier. Paris, 1658, 2 vols.
Translated into Latin with a Revised Arabic Edition, by S. H. Manger. Leeuwarden, 1767–1772, 2 vols.
Translated into English by J. H. Sanders. London, 1936.

Ibn Juljul, al-Andalusī, Abū Dāwūd Sulaymān b. Ḥassân
Les générations des médecins et des sages, edited by Fu'ād Sayyid. Cairo, 1955.

Ibn aṣ-Ṣiddîq, A.
Ibrāz al-wahm al-maknūn min kalām Ibn Khaldūn
Damascus, 1929.

Ibrāhīm-Hilmy
The Literature of Egypt and the Soudan, from the Earliest Times to 1885, a Bibliography
London, 1886, 2 vols.; I, 316–317.

Ibrāshī, Muḥammad 'Aṭīya al-, and Abu' l-Futūḥ at-Tawānisī
Silsilat Tarājim.
Cairo, 1957, II, 89–142.

Iorga, N.
Geschichte des Osmanischen Reiches
Gotha, 1908 ff., I, 317–338.

Iqbal, Sir Mohammad
The Reconstruction of Religious Thought in Islam
Oxford, 1934.

Irving, T. B.
"The World of Ibn Khaldūn"
Islamic Literature (Lahore, 1957), IX, no. 6, 347–351, no. 8–9, 473–477.

"Peter the Cruel and Ibn Khaldūn"
Islamic Literature (Lahore, 1959), XI, 5–17.

"A Fourteenth Century View of Language (Ibn Khaldūn)"
The World of Islam, Studies in Honour of Philip K. Hitti, edited by J. Kritzeck and R. B. Winder. London, 1959, pp. 185–192.

Iskandarī, Aḥmad al-
"Ibn Khaldūn"
Revue de l'académie arabe (Damascus, 1929), IX, 421–432, 461–471.

'Issa, 'Alī Aḥmad,
The Arabic Society: Experimental Sociological Studies
Cairo, 1961, pp. 179–191.

Issawi, Charles
An Arab Philosophy of History, Selections of the Prolegomena of Ibn Khaldūn of Tunis (1332–1406)
Wisdom of the East Series. London, 1950, no. 100.

"Arab Geography and the Circumnavigation of Africa"
Osiris (Bruges, 1952), X, 117–128.

Ivanov, N. A.
"Ibn Khaldūn's 'Kitāb al-'Ibar' as a Source for the History of North African Lands in the 14th Century" (in Russian)
Arabskii Sbornik (Moscow, 1959), XIX, 3–45.

Jabrī, Shafīq
"Muṣṭalaḥāt Ibn Khaldūn"
Revue de l'Académie Arabe (Damascus, 1951), XXVI, 370–376.

Jaffar, S. M.
History of History
Peshawar City, 1961, I, 44–47.

Julien, Ch. André
Histoire de l'Afrique du Nord
2nd ed., par R. Le Tourneau. Paris, 1952, pp. 134–135.

Jum'a, Muḥammad Luṭfī
Ta'rīkh falāsifat al-Islām fi'l Mashriq wa'l Maghrib
Cairo, 1927, pp. 225–252.

Karrou, 'Abdul-Qāsim
Al-'Arab wa-ibn Khaldūn
Tunis, 1956.

Kay, Henry Cassels
Yaman: Its Early Medieval History by Nājm ad-dīn 'Omârah al-Ḥakamı, also The Abridged History of Its Dynasties by Ibn Khaldūn
London, 1892, pp. 138–190.

Kerr, Malcolm H.
Islamic Reform. The Political and Legal Theories of Muḥammad 'Abduh and Rashīd Riḍā
Berkeley and Los Angeles, 1966.

Khadduri, Majid
War and Peace in the Law of Islam
Baltimore, 1955.

Khadduri, Majid and Herbert J. Liebesny, editors
Law in the Middle East
Washington, 1955, I.

Khalifé, Ignace-Abdo, S. J.
"Un nouveau traité mystique d'Ibn Ḥaldūn"
Proceedings of the 24th International Congress of Orientalists. München-Wiesbaden, 1959, pp. 330–333.

Khemiri, T.
"Der 'Aṣabīja-Begriff in der Muqaddima des Ibn Ḫaldūn"
Der Islam (Berlin, 1936), XXI, 163–188.

Khimsī, Na'im, al-
"Al-Balāgha bayn al-lafz wa'l ma'na"
Revue de l'Académie Arabe (Damascus, 1950), XXV, 447–448.

Khuḍr at-Tunīsī, Muḥammad
Ḥayātu Ibn Khaldūn
Cairo, 1925.

Khūri, Ra'īf
"Ibn Khaldūn wa-Hegel"
aṭ-Ṭarīq. Beirut, 1944, III, fasc. 3, p. 5.

Köbert, R.
"Gedanken zum Semitischen Wort- und Satzbau, 'Ibar = I'tibār"
Orientalia (Rome, 1946), n.s. XV, 151–154.

Krachkovsky, Ignace Y.
"La géographie au Maghrib"
Œuvres choisies. Moscow-Leningrad, 1955–1957, IV, 431–438.

Kramers, J. H.
"L'Islam et la démocratie"
Orientalia Neerlandica (Leiden, 1948), pp. 223–239.

Kremer, Alfred von
"Ibn Chaldūn und seine Culturgeschichte der islamischen Reiche"
Sitzungsberichte der Kaiserlichen, Akademie der Wissenschaften, Phil-hist. Klasse. Vienna, 1879, XCIII, 581–634.

Kritzeck, James, editor
Anthology of Islamic Literature, from the Rise of Islam to Modern Times
New York, 1964; Mentor Books, New York, 1966.

Kurd, 'Alī Muḥammad
"Ibn Khaldūn"
Revue de l'académie arabe (Damascus, 1946–1947), XXI–XXII, 396–404.

"Ibn Khaldūn wa-Tīmūrlank (according to Ibn az-Zamlakānī)"
Revue de l'académie arabe (Damascus, 1948), XXIII, 159.

Kuroda, Toshirō
"Ibun-Harudon 'rekishi josetsu' no hōhō (La méthode de 'l'introduction a l'histoire' d'ibn Haldun)"
Isuramu seikai (Tokyo, 1963), I, 68–72.

Labīb, Ṣubḥī Y.
Handelsgeschichte Ägyptens im Spätmittelalter (1171–1517)
Wiesbaden, 1965.

Labica, Georges
"Esquisse d'une sociologie de la Religion chez Ibn Khaldoun"
La Pensée (Paris, 1965), pp. 3–23.

Labica, Georges and Bencheikh Jamel-Eddine
Le Rationalisme d'Ibn Khaldoun, Extraits de la Muqaddimah
Paris, 1965.

Lacoste, Yves
"La grande œuvre d'Ibn Khaldoun"
La Pensée (Paris, 1956), LXIX, pp. 10–33.

Ibn Khaldoun, Naissance de l'histoire passé du tiers-monde
Paris, 1966.

Lanci, M. A.
Dissertazione storico-critica: Eben Caliduno intorno all arabesca Paleografia
Rome, 1820.

Laoust, H.
Essai sur les doctrines sociales et politiques de Taḳī-d-Dīn b. Taimīya
Cairo, 1939.

Le Strange, G.
The Lands of the Eastern Caliphate
Cambridge, 1905.

Levi Della Vida, Giorgio
"The 'Bronze Era' in Moslem Spain"
Journal of the American Oriental Society (Baltimore, 1943), LXIII, no. 3, 183–191.

"La traduzione araba delle Storie di Orosio"
Miscellanea Giovanni Galbiati. Fontes ambrosiani, 25–27. Milan, 1951, 3 vols; III, 185–203.
Spanish translation, with additions. *al-Andalus.* Madrid-Granada, 1954, XIX, 257–293.

"Ibn Khaldūn"
Collier's Encyclopedia. New York, 1952, X, 326.

"Review of Franz Rosenthal's English translation of the Muqaddimah"
Oriente Moderno (Rome, 1958), XXXVIII, 1005–1007.

Lévi-Provençal, E.
"Note sur l'exemplaire du Kitāb al-'Ibar offert par Ibn Ḫaldūn à la Bibliothèque d' al-Karawīyīn à Fez"
Journal Asiatique (Paris, 1923), CCIII, 161–168.

Extraits des Historiens Arabes du Maroc
3rd ed., Paris, 1948.

Histoire de l'Espagne Musulmane
Paris-Leiden, 1950–1953, 3 vols.

Levin, I.
"Ibn Khaldūn, an Arab Sociologist of the 14th Century" (in Russian)
Novyi Vostok. Moscow, 1926, XII, 241–263.

Levy, Reuben
The Social Structure of Islam
2nd ed., Cambridge, 1957.

Lewis, Bernard
The Arabs in History
London, 1960.

"The Muslim Discovery of Europe"
Bulletin of the School of Oriental and African Studies (London, 1957), XX, 409–416.

"The Use of Muslim Historians of Non-Muslim Sources"
Historians of the Middle East. Historical Writing on the Peoples of Asia. London, 1962, IV, 180–191.

Lichtenstädter, Ilse
"Arabic and Islamic Historiography"
Muslim World (Hartford, 1945), XXXV, 126–132.

Liebling, A. J.
"The Round of History"
The New Yorker (New York, 1959), XXXV, 213–241.

Luciani, J. D.
"La théorie du droit musulman (Ouçoul el-fiqh) d'après Ibn Khaldoun"
Revue Africaine (Algiers, 1928), LXIX, 49–64.

Macdonald, D. B.
Aspects of Islam
New York, 1911, pp. 309–319.

The Religious Attitude and Life in Islam
2nd ed., Chicago, 1912.

"al-Mahdī (according to Ibn Khaldūn)"
Encyclopaedia of Islam. Leiden, 1928, III, 113–115.

Ibn Khaldūn: A Selection from the Prolegomena of Ibn Khaldūn, with Notes and an English-German Glossary
Semitic Study Series IV. Leiden, 1948.

Macdonald, J.
"An Arab's Appreciation of Ibn Khaldūn and Western Criticism of Islam"
Islamic Literature (Lahore, 1959), XI, 187–195.

Machado, Oswaldo A.
"La historia de los Godos segun Ibn Jaldūn"
Cuadernos de Historia de España. Buenos Aires, 1944, I–II, 139–153.

"Historia de los Arabes de España por Ibn Jaldūn"
Cuadernos de Historia de España. Buenos Aires, 1946–1948; IV, 136–147; VI, 146–153; VII, 138–145; VIII, 148–158.

Machado, Pedro José
"A Língua Arábica do Andaluz segundo os 'Prolegómenos' de Iben Caldune"
Boletim de Filologia (Lisbon, 1944), VII, 401–418.

Machuel, L.
Les Auteurs Arabes (Pages choisies des Grands Ecrivains)
Paris, 1912, pp. 342–348.

Madelung, W. von
"Fatimiden und Baḥrain qarmaṭen"
Der Islam (Berlin, 1959), XXXIV, 34–88.

Magali-Boisnard, Mme.
"La vie singulière d'Ibn Khaldoun, historien des Arabes et des Berbères"
Bulletin de la Société de Géographie d'Alger et de l'Afrique du Nord (Algiers, 1929), no. 120, pp. 497–514.

Le roman de Khaldoun
Paris, 1930.

Maghribī, 'Abd al-Qādir, al-
"Ibn Khaldūn bi-l-madrasah al-'Ādilīyah bi-Dimashq"
Muḥammad wa-l-Mar'ah. Damascus, 1347 H. (1929 A.D.), pp. 38–82.

Mahdi, Muḥsin
"The Foundation of Ibn Khaldūn's "ilm al-'umrān" in Classical and Islamic Political Philosophy"
Proceedings of the 23rd International Congress of Orientalists. Cambridge, 1954.

Ibn Khaldūn's Philosophy of History, A Study in the Philosophic Foundation of the Science of Culture
London, 1957; Chicago, 1964.

"Die Kritik der islamischen politischen Philosophie bei Ibn Khaldūn"
Wissenschaftliche Politik: Eine Einführung, Grundfragen ihrer Tradition and Theorie. Freiburg (Breisgau), 1962, pp. 117–151.

"Ibn Khaldūn"
Approaches to the Oriental Classics, edited by Wm. Theodore de Bary. New York, 1959, pp. 68–83.

"Ibn Khaldūn"
International Encyclopedia of the Social Sciences. New York, 1967.

Maḥmassānī, Ṣobḥī
Les idées économiques d'Ibn Khaldoun, Essai, historique, analytique et critique
Lyon, 1932.

Mahrajān Ibn Khaldūn
Proceedings (A'māl) of a Symposium on Ibn Khaldūn, held in Cairo. Cairo, 1962.

Colloque organisé par la Faculté des Lettres à Rabāṭ (Université Mohammad V).
Casablanca, 1962.

Maitrot de la Motte-Capron, A.
"Essai sur le nomadisme"
Revue Internationale de sociologie (Paris, 1939), XLVII, 321–326.

Mallāḥ, Maḥmūd, al-
Daqā'iq wa-haqā'iq fī muqaddimat Ibn Khaldūn
Baghdad, 1955.

Naẓarat thāniyat fī muqaddimat Ibn Khaldūn
Baghdad, 1956.

Maqqarī, Aḥmad b. Muḥammad al-
Analectes sur l'histoire et la littérature des Arabes d'Espagne, edited by R. Dozy and others
Leiden, 1855–1860, I; 1858–1861, II.

The History of the Mohammedan Dynasties in Spain, translated by P. de Gayangos
London, 1840, I, Appendix B, pp. xxvii–xlii; London, 1843, II, Appendix D, pp. xlix–lxxx.

Marçais, Georges
"La guerre vue par Ibn Khaldoun"
Bulletin d'Information du Gouvernement Générale de l'Algérie. Algiers, 1939, pp. 293–295.

"Les idées d'Ibn Khaldoun sur l'évolution des sociétés"
Bulletin d'Information du Gouvernement Générale de l'Algérie. Algiers, 1940, pp. 465–468.

"Les idées d'Ibn Khaldoun sur l'histoire"
Bulletin des études Arabes (Algiers, 1941), no. 1, pp. 3–5.

La Berbérie Musulmane et l'Orient au Moyen Age
Paris, 1946.

"Ibn Khaldoun et le livre des Prolégomènes"
Revue de la Méditerranée (Paris-Algiers, 1950), IV, 406–420; 524–534.

Marçais, W.
Review of E. F. Gautier, "Les siècles obscurs du Maghreb"
Revue critique d'histoire et de littérature (Paris, 1929), XCVI, 255–270.

Margoliouth, D. S.
Lectures on Arabic Historians
Calcutta, 1930, pp. 156–158.

"Ibn Khaldūn"
Encyclopaedia of the Social Sciences.
New York, 1942, VII, 564–565.

Marías, Aguilar J.
La filosofía en los textes
Barcelona, 1950, I, 450–463.

Massé, Henri
"Les études arabes en Algérie de 1830 à 1930"
Revue Africaine (1933), LXXIV, 208–258, 458–505.

Mas'ūdī, al
Millenary Commemoration Volume, edited by S. Maqbūl Aḥmad and A. Raḥmān
Aligarh, 1960.

Matteo, Ignazio di
"Il taḥrif od alterazione della Bibbia secondo i musulmani"
Bessarione. Rome, 1922, XXVI, 242–243.

Maunier, René
"Les idées économiques d'un philosophe arabe, Ibn Khaldoun"
Revue d'Histoire économique et sociale (Paris, 1912), VI, 409–419.

"Les idées sociologiques d'un philosophe arabe au XIVᵉ siècle"
Revue Internationale de Sociologie (Paris, 1915), XXIII, 142–154; also *l'Egypte contemporaine* (Cairo, 1917), VIII, 31–43.

Mélanges de Sociologie nord-africaine
(Contains the two preceding titles.) Paris, 1930, pp. 1–35.

Menasce, Jean de
"Arabische Philosophie"
Bibliographische Einführungen in das Studium der Philosophie. Bern, 1948, p. 24.

Merad, 'Alī
"L'Autobiographie d'Ibn Khaldūn"
Institut des belles lettres arabes (Tunis, 1956), XIX, 53–64.

Mercier, E.
Histoire de l'établissement des Arabes dans l'Afrique septentrionale selon les documents fournis par les auteurs arabes et notamment par l'histoire des Berbères d'Ibn Khaldoun
Constantine, 1875.

Histoire de l'Afrique septentrionale
Paris, 1888, 1891, 3 vols.

Meyer, Eduard
Geschichte des Altertums
3rd ed., Berlin, 1902–1939, I, 83–84.

Meyerhof, Max
"An early mention of sleeping sickness in Arabic Chronicles"
Journal of the Egyptian Medical Association (Cairo, 1941), XXIV, 284–286.

Miège, J. L.
"La modernité d'Ibn Khaldoun"
Mahrajān. Rabāṭ, 1962, pp. 13–19.

Mignanelli, B. de
Ascensus Barcoch, s.v. Fischel.

Vita Tamerlani, s.v. Fischel.

Montagne, R.
La civilization du desert
Paris, 1947.

Muḥāsib, Jamāl al
"La théorie de l'education chez Ibn Khaldoun, (at-Tarbīya 'ind Ibn Khaldūn)"
al-Mashriq. Beirut, 1949, XLIII, 365–399.

Muhtadī, Shukrī
" 'Abd-ar-Raḥmān Ibn Khaldūn"
al-Muqtaṭaf. Cairo, 1927, II, 167–173, 270–277.

Müller, A.
Der Islam im Morgen- und Abendland
Berlin, 1885–1887, II, 666–670.

Muller, Herbert J.
The Loom of History
New York, 1958.

Muqtaṭaf, Majallat al-
Ibn Khaldūn al-Maghribī wa-Herbert Spencer al-Anglīzī
Cairo, 1886, X, 513–522.

Mûsâ, Munîr M.
General Sociology
Damascus, 1959, I, 27–36.

Nadvī, Muḥammad Khanīf
Afkār-i Ibn Khaldūn (in Urdu)
Lahore, 1954.

Nafīsī, Sa'īd
"Ibn Khaldūn"
Farhang nāmah i Pārsī (A Persian Encyclopaedia). Teheran, 1940, I, 528–532.

Nakosteen, Mahdi
History of Islamic Origins of Western Education
Boulder, Colorado, 1964.

Nasha't, Muḥammad 'Alī
The Economic Ideas in the Prolegomena of Ibn Khaldūn
Cairo, 1944.

"Ibn Khaldoun, Pioneer Economist"
L'Egypte Contemporaine (Cairo, 1945), XXXV, 375–490.

Nāṣirī, Aḥmad b. Khālid an-
Kitāb al-Istiqçā' li-akhbār douwal el-maghrib el-aqça
Casablanca, 1954–1955, 4 vols. (French translation of vol. IV in *Archives marocaines* (1934), XXIII, "Les Mérinides", by I. Hamet.)

Nassar, Nassīf
"Le Maître d'Ibn Khaldūn: al-Ābilī"
Studia Islamica. Paris, 1965, XX, 103–114.

Nicholson, R. A.
Translations of Eastern Poetry and Prose
Cambridge, 1922, pp. 176–185. Republished in *Introduction to Islamic Civilization* (Course Syllabus and Selected Reading) by M. G. S. Hodgson. Chicago, 1958, II, 490–501.

A Literary History of the Arabs
London, 1923, pp. 437–440; 2nd ed., London, 1930.

Noël des Vergers, M. J.
Histoire de l'Afrique sous la dynastie des Aghlabites et de la Sicile sous la domination musulmane. Texte arabe d'Ebn Khaldoun, accompagné d'une traduction française et de notes.
Paris, 1841.

Nūr, Muḥammad 'Abd al Mun'im
An Analytical Study of the Sociological Thought of Ibn Khaldūn
Cairo, 1960.

Oppenheimer, Franz
System der Soziologie: Der Staat
Jena, 1926, II, 173–174 ff.; IV, 251 ff.

Ortega y Gasset, J.
"Abenjaldūn nos revela el secreto"
El-Espactador, Revista de Occidente (Madrid, 1934), VIII, 9–53.

Pearson, J. D.
Index Islamicus, Supplement, 1956–1960
Cambridge, 1962.

Pearson, J. D. and J. F. Ashton, editors.
Index Islamicus, 1906–1955. A catalogue of articles on Islamic subjects in periodicals and other collective publications.
Cambridge, 1958.

Pellat, Charles
Langue et Littérature Arabes
Paris, 1952, pp. 177–180.

Pérès, Henri
Ibn Khaldoun (1332–1406), Extraits choisis de la "Muqaddima" et du "Kitāb al-'Ibar"
Algiers, 1947.

"Ibn Khaldoun: sa vie et son œuvre" (Bibliographie)
Bulletin des études Arabes (Algiers, 1943), pp. 55–60, 145–146.

"Essai de bibliographie d'Ibn Ḫaldūn"
Studi Orientalistici in onore di G. Levi Della Vida. Rome, 1956, II, 304–329.

"Le Siècle d'Ibn Khaldoun (VIIIe–XIVe)"
Bibliothèque de l'Institut d'Etudes Supérieures Islamique d'Alger. Algiers, 1960, XVI.

Perlmann, Moshe
"Ibn Khaldūn on Sūfism"
Bibliotheca Orientalis. Leiden, 1960, XVII, 222–223.

Piquet, V.
Les Civilizations de l'Afrique du Nord
Paris, 1909.

Pizzi, I.
Letteratura Araba
Milan, 1903, pp. 333–337.

Plessner, M.
"Beiträge zur islamischen Literaturgeschichte"
Islamica (Leipzig, 1931), IV, 538–542. See also *Orientalistische Literaturzeitung* (1933), XXXVI, 111–115.

Poncet, J.
"L'évolution des 'genres de vie' en Tunisie: autour d'une phrase d'Ibn Khaldoun"
Cahiers de Tunisie (1954), II, 315–323.

Pons-Boigues, Francisco
Ensayo bio-bibliográfico sobre los historiadores y geógrafos Arábigo-Españoles
Madrid, 1898, pp. 350–362.

Popper, William
Egypt and Syria under the Circassian Sultans, 1382–1469 A. D. Systematic Notes to Ibn Taghrī Birdī's Chronicles of Egypt
University of California Publications in Semitic Philology (1955–1957), XV–XVI.

Indicies to Ibn Taghrī Birdī's History of Egypt 1382–1469 A. D.
University of California Publications in Semitic Philology (1963), XXIV.

Prakash, Buddha
"Ibn Khaldun's Philosophy of History"
Islamic Culture (Hyderabad, 1954), XXVIII, 492–508; 1955, XXIX, 104–119, 184–190, 225–236.

The Modern Approach to History
New Delhi, 1963.

Qādir, 'Abd al-
"The Social and Political Ideas of Ibn Khaldūn"
The Indian Journal of Political Science (Allāhabād, 1941), III, 117–126.

"The Economic Ideas of Ibn Khaldūn"
The Indian Journal of Economics (Allāhabād, 1942), XXII, 898–907.

Qamīr, Yuḥannā
Muqaddimat Ibn Khaldūn: dirāsah-mukhtārāt
Beirut, 1947.

Quiros Rodriquez, C.
"Ibn Jaldūn, político e historiador"
Archivos del Instituto de Estudios Africanos. Madrid, 1952, VI, 7–19.

Raliby, Osman
On the Political and Social Ideas of Ibn Khaldūn (Indonesian text)
Djakarta, 1963.

Rappoport, Ch.
Zur Characteristik der Methode und Hauptrichtungen der Philosophie der Geschichte
Bern, 1896, pp. 75–79.

La philosophie sociale de l'histoire comme science de l'évolution
Paris, 1903; 2nd ed., 1925, pp. 78–88.

Reinaud, J. T.
"Ibn Khaldoun"
Nouvelle Biographie Générale, edited by Didot. Paris, 1877, XXV, 740–747.

Renaud, H. P. J.
"Divination et histoire nord-Africaine aux temps d'Ibn Khaldoun"
Hespéris (Paris, 1943), XXX, 213–221.

"Sur un passage d'Ibn Khaldoun relatif à l'histoire de mathématique"
Hespéris (Paris, 1944), XXXI, 35–47.

Ribera y Tarragó, J.
La ensenañza entre los Musulmanes españoles
Saragossa, 1893.

Richter, G.
"Medieval Arabic Historiography"
Islamic Culture (Hyderabad, 1960), XXXIV, 148–151.

Riḍwān, Ibrāhīm
Muqaddimah, Selections, edited by Aḥmad Zaqī
Cairo, 1960.

Ritter, Hellmut
"Irrational Solidarity Groups: A socio-psychological study in connection with Ibn Khaldūn"
Oriens (Leiden, 1948), I, 1–44.

"Autographs in Turkish Libraries"
Oriens (Leiden, 1953), VI, plate 17 and p. 83.

Riẓā, Ḥamīd
"Ibn Khaldūn, the philosopher of history"
Islamic Review (Woking, 1938), XXVI, 267–271.

Roemer, H. H.
"Neuere Veröffentlichungen zur Geschichte Timurs und seiner Nachfolger"
Central Asiatic Journal (The Hague, 1956), II, 219–232.

Rosenthal, Erwin I. J.
Ibn Khaldūn Gedanken über den Staat, Ein Beitrag zur Geschichte der mittelalterlichen Staatslehre
Munich-Berlin, 1932.

"Ibn Khaldūn: A North African Muslim Thinker of the 14th Century"
Bulletin of the John Rylands Library (Manchester, 1940), XXIV, 307–320.

"Some Aspects of Islamic Political Thought"
Islamic Culture (Hyderabad, 1948), XXII, 1–17.

"Ibn Jaldūn's attitude to the Falāsifa"
al-Andalus. Madrid-Granada, 1955, XX, 75–85.

Political Thought in Medieval Islam
Cambridge, 1962, pp. 84–109; 260–268.

Rosenthal, Franz
"Die arabische Autobiographie"
Studia Arabica, Vol. I (*Analecta Orientalia*). Rome, 1937, XIV, 1–40.

"The Technique and Approach of Muslim Scholarship"
Analecta Orientalia. Rome, 1947, XXIV.

A History of Muslim Historiography
Leiden, 1952. (Arabic translation, Baghdad, 1963.)

"The Use of Arabic Writing"
Ars Orientalis. Washington, 1961, II, 16–23.

"The Influence of the Biblical Tradition on Muslim Historiography"
Historians of the Middle East, edited by B. Lewis and P. M. Holt. London, 1962, pp. 35–45.

Rossi, G. B. de
Dizionario storico degli autori arabi
Parma, 1807, p. 56.

Roy, B.
Extrait du Catalogue des manuscript et des imprimés de la Bibliothèque de la Grande Mosquée de Tunis
Tunis, 1900, no. 6216.

Rushdī, Ṣāliḥ
Rajulun fi'l-Qāhira (A Man in Cairo)
Kutub li'l-jamī'a. Cairo, 1957, no. 115.

Rubio, P. Luciano
"En torno à los "Prolegómenos" de Abenjaldūn, Muqaddima o Muqaddama?"
La Cuidad de Dios (Madrid, 1950), no. 162, pp. 171–178.

Rus'an, H.
Ibnu Chaldun tentang sosial ekonomi
Djakarta, 1963.

Saab, Ḥasan
"Ibn Khaldūn"
Encyclopedia of Philosophy. New York, 1967, IV, 107–109.

Sacy, Antoine Isaac Silvestre De
"Extraits des Prolégomènes d'Ebn-Khaldoun"
Relation de l'Egypte, par Abd-Allaṭīf. Paris, 1810, pp. 509–524 (translation); pp. 558–564 (Arabic text).

Chrestomathie Arabe, ou Extraits de divers écrivains arabes
2nd ed., Paris, 1826–1827, I, 370–411; II, 168–169, 257–259, 279–336; III, 342–346.

Anthologie grammaticale arabe
Paris, 1829, pp. 167–186, 408–447, 472–476.

"Eben Khaldoun sur Sofisme"
Notices et Extraits. Paris, 1831, XII, 293–305.

Le Soufisme d'après les Prolégomènes d'Ebn Khaldoun
Libres Études, edited by E. Bailly. Paris, 1909–1910, pp. 6–9.

"Ibn Khaldoun"
Biographie universelle ancienne et moderne . . . , edited by Michaud. 2nd ed., Paris, 1843 ff., XX, 268–271.

Saeed Sheikh, M.
"Ibn Khaldūn"
Iqbal (Lahore, 1960), IX, 14–22.

Ṣalībi, J. and K. 'Ayād
Ibn Khaldoun: morceaux choisis (*Muntaḥabāt*)
Damascus, 1933.

Ṣalībi, Kamal S.
"Listes chronologiques des grands cadis de l'Egypte sous les Mamelouks"
Revue des Etudes Islamiques (Paris, 1957), XXV, 81–125.

Sāmī al-Kayālī
"Ibn Khaldun wa l-'Arab"
al-Fikr al-'Arabīyah. Cairo, 1943, pp. 13–26.

Samīhī, 'Abdul Karīm
"Ibn Khaldūn and his Ta'rīf"
Revue al-Anwār (Tetuan, 1951), no. 26, pp. 12–13, 19–20.

Sánchez-Albornoz, Claudio
"Ben Jaldūn ante Pedro El Cruel," in *La España Musulmana según los autores islamitas y cristianos medievales*
Buenos Aires, 1946, II, 422–423.

Sanders, J. H.
Tamerlane, or Timur the Great Amir (From the Arabic Life of Aḥmad Ibn Arabshāh)
London, 1936.

Santillana, David
Istituzioni di Diritto musulmano malichita, con riguardo anche al sistema sciafiita
Rome, 1926–1938, 2 vols.

Sarkis, Joseph E.
Dictionnaire encyclopédique de Bibliographie Arabe
Cairo, 1928–1931, XCV–XCVII.

Sarton, G.
Introduction to the History of Science
Baltimore, 1948, III, 1767–1779.

"Arabic Scientific Literature"
I. Goldziher Memorial Volume, Part I. Budapest, 1948, pp. 55–72.

Saunders, J. J.
"The Problem of Islamic Decadence"
Cahiers d'Histoire mondiale (Paris, 1963), VII, 701–720.

Sauvaget, J.
"Historiens arabes (pages choisies et traduites)" *Initiation à l'Islam*
Paris, 1946, V, 137–146.

Introduction to the History of the Muslim East. A bibliographical guide
As recast by Claude Cahen
Berkeley–Los Angeles, 1965.

Schimmel, A.
Ibn Chaldun, Aus dem Arabischen, Augewählte Abschnitte aus der Muqaddima
Tübingen, 1951.

Schmid, Johan von
"Ibn Khaldoun, Philosophe et Sociologue Arabe (1332–1406)"
Revue de l'Institut de Sociologie (Bruxelles, 1951), pp. 3–19.

Schmidt, Nathaniel
"The Manuscripts of Ibn Khaldūn"
Journal of the American Oriental Society (Baltimore, 1926), XLVI, 171–176.

"Ibn Khaldūn"
The New International Encyclopedia. New York, 1930, II, 716–717.

Ibn Khaldūn, Historian, Sociologist, and Philosopher
New York, 1930.

"Ibn Khaldūn and his Prolegomena"
Muslim World (Hartford, 1932), XXII, 61–63.

Schreiner, M.
"Zur Geschichte der Aussprache des Hebräischen bei Ibn Chaldūn"
Zeitschrift fur die Alttestamentliche Wissenschaft (Giessen, 1886), VI, 251–255.

Schulz, F. E.
"Sur le grand ouvrage historique et critique d'Ibn Khaldoun . . ."
Journal Asiatique (Paris, 1825), 1. sér., VI–VII, 213–226, 279–300.

"Extrait du grand ouvrage historique d'Ibn Khaldoun"
Journal Asiatique (Paris, 1828), 2. sér., II, 117–142.

Şerefeddin, M.
"Ibni Haldun Vesilesiyle Islâm ve Türkler"
Iş Meçmuasi (Istanbul, 1938), no. 15–16, pp. 67–71.

Shafaq, Rīẓa Zādeh
"Ibn Khaldūn and the history of philosophy" (in Persian)
Revue de la Faculté des Lettres de Tabriz, edited by Adīb Ṭuṣi (Tabrīz, 1950), III, pp. 360–369.

Sharīf, M. M., editor
A History of Muslim Philosophy
Wiesbaden, 1967, II, chaps. 46 and 49.

Shaykh al-Arḍ, Taysīr
Ibn Khaldūn
Beirut, 1966.

Sherwani, H. Kh.
"Political theories of certain early Islamic writers"
The Indian Journal of Political Science (Allāhabād, 1942), III, 225–236.

Studies in Muslim political Thought and Administration
Lahore, 1945, pp. 181–193.

"The genesis and progress of Muslim socio-political thought"
Islamic Culture (Hyderabad, 1953), XXVII, 144–148.

"Ibn Khaldūn—a Life Sketch"
Indian Journal of the History of Medicine (Madras, 1959), IV, 9–12.

Shiber, Saba G.
"Ibn Khaldūn—An Early Town Planner"
Middle East Forum (Beirut, 1962), XXXVIII, 35–39.

Sikirič, Šacir
"Ibn Haldunova Prolegomena (Les Prolégomènes d'Ibn Ḥaldūn)"
Prilozi za orijentalnu filologiju i istoriju jugoslovenskih naroda pod turskom vladivinom (*Revue de Philologie orientale et d'Histoire des Peuples yougoslaves sous la Domination turque*) (Sarajevo, 1954–1955), V, 233–240. (French summary, p. 250.)

Simon, Heinrich
Ibn Khaldūn's Wissenschaft von der menschlichen Kultur
Beiträge zur Orientalistik. Leipzig, 1959, II.

Simon, Marcel
"Le Judaisme berbère dans l'Afrique ancienne"
Revue d'Histoire et de Philosophie Religieuses (Strasbourg, 1946), XXVI, 1–31, 105–145.

Slane, William MacGuckin, Baron de
"Autobiographie d'Ibn Khaldoun" (translated)
Journal Asiatique (Paris, 1844), 4. sér., III, 5–60, 187–210, 291–308, 325–353; corrected and republished in *Notices et Extraits* (Paris, 1863), XIX, vi–lxxxii ff.

Catalogue des manuscripts arabes dans la Bibliothèque Nationale
Paris, 1883–1895.

Ibn Khaldoun: Histoire des Berbères et des dynasties musulmanes de l'Afrique septentrionale, texte arabe
Algiers, 1847–1851, 2 vols.

Ibn Khaldoun: Histoire des Berbères et des dynasties musulmanes de l'Afrique septentrionale. Traduite de l'Arabe.
Algiers, 1852–1856, 4 vols.; new ed. by Paul Casanova, Paris, 1925–1956, 4 vols.

Somogyi, Joseph de
"The Development of Arabic Historiography"
Journal of Semitic Studies (Manchester, 1958), III, 373–387.

Sorokin, P. A.
Social Philosophies of an Age of Crisis
Boston, 1951.

Sorokin, P. A., C. C. Zimmerman, and others, editors
A Systematic Source-Book in Rural Sociology
Minneapolis, 1930, I, 54–68.

Spuler, Berthold
"Remarks on Ibn Khaldūn"
Vierteljahrschrift für Social- und Wiltschaftsgeschichte. Wiesbaden, 1953, XL, 63–67.

"Ibn Khaldoun, the Historian"
Proceedings of Mahrajān. Cairo, 1962, pp. 349–356.

Spuler, Berthold and L. Forrer.
Der Vordere Orient in *Islamischer Zeit, Wissenschaftl Forschungsberichte*
Bern, 1954.

Subba Reddy, D. V.
"Sociology of Medicine in the Muqaddimah of Ibn Khaldūn"
Indian Journal of the History of Medicine (Madras, 1959), IV, 13–23; (1960) V, 10–21.

Ṣubḥī Pāshā, 'Abdul-Laṭīf
Miftāḥ al-'Ibar, Turkish translation of parts of Ibn Khaldūn's *'Ibar*
Istanbul, 1276 H., 4 vols.

Surdon, G. and L. Bercher
Recueil de textes de sociologie et de droit public musulman contenus dans les "Prolégomènes" d'Ibn Khaldoun, choisis et traduits
Algiers, 1951.

Syrier, M.
"Ibn Khaldūn and Islamic Mysticism"
Islamic Culture (Hyderabad, 1947), XXI, 264–302.

Tamura, Jitsuzō
"Isurāmu bummei hihyōka Ibun-Harudōn no keizaikan: 'Seikaishi josetsu' wo tsujite mita (Les vues economiques du critique musulman Ibn Haldun; a propos de 'l'introduction a l'histoire universelle')
Ajia keizai (Tokyo, 1963), IV, fasc. 9, pp. 9–15.

Ṭanjī, Muḥammad b. Tāwīt aṭ-
"Prolégomènes d'Ibn Khaldoun"
Proceedings of the 22nd International Congress of Orientalists in Istanbul.
Leiden, 1957, II, 262–263.

Tawānisī, Abu'l Futūh M. al-
Ibn Khaldūn
Cairo, 1961.

Tekindağ, M. C. Şehabeddin
Berkuk Devrinde, Memlūk Sultanliği
Istanbul, 1961.

Terrasse, H.
Histoire du Maroc
Paris, 1949–1950, 2 vols.

Tiesenhausen, V. G.
"Die Geschichte der 'Oqailiden-Dynastie"
Mémoires de l'Académie Impériale des Sciences. St. Petersburg, 1859, VIII, 129–172.

"Recueil de matériaux relatifs à l'histoire de la horde d'or"
Mémoires de l'Académie Impériale des Sciences. St. Petersburg, 1884, I, 365–394, texte et traduction.

Togan, Zeki Velidi, A.
"Ibn Khaldūn et l'avenir de l'état musulman"
Bilgi Meçmuasi. Istanbul, 1941, pp. 733–743.

Tarihde Usul
Istanbul, 1950, no. 449, esp. pp. 170–187.

"Kritische Geschichtsauffassung in der Islamischen Welt des Mittelalters"
Proceedings of the 22nd International Congress of Orientalists. Istanbul, 1953, I, 76–85.

Tornberg, C. J.
"Ibn Khalduni Narratio de Expeditionibus Francorum in Terras islamismo subjectas"
Nova Acta regiae societatis scientiarum Upsaliensis. Upsala, 1844, XII, 1–154.

"Notitiae de populo Berberorum ex Ibn Khalduno in Primordia dominationis Murabitorum . . ."
Nova Acta regiae societatis scientiarum Upsaliensis. Upsala, 1844, XII, 315–336, 398–400.

"Geschichte der Franken"
Quellenbeiträge zur Geschichte der Kreuzzüge, R. Röhricht, editor. Berlin, 1875, pp. 5–31.

Toynbee, A. J.
"The Relativity of Ibn Khaldūn's Historical Thoughts"
A Study of History. London, 1935, III, 321–328, 473–476; 1954, X, 84–87.

Tritton, A. S.
Materials on Muslim Education in the Middle Ages
London, 1957

Tyan, E.
Histoire de l'organisation judiciaire en pays d'Islam
Lyon, 1938–1943, 2 vols.; new ed., Leiden, 1960.

Institutions du droit public musulman; Le Califat
Paris, 1954, I.

Ülken, Hilmi Ziya
La Pensée de l'Islam
Istanbul, 1953, pp. 557–576.

"Ibn Khaldoun. Initiateur de la sociologie"
Proceedings of Mahrajān. Cairo, 1962, pp. 29–40.

Ülken, Hilmi Ziya and Z. V. Findikoğlu
Ibni Haldūn
Istanbul, 1940.

Vera, Fr.
La cultura española medieval
Madrid, 1933, I, 102–108.

Villenoisy, Cosseron de
"Un homme d'etat, historien et philosophe du XIVe siècle (Ibn Khaldoun)"
La Nouvelle Revue (Paris, 1886), XL, 545–578.

Wāfī, 'Alī 'Abd al-Wāḥid
" 'Abd ur-Raḥmān Ibn Khaldūn"
Collection A'lām al-'Arab. Cairo, 1962.

Wajdī, Muḥammad Farīd
"Ibn Khaldūn fi-l Mizān"
Hilāl (Cairo, 1932), XL, 1234–1242.

Walzer, R.
"Aspects of Islamic Political Thought"
Oriens (Leiden, 1963), XVI, 40–60.

Wardī, 'Alī al-
Manṭiq Ibn Khaldūn (*Lectures on the Logic of Ibn Khaldūn*)
Cairo, 1962.

Weil, Gustav
Geschichte des Abbasidenchalifats in Egypten
Stuttgart, 1862, II, 63–83, 89.

Welch, Galbraith
North African Prelude: The first 7000 years
New York, 1949, pp. 173–174, 390–392.

Wesendonk, O. G. von
"Ibn Chaldun, ein arabischer Kulturhistoriker des 14. Jahrhunderts"
Deutsche Rundschau. Berlin, 1923, Jahrgang 49, pp. 45–53. (Arabic translation by M. A. 'Enān, Cairo, 1933.)

White, Hayden V.
"Ibn Khaldūn in World Philosophy of History"
Comparative Studies in Sociology and History. The Hague, 1960, II, 110–125.

Wiet, Gaston
Les Biographies du Manhal Ṣāfī, Mémoires présentés à l'Institut d'Egypte
Cairo, 1932, XIX, no. 1383.

"L'Egypte Arabe de la conquête Arabe à la conquête Ottomane (642–1517)"
Histoire de la nation égyptienne, edited by Gabriel Hanotaux. Paris, 1931–1940, 7 vols.; IV, 530.

Grandeur de l'Islam: de Mahomet à François I
Paris, 1961.

Cairo, City of Art and Commerce, translated by S. Feiler
The Centers of Civilization Series, no. 16. Norman: University of Oklahoma, 1964.

Wright, William, editor
The Paleographical Society: Facsimiles of Manuscripts and Inscriptions Oriental Series. London, 1875–1883, cf. pl. 84.

Wolfson, Harry Austryn
"Ibn Khaldūn on Attributes and Predestination"
Speculum. Cambridge, 1959, XXXIV, 585–597; republished *Religious Philosophy, A Group of Essays,* Harvard, 1961, pp. 177–195.

Wüstenfeld, H. F.
"Die Geschichtschreiber der Araber und ihre Werke"
Abhandlungen der Gesellschaft der Wissenschaften. Hist.-Philol. Klasse. Göttingen, 1882, XXIX, no. 456, 26–31.

Zahida, H. Pāshā
"Ibn Khaldoun—Sociologist"
Actes du XVe Congrès international de sociologie. Istanbul, 1952.

Zaydān, J.
Ta'rīkh adab al-lughah al-'arabīya
Cairo, 1913, III, 210–214.

Zmerli, S.
"La vie et les œuvres d'Ibn Khaldoun"
Revue Tunisienne (Tunis, 1911), XVIII, 532–536.

INDEX

Abaghā Khān, 90
'Abbāsid Caliphate, 47, 57–58, 91
'Abdullāh b. Salām, 55
'Abd al-'Azīz (Sultan), 16
'Abd al-Jabbār b. an-Nu'mān al-Khwārizmī, 48
al-Ābilī Muḥammad b. Ibrāhīm, 56
Abū'l-'Abbās, 16, 17, 21, 22
Abū 'Alī b. Bādīs, 56
Abū 'Inān Fāris, 15, 16
Abū Isḥāq, 15
Abū Sa'īd, Il-Khān, 86, 91
Abū Sa'īd 'Uthmān b. 'Abdu'l-'Abbās, 102
Abū Sālim, 16, 31
Abū Shākir Buṭrūs, 117
Abū Ya'qūb al-Bādisī, 57
Abū Yāzīd (Bāyāzīd), 100
Abū Zakarīyā' Yaḥyā, 21
Achaemenid Persia, 121–122, 123
'Ād, 150
'Ādilīya Madrasah, 43, 96
Afrāsiyāb, 53, 122
Afrīdūn, 53, 122
ahl adh-dhimma, 78
ahl al-kitāb, 125, 150–151
Aḥmad b. 'Ajlān, 35
Aḥmad b. Uways, 93
'Akkā, 67
Alamūt, 91
Aleppo, 42, 49, 64, 78, 80, 83, 95, 99, 101, 105–107
Alexander, 53–54, 121, 131, 143, 151, 152
Alexandria, 15, 18, 21, 36, 49, 76, 107, 117, 135, 138, 147, 151
'Alī, 58, 104
Alṭunbughā al-Jūbānī (Emir), 20, 36, 38–39, 76, 164
Amalikites, 139
amān, 60
Ānas al-Jarkāsī, 74
Antioch, 135
Antipater, 143
Apocrypha, 116, 131, 142, 146
Apocryphal Gospels, 116, 131
Apostles, 132–133, 145
Ardashīr, 122
Ardashīr b. Babak, 123
Arghūn Khān, 90–91
Aristeas, 147
Artaxerxes, 122–123
'aṣabīya, 26, 52, 88, 103, 153–154
Asanbughā (Emir), 95
Ashraf ash-Sha'bān, 74
aṭābak, 38, 75
Aṭlmish, 101
Avesta, 124, 126, 128, 132, 147
Aybak, 73
'Ayn Jālūt, 91
Aytamish, 77–78
Azerbaijān, 125
Azhar Mosque, 26, 32

Ba'albek, 101
bābā, 134
Bāb an-Naṣr, 68
Baghdād, 58, 88, 91, 93, 94, 109, 147
Bahrām, 122
Bahrām b. Hormuz, 128
Baḥrī Mamlūks, 73
Baisaq ash-Shaikhī, 101
Balkh, 126
Banū Jaghaṭāi, 46, 47, 90, 93, 103–104
Banū Khaldūn, 15, 21, 161
Baraka, 74–75
Bar Dayṣān, 135

Barqūq (Sultan), *passim*
al-Barqūqīya, 27
Barūkh, 126
baṭrīk, 134
Baybarsīya Khānqa, 27, 28, 35, 36, 37, 38, 76
Bayn Qaṣrain street, 27, 31
Berbers, 16, 26, 51, 71, 72, 111
Bethlehem, 42, 131, 136
Biblical books, 116, 118, 123, 133, 145–146
Biblical prophets, 122, 125–126, 139, 146, 147
al-Bīrūnī, 47, 131, 145, 147, 151
Biskra, 16, 21
Bougie, 16
al-Burda, 47
Burhān ad-Dīn al-Khwārizmī, 84
Burhān ad-Dīn al-Maḥallī, 80
Byzantine historians, 106–107
Byzantines, 124, 127, 130, 131, 133, 135

cadi, *passim*
Caesar, 53–54, 151, 152
Cairo, *passim*
Caliphate, 49, 57–58, 83, 88, 89, 91
Canaanite tribes, 139
Carthage, 151
Ceuta, 50
Chaldaens, 155
Chalcedon, 134
Children of Israel, 115, 126, 138, 140, 143, 149–150, 153
China, 84, 88, 111
Christian Canon, 116, 130, 131, 132–133
Christianity, 6, 35, 105–106, 110, 115–118, 120, 124, 127, 130–137
Chronicle of Yosiphon, 139–144, 145, 146, 147, 152, 154
Circassian, 71, 72, 74, 80, 162
Citadel (of Damascus), 44, 46, 98–99
Clement, 133, 145
Cleopatra, 151, 152
Constantine, 21, 56, 124, 127, 133–134
Constantinople, 134
Copts, 115, 117, 146
Cyrus the Great, 123, 139

Damascus, 4, 23, 25, 38, 39, 42–67 *passim*, 75, 77, 78, 81, 83, 94–100 *passim*, 101, 103, 105–107, 162
Darius, 122, 123, 139
daulat al-atrāk, 72
Delhi, 95
Democrit, 110
Dhū Nuvās, 127

Dīn al-Barāham, 90
Dīn al-Majūsīya, 89, 90, 123–129
Dīn an-Naṣrānīya, 132
Dīn an-Nigushīya, 89
Dīn aṣ-Ṣābi'a, 115n
Diocletian, 151
Druzes, 66
Dūshī Khān, 88–89

Ecumenical Councils, 134
Emmanuel Piloti, 107
Ephesus, 134
Eutychius (Sa'īd b. Biṭrīq), 117, 147

Faraj (Sultan), 19, 25, 40, 42–44, 45, 59, 64, 67, 71, 77, 81, 92, 94, 95–96, 98, 100, 101, 102, 107, 161
Fāṭimid, 56–57
Fayyūm, 40
fetwā, 34–37, 39, 76
Fez, 15, 16, 24, 25, 50, 51, 56, 102, 160
fiqh, 26

Galen, 109, 123
Gāzā, 44, 67, 101
Ghāzān Khān, 91–92
Gibraltar, 16, 50
Gospels, 116, 131, 133, 147
Greek-Iranian synchronism, 123, 131

ḥadīth, 15, 27, 116
Ḥaḍraumaut, 15
Ḥafṣid Dynasty, 15, 16, 17, 42
ḥājib, 32, 72
al-Ḥakam II al-Mustanṣir, 118
ḥalāwa, 47
Ham, 150
Hamā, 101
Ḥasīdīm, 149
Hasmoneans, 132, 140, 142, 143, 148, 154
Hebrew Canon, 133, 138–139, 145–146
Hebrew-Iranian synchronism, 122–123, 131
Hebrew language, 126, 148–149
Hebron, 42, 136
Hegesippus, 141, 142
Helen, 127, 133–134
Herod (House of), 131–132, 140, 142, 143
ḥidthān, 55
Ḥomṣ, 78
Hūd, 150
Hūlāgū Khān, 58, 89, 90, 91, 92, 124, 159
Hyrcanus, 143, 148

'Ibādites, 149
Ibn al-'Amīd (Jirjis al-Makīn), 117, 133, 144, 147
Ibn 'Arafah, 17
Ibn ad-Duwaydārī, 66
Ibn Baṭṭūṭah, 84, 162
Ibn al-Jubayr, 162
Ibn al-Khaṭīb (Lisān ad-Dīn), 16, 159, 163
Ibn Mufliḥ (Taqī ad-Dīn; Burhān ad-Dīn), 44–46, 57, 97
Ibn al-Muqaffā', 125
Ibn Musabbiḥī, 117
Ibn ar-Rāhib, 117, 133, 144
Ibn Zarzar Ibrāhīm, al-Yahūdī, 56
al-Idrīsī, 84, 100
Ifrīqiya, 50
ijtihād, 58
Imamate, 58
Iṣfāhān, 94
Isra'īliyāt, 118, 150
Ishkanīya, 122
Iṣṭakhr, 126

Jacobites, 135–136
Jaghaṭāi, 88–89, 94
al-jalwā al-kubarā, 140, 148, 152
Jamāl ad-Dīn al-Aqfahsī, 67
Jamal ad-Dīn Maḥmūd b. 'Alī al-Ustādār, 79, 164
Jāmasp, 126, 128
al-Jarkāsī, 96
Jenghiz Khān, 6, 83–90, 93, 103, 124, 159
Jeremiah, 126
Jerusalem, 42, 123, 131, 133, 135, 136, 141, 143, 147, 148, 151, 152, 153, 162
Jesus and family, 123, 124, 130–135
Josephus Flavius, 141–142
Judaism, 6, 110, 115–116, 117–118, 120, 127, 132, 138–155

Ka'b al-Aḥbār, 119
Karak, 75–76, 78
Karaites, 148
Kārimites, 80
Kawādh b. Peroz, 128
Kayqāwūs, 121
Kaystasp, 126–127, 128
Kayyanids, 122
khānqa, 27, 28, 29, 37, 39
Khārijites, 58, 136
al-Khāṣṣakī, 74
Khawājā 'Uthmān, 74
khil'a, 60
Khosraw, 53–54, 122
Khūrāsān, 53, 84, 88, 89, 94, 95
Khwārizm, 84, 89, 94
Khwārizm Shāhs, 85, 88
kitābīya, 74
Kōhen, 148, 154
kufr, 135
Kumerat, 122

Maccabees, 146
madrasah, 26, 27, 32, 35, 43, 73, 96
Maghrib (various divisions), 49–52, *passim*
Magians, 124, 133
Maḥmūd (Emir), 79
Mahrajān, 127
malāḥim, 55
Mālik b. Anas (al-Muwatta), 27
Malik al-Manṣūr Ḥājjī, 35, 75
Malik aṣ-Ṣāliḥ Ḥājjī, 75
Malikite Chief Cadi, 3, 30–41, 42, 43, 50, 67–68, 73, 78
Mamlūks, 3, 5, 15–108 *passim*, 160, 162
Mangū Khān, 91
Mānī, 128
Manṣūr (Caliph), 125
Manūshihr, 53, 122, 125, 126
Marcion, 135
al-Mas'ūdī, 111, 114, 116, 125, 127, 130, 139, 145, 149, 150
al-Māwardī, 31
maẓālim, 16, 31
Māzāndarān, 88, 94
Mazdak, 128
Mecca, 4, 17, 18, 19, 23, 27, 35, 42, 50, 82, 161, 162
Melchites, 117, 135–136
Merinid Dynasty, 15, 16, 31, 42, 51
Miganelli, Bertrando de, 107
Minṭāsh, 35–36, 37, 38, 39, 75–76
Moabites, 139
Mōbedhān, 124, 128
Mongolian language, 51
Moses, 53, 122, 138, 139, 149, 153
mufti, 17, 32, 34
Muḥammad b. 'Arafah, 34
Muḥammad b. 'Ammār, 28
Muḥammad V of Granada, 16
mulāḥid, 91
al-Muwaṭṭa, 27

Nabaṭaens, 53, 54, 115
nā'ib, 91
nā'ib al-qala', 46
Naṣīr ad-Dīn aṭ-Ṭūṣī, 86
Naurūz, 127
Nazareth, 132

Nebuchadnezzar, 53–54, 122, 123, 140, 151, 152
Nestorians, 135–136
Nestorius, 135
niblah, 127
Nicea, 134
Nicholaus of Damascus, 142
Normans (Norsemen), 124
Nūr ad-Dīn al-Kharrūbī, 80

Ogatāi Khān, 88–89
Omayyad Mosque, 44, 45, 98
Orosius, Paulus, 117–118, 139, 144

Palestine, 42, 53, 67, 125, 136
Parthians, 122
Patriarchs, 134, 135, 136, 138
Pedro of Seville, 16
Perushim, 149
Philistines, 139
Philo, 147
Pishdādiyān, 122
Pontius Pilate, 132
Pope, 134–135
Ptolemaens, 143
Ptolemy, 109, 147
Pythagoras, 110, 123

Qal'at Ibn Salāmah, 17
Qamḥīya Madrasah, 26, 32
Qarawīyīn Mosque, 56
Qarakorum, 89
Qāsim b. Aṣbagh, 118
al-Qiyāma (al-Qumāma), 134
Qubilāi, 89

Rabbanim, 148
ar-Rakrākī, Shams ad-Dīn Muḥammad b., 36, 38
Rashīd ad-Dīn (ad-Daulah), 87
Rāydānīya, 43
riḥla, 84, 159
Riyāsat al-jālūt, 148
Roger, King of Sicily, 84
ar-Ruhā', 95
Rustum, 122

Ṣabaens, 115
Sa'd al-Yahūdī, 91
Ṣadr ad-Dīn al-Munāwī, 59, 101
Saduqim, 149
Ṣafad, 64, 66, 78
Saint Augustine, 151
Saladin (Ṣalāḥ ad-Dīn), 26, 72, 83
Ṣalāḥīya Madrasah, 31
Samaritans, 139, 149
Samarqand, 59, 61, 64–65, 89, 95, 104, 106
Ṣarghitmishīya Madrasah, 27, 35
Sassanid Persia, 121–123, 131
Sayf ad-Dīn Anas al-Jarkasī, 74
Seleucides, 143
Seljūqs, 88
Septuagint, 146–148
Shāh Malik, 59–60
Shaikh Sayf ad-Dīn Lājīn al-Jarkasī, 96
Shajar ad-Durr, 73
Shams ad-Dīn al-Bākharzī, 89
Shams ad-Dīn al-Iṣfahānī, 86
Shāpūr, 123, 128, 131
Shaqḥab, 66, 76, 92
Sharī'a, 90
Shihāb ad-Dīn b. al-'Izz, 49
Shihāb ad-Dīn al-Muslim, 80
Shi'ites, 58, 136
Shīrāz, 94
shūhūd, 32, 41
Sicily, 110
Sijilmāsah, 51
Sīstān, 104
Sīwās, 95, 96
Spain, 2, 15, 16, 19, 21, 23, 50, 61, 72, 101, 110–111, 124, 161, 162
Stoa, 109
aṣ-Ṣubayba, 66
Sūdūn ash-Shaikhūnī (Emir), 36–38
Ṣūfi, 28
Sunnites, 58
Ṣūyūrghatmish Khān, 54, 103–104

Tabāristān, 94
aṭ-Ṭabarī, 54–55, 112, 116, 125–126, 127, 131, 139
tabdīl, 151
Tabrīz, 94
taḥrīf, 151
Takīna Khatūna, 53
Tamerlane, 3, 6, 25, 38, 42–65, 66, 71, 80, 83, 90, 92, 93–108, 159, 161
Tamūcin, 88
Tanam, 77
Tangier, 50
Tarāghāi, 103
Taurāt, 24, 118, 122, 132, 138, 144–145, 147, 148, 149, 150, 151, 152
ta'wīl, 151
Thamūd, 150
Titus, 119, 123, 139, 140, 141, 143, 152

Tlemcen (Timilsān), 16, 21, 24, 50
Tripoli, 78
Troy, 151, 152
Ṭūlī Khān, 88–89
Tunis, 2, 15, 17, 18, 21–22, 23, 24, 34, 160

al-'Umarī, 86
urdū, 59

Vespasian, 140, 141
Vulgate, 143

Wahb b. Munabbih, 119

Yaḥyā, 131
Yaḥyā b. 'Abd Allāh, 56
Yalbughā al-Khassākī an-Nāṣirī, 28, 35–36, 38, 74, 75–76
Yashbak ash-Sha'bānī (Emir), 43, 96
Yastāsb, 121
Yāsā, 90, 103
Yazdigird, 122, 151
Yazzadār, 99
Yūsuf b. 'Alī b. Ghānem, 23
Yūsuf b. Khālid al-Bisāṭī, 67–68
Yūsuf ibn Kuryūn, 119, 140–141, 144, 146, 148, 152, 153

aẓ-Ẓāhir Baybars (Sultan), 58, 73
aẓ-Ẓāhirīya, 27
Zakarīyā' b. Sa'īd al-Isrā'īlī, 143
Zanātah, 26, 50
Zane, Paole, 107
Zarādusht, 127
Zindīq, 128
Zoroastrianism, 6, 110, 115–116, 123–129, 132

www.ingramcontent.com/pod-product-compliance
Lightning Source LLC
Chambersburg PA
CBHW021705230426
43668CB00008B/737